Indigenous Aspirations and Rights

INDIGENOUS ASPIRATIONS AND RIGHTS

The Case for Responsible Business and Management

Edited by **Amy Klemm Verbos, Ella Henry**
and **Ana Maria Peredo**

Routledge
Taylor & Francis Group

LONDON AND NEW YORK

First published 2017
by Routledge
2 Park Square, Milton Park, Abingdon, Oxon OX14 4RN
and by Routledge
711 Third Avenue, New York, NY 10017
Routledge is an imprint of the Taylor & Francis Group, an informa business

Cover by Sadie Gornall-Jones.

British Library Cataloguing in Publication Data:
 A catalogue record for this book is available from the British Library.

Library of Congress Cataloging in Publication Data:
 A catalog record for this title has been applied for.

 ISBN-13: 978-1-78353-323-7 [hardback]
 ISBN-13: 978-1-78353-399-2 [paperback]
 ISBN-13: 978-1-78353-324-4 [PDF ebook]
 ISBN-13: 978-1-78353-400-5 [ePub ebook]

Typeset in Franklin and Utopia by OKS Group

Contents

>
> Amy Klemm Verbos, University of Wisconsin-Whitewater, USA
> Ella Henry, Auckland University of Technology, New Zealand
> Ana Maria Peredo, University of Victoria, Canada

>
> Carma M. Claw, New Mexico State University, USA
> Deanna M. Kennedy, University of Washington Bothell, USA
> Deborah Pembleton, St. John's University, USA

>
> Dennis Foley, University of Canberra, Australia

>
> Ella Henry, Auckland University of Technology, New Zealand
> Hugh Sayers, Motiti Rohe Moana Trust, New Zealand

>
> Benedict Y. Imbun, Western Sydney University, Australia

Acknowledgments

Our thanks to Greenleaf editors for trusting us, and for their unfailing help and support as we carried out this project. Victoria Halliday has been our mainstay in maintaining an overall sense of the project, and in keeping track of details. We appreciate the Native, Aboriginal and Indigenous Caucus for their support as our home at the Academy of Management. We acknowledge the Diversity and Inclusion Theme Committee and Management Education Division for sponsoring the professional development workshop at the 2015 Academy of Management which inspired this book. Our gratitude extends to all contributors to this volume, who brought stories from around the globe to further our understanding of the relationship between business and Indigenous peoples. We also thank Jonas Haertle, Head of the PRME Secretariat in the UN Global Compact office and his entire team for supporting this volume, for their tireless efforts to improve management education, and for their explicit inclusion of Indigenous rights in this effort. Finally, we would like to thank our spouses and families for their patience as we carried out the work of putting this volume together. We have endeavored in this effort to honor our ancestors, all Indigenous peoples, and future generations.

The Ten Principles of the United Nations Global Compact

Source: https://www.unglobalcompact.org/what-is-gc/mission/principles

Human Rights

Principle 1: Businesses should support and respect the protection of internationally proclaimed human rights; and

Principle 2: make sure that they are not complicit in human rights abuses.

Labour

Principle 3: Businesses should uphold the freedom of association and the effective recognition of the right to collective bargaining;

Principle 4: the elimination of all forms of forced and compulsory labour;

Principle 5: the effective abolition of child labour; and

Principle 6: the elimination of discrimination in respect of employment and occupation.

Environment

Principle 7: Businesses should support a precautionary approach to environmental challenges;

Principle 8: undertake initiatives to promote greater environmental responsibility; and

Principle 9: encourage the development and diffusion of environmentally friendly technologies.

Anti-Corruption

Principle 10: Businesses should work against corruption in all its forms, including extortion and bribery.

The Six PRME Principles

Source: http://www.unprme.org/about-prme/the-six-principles.php

Principle 1 | Purpose: We will develop the capabilities of students to be future generators of sustainable value for business and society at large and to work for an inclusive and sustainable global economy.

Principle 2 | Values: We will incorporate into our academic activities and curricula the values of global social responsibility as portrayed in international initiatives such as the United Nations Global Compact.

Principle 3 | Method: We will create educational frameworks, materials, processes and environments that enable effective learning experiences for responsible leadership.

Principle 4 | Research: We will engage in conceptual and empirical research that advances our understanding about the role, dynamics, and impact of corporations in the creation of sustainable social, environmental and economic value.

Principle 5 | Partnership: We will interact with managers of business corporations to extend our knowledge of their challenges in meeting social and environmental responsibilities and to explore jointly effective approaches to meeting these challenges.

Principle 6 | Dialogue: We will facilitate and support dialog and debate among educators, students, business, government, consumers, media, civil society organisations and other interested groups and stakeholders on critical issues related to global social responsibility and sustainability.

Business's effects on Indigenous aspirations and rights

An introduction

Amy Klemm Verbos, Ph.D.
University of Wisconsin-Whitewater, USA

Ella Henry, Ph.D.
Auckland University of Technology, New Zealand

Ana Maria Peredo, Ph.D.
University of Victoria, Canada

In accordance with Indigenous prophecies, 13 Indigenous grandmothers from several continents met and formed an International Council of Thirteen Indigenous Grandmothers to bring Indigenous teachings and prayer to heal the world (Schaefer, 2006). Beginning in 2005, they held a cycle of 13 subsequent official gatherings, with each grandmother holding a gathering in her home place (International Council of Thirteen Indigenous Grandmothers, n.d.). The grandmothers offered a hopeful vision for mother Earth if we begin to remember our interconnectedness and the need to live in peace and harmony with each other and with nature (Schaefer, 2006). Nevertheless, the wisdom, knowledge, culture, spirit, and the very lives of the world's approximately 370 million Indigenous peoples in about 90 countries remain at risk (see, for example, Reading, 2015).

Following decades of discussion and negotiation, the United Nations General Assembly adopted the Declaration on the Rights of Indigenous Peoples (DRIP) on September 13, 2007. The vote was 143 states for, Australia, Canada, New Zealand and the United States opposed, and 11 states abstained (Azerbaijan, Bangladesh, Bhutan, Burundi, Colombia, Georgia, Kenya, Nigeria, Russian Federation, Samoa and Ukraine) (United Nations Human Rights, 2016). Australia, Canada, New

Zealand,[1] and the United States subsequently changed their positions to support the DRIP, although future policy shifts are possible.

The DRIP's 46 Articles affirm, reaffirm, recognize, and acknowledge Indigenous peoples' political, legal, economic, cultural, human, labor, land, spiritual, religious, language, and educational self-determination rights, other inherent rights, rights granted in international law or elsewhere, citizenship rights, cultural protection against forced assimilation, and a right to free, prior, and informed consent to matters that may affect them. Article 33 is of particular note, as it gives Indigenous peoples the right of self-identification, deciding through their own procedures who does or does not have membership in their institutions. For that reason, we do not define Indigenous peoples here, but defer to the United Nations approach instead. The legal status of Indigenous peoples as Indigenous within the countries in which they dwell has significant consequences with respect to their rights, as Kayseas *et al.* explain in Chapter 5.

The DRIP acknowledges that Indigenous peoples have been systematically denied their rights the world over and calls upon states to support, protect, and defend them (United Nations, 2008). Indigenous peoples' rights are often denied under color of law. States may act on behalf of, in concert with, or turn a blind eye to actions by business. Both legal and illegal actions quash Indigenous rights and aspirations in alarming ways throughout an increasingly global business environment. It is our intention not only to surface some of these issues but to offer some guidance to move toward more positive futures when business action intersects with Indigenous peoples' rights under the DRIP. The United Nations (UN) Global Compact and its educational initiative, the Principles for Responsible Management Education (PRME), present an institutional framework for voluntary action and a way to direct corporate attention toward this much neglected area of corporate social responsibility.

UN initiatives and the need for this book

The UN Global Compact began in 2000 as an ambitious, voluntary, global corporate social responsibility initiative centered on Ten Principles relating to the intersection of business and human rights, labor rights, environmental degradation, and corruption. As of this writing, 9,000 businesses and 3,000 non-business organizations are committed to the Principles, to continuously improving human and labor rights practices and reducing environmental degradation and corruption in the global economy, and to reporting on their progress (United Nations Global Compact, 2017b).

---

1 The Māori Party, the indigenous political party, held the balance of power and was able to negotiate a change of heart in 2010.

Through this initiative, a perceived need surfaced to alter business education in such a way that future managers become aware of the potential negative impacts of business activities and embrace the need for business to contribute toward solving some of the most vexing problems facing humanity across the globe. In 2007, a 60-person Steering Committee including major business school deans and/or other academic representatives, co-convened with the UN Global Compact, AACSB International, European Foundation for Management Development (EFMD), The Aspen Institute Business and Society Program, European Academy of Business in Society (EABIS), Globally Responsible Leadership Initiative (GRLI), and Net Impact, a business student organization, to craft and publish the Principles for Responsible Management Education (PRME) (PRME Secretariat, 2017a). The PRME engage business educators, students, and the business community to develop future corporate leaders' capabilities to work toward a more sustainable future for business and society, and to build a more inclusive and sustainable global economy. To date, more than 650 educational institutions are signatories to the PRME, bringing about change in management education by committing to the Principles, continuous improvement toward realizing this purpose, and sharing progress (PRME Secretariat, 2017b).

Under both the UN Global Compact and the PRME, participants report on progress toward their continuous improvement commitments to the respective principles. Each participant is not required to do all things well, but focus attention according to its priorities. Most participants in these initiatives, corporate managers, professors, instructors, and students who will be future managers, could learn from Indigenous perspectives and do much more to understand, respect, and uphold Indigenous peoples' rights (see, e.g., Verbos *et al.*, 2011; Verbos and Humphries, 2014, 2015a, 2015b). This volume is an effort to assist in this process.

Notably, the UN Global Compact acknowledges the role of business relative to the plight of Indigenous peoples, and connects the DRIP to Human Rights Principles 1 and 2 in its Business Reference Guide to the DRIP (BRG), published in 2013. The UN Global Compact has subsequently published cases and webinars in an effort to engage the business community in recognizing Indigenous rights (see, for example, United Nations Global Compact, 2017a). It is the confluence of these UN initiatives, the Global Compact, the PRME, the DRIP, and the BRG, that inspired this volume.

The BRG places a strong focus on the full, prior, and informed consent aspect of dealing with Indigenous peoples. This is certainly a good start and several chapters of this book demonstrate a great need for better practices in interactions between business and Indigenous peoples relative to this consent. Moreover, and perhaps more importantly, there is a need for greater understanding of not only Indigenous peoples' rights, but also their aspirations. In this, Western assumptions of economic development and progress do not necessarily apply (Peredo and McLean, 2013). Many Indigenous peoples are not acquisitive and do not want to trade their traditional livelihoods for Western-style employment, especially at the expense of their respective territories, sacred spaces, cultural practices, and the health of the natural environment.

The chapter authors have undertaken to tell stories through cases about how business intersects with Indigenous peoples from an Indigenous perspective. This is something that is missing in management education (Verbos and Humphries, 2015a, 2016), yet is vital to understanding Indigenous peoples' aspirations, and to enabling better understanding, positive change, and greater self-determination when business intersects with Indigenous peoples' territories, sacred and cultural places, and the land and environment that sustains them.

It would be impossible to cover the entire landscape of issues emerging from how businesses deal with Indigenous peoples when rights collide, coexist, or coincide. In the three sections of this book we have endeavored to provide scholarly cases from various continents, industries and, to the extent possible, through Indigenous scholars. We also appreciate our non-Indigenous chapter authors and their respectful research bringing to light Indigenous perspectives. In the first section, the cases are, from an Indigenous perspective, failures by businesses in relationship to Indigenous peoples. The second section examines ongoing challenges faced by Indigenous peoples dealing with global business, and includes some frameworks for better understanding and engagement. The third section delves into areas in which Indigenous aspirations and rights may align with business interests to produce positive outcomes. These come with appropriate doses of caution. The book concludes with how these cases may inform businesses intersecting Indigenous peoples' rights and aspirations, what might be done toward greater understanding and support for these rights by participants and non-participants in the UN Global Compact, and a call for greater education in business schools and beyond in order to protect, support, and defend the rights of Indigenous peoples under the DRIP, most especially the right to self-determination for Indigenous peoples.

Section I: Indigenous perspectives on failures

This section casts an eye across different regions, peoples, and industry sectors. These chapters reflect on Indigenous experiences, and explore how the manner in which business and government intersect with Indigenous peoples can lead to failures. It acknowledges the ways that Indigenous peoples assess failure in these instances. The aim is to offer case studies providing new insights for business students and business organizations, about ways that they can adopt more responsible behavior, strategies, policies and programs for their interaction with Indigenous peoples. The fundamental premise of this section is that such changes will achieve more mutually beneficial outcomes. Although not all of these cases resulted in catastrophic failure, they exemplify how business and/or government do not fully appreciate, recognize, respect, and protect Indigenous aspirations and wellbeing, despite the DRIP.

Chapter 1, "A Business Case Examined through an Indigenous Lens" by Carma Claw, Deanna Kennedy, and Deborah Pembleton, explores how Pendleton Woolen Mills' business decisions have, over time, impacted its Native American customer base. Pendleton, renowned by Native Americans for its blankets and clothing using Native and Native-inspired designs, served its Native customers well for over one hundred years. However, recent changes in strategy have made its products increasingly unaffordable for many of its traditional Indigenous customers. Claw *et al.* consider these issues from the business side, and the theory of corporate social responsibility. They use an Indigenous lens to consider cultural appropriation and issues it invokes, noting "the lack of attention to Indigenous perspectives when Indigenous culture is appropriated or affected is a failure on the part of corporate social responsibility" (p. 20).

In Chapter 2, "The Dark Side of Responsible Business Management," Dennis Foley explores the less researched harmful effects of emulating Western business practices in Indigenous enterprise. He acknowledges the critical role of business in Indigenous economic development. However, Foley explains that business enterprise may not be a panacea for Indigenous peoples, given the devastating impacts that business can have on those attempting to inculcate and replicate the Eurocentric, capitalist business model. Among other problems, he identifies high levels of stress, early death, and alienation, which temper the positive effects of increased self-determination. In terms of Aboriginal business development, "Government may have good intentions but realistically they are blind in policy development, lacking empirical data and/or community interaction to understand the impact of modern enterprise creation" (p. 22), which Foley labels the dark side of Indigenous entrepreneurship.

Chapter 3, "Environmental Crisis in New Zealand: Tribal, Government and Business Responses to the Sinking of the MV *Rena*," is by Ella Henry and Hugh Sayers who explore the 2011 grounding of an international vessel in New Zealand waters and its impacts on the small, local tribe whose island is closest to the reef upon which the ship went aground. The sinking of the *Rena* has been described as New Zealand's worst maritime environmental disaster. This event brought together the vessel owners, Greek shipping company Costamare, local tribes, and a wide range of New Zealand governmental agencies charged with managing different aspects of the event: marine, social, judicial, and those relating to Māori. Henry and Sayers find that

> This case highlights the ongoing need for vigilance on the part of Indigenous peoples to protect their rights and resources. It also focuses on the need for governments to adhere to international agreements to which they are party. Finally, it invokes businesses to deal with Indigenous peoples in a respectful way (p. 45).

Benedict Imbun's chapter, "The Chinese, Political CSR, and a Nickel Mine in Papua New Guinea," builds on the work of Scherer and Palazzo (2011) on political corporate social responsibility, focusing on the increasingly important role played by large multinational corporations in countries characterized by a weak state. Imbun looks at the Chinese-operated Ramu Nickel Mine (RNM) in an isolated region of Papua New Guinea. He analyzes the pressures and challenges faced by local communities, despite RNM's Community Development Strategy. He concludes,

> RNM management recognize the growing criticisms of its operations and expectations of greater benefits for the local communities. They have wielded political corporate social responsibility as a corporate strategy to satisfy government and appease local communities. Members of those communities believe that RNM has a moral obligation to contribute as much energy to their economic and social development needs as it does to exploiting the local communities for its mining endeavors (p. 57).

Notably, Papua New Guinea was not present for the vote on the DRIP.

Section II: Business and ongoing challenges to Indigenous aspirations and rights

The second section of the book addresses some of the daunting ongoing challenges faced by Indigenous peoples worldwide and the inadequacy of current forms of justice and engagement. Although the chapters are largely from the Americas, the issues raised occur the world over. Chapter 5, "Indigenous Rights Capital: The Basis for Sustainable Enterprise Creation," is a collaborative effort by Bob Kayseas, Bettina Schneider, Raquel Pasap, Moses Gordon, and Robert Anderson. They recount a brief historical and legal overview of Indigenous Canadians' rights, from the First Nations relationships with the Canadian Government, legal impediments to full recognition of First Nations rights, and the rights issues impacting First Nations' economies. Kayseas *et al.* highlight the complexities and paradoxes faced by Indigenous peoples dealing with the legacies of colonialism while working to maintain their Indigenous identities as participants in the modern world. Then, they examine the case of the Fishing Lake First Nation vis-à-vis the Canadian Government, the province of Saskatchewan, and with respect to a potash mine planned for the areas near their territory. Kayseas *et al.* find that the voice given the Fishing Lake First Nations by law, treaty, and inherent sovereign rights resulted in a confidential agreement with the mining company that will give the people, among other things, joint venture opportunities to provide services to the company as well as undisclosed community development benefits.

In Chapter 6, "Indigenous Human Rights Perils as an Ongoing Challenge," Amy Klemm Verbos focuses on human rights violations against Indigenous peoples, by or for the benefit of businesses, and limited legal redress available to them. The first case is that of Honduran Indigenous human rights and environmental activist Berta Cáceres, murdered on March 3, 2016 for her work in opposition to the Agua

Zarca Dam on behalf of the Lenca people. Cáceres is but one higher profile murder in a global murder epidemic of Indigenous and non-Indigenous land and environmental protectors. In the second case, Verbos turns attention to Texaco, Inc., its successor Chevron Corporation, and legal strategies to avoid redress to Indigenous Peruvian and Ecuadorian people for its environmentally disastrous spill of 18 billion gallons of oil and toxic waste in the Amazon. It highlights United States court rulings in delaying and defeating these claims over the period of 1993 to 2016. This chapter demonstrates that Indigenous people may find justice under the law elusive and there is a great need to educate the corporate sector, bring greater visibility to the plights of Indigenous peoples, and move corporations toward respect for Indigenous peoples' rights and more constructive action in keeping with the DRIP and the BRG.

Finnish scholar, Susanna Myllylä gives Indigenous perspectives on Finnish logging in Brazil in Chapter 7, "Reclaiming Pluriverse in CSR: Brazilian Indigenous Peoples and the Finnish Forest Cluster." Using a bottom up qualitative method, she explores how Finnish companies engaged with the Tupinikim, Guaraní, and Pataxó peoples, including how Indigenous and Western perspectives were not consonant. She explains that a "pluriverse" is a world in which many worlds fit harmoniously. Her corporate-community relations framework with 22 responsibilities of engagement intends to move the status quo from corporate dominance and Indigenous resistance to positive integration of differing perspectives of business and Indigenous peoples.

In the last chapter in this section, Chapter 8, "Community–Business Dialogues," Natalia Delgado outlines international law relative to biological Indigenous knowledge and how it relates to the UN Global Compact and BRG, among other international initiatives. She critically examines three pilot cases from Peru, Brazil, and Madagascar that implemented participatory and dialogic practices toward the concept of free, prior, and informed consent, but did not achieve the hoped-for results. In part, this is because the corporate and community worldviews and objectives did not align. Delgado concludes "it is critical that efforts aiming at integrative and transformative types of interaction respectfully recognize the political and cultural needs and aspirations of communities in order to promote community rights in practice" (p. 113).

Section III: Modelling success for Indigenous and business interests

The third section of the book, "Modelling success for Indigenous and business interests," includes four case studies that document and analyze forms of business or engagement that could be considered successful from an Indigenous perspective. Chapter 9, "A Business Quest for Peace," is by Nigerian Yoruban researchers

Douglas Adeola and Ogechi Adeola. They record the peace process aimed at ending the petro-violence in the oil-rich Niger Delta. The chapter outlines the ways that the Ijaws, Itsekiris, and Ilajes Indigenous people advocated for their rights, and how the company responded through community engagement.

In Chapter 10, titled "Everything is One? Relationships between First Nations and Salmon Farming Companies," Norwegian scholar Lars Huemer asks "can this sense of unity and shared destiny be developed between First Nations and corporations?" (p. 130). Salmon farming is controversial, but can community good be facilitated through corporate relationships? Huemer documents the evolution of two types of relationships, and the different types of learnings that arose in the collaboration between the Ahousaht and Tla-o-qui-aht First Nations and salmon farming corporations.

Chapter 11, "Strong Indigenous Communities: Indigenous Worldviews and Sustainable Community Development," is provided by American Indian scholars, Keith James and Mark Blair. They present a case study of a multiple party, sustainable development collaboration in the interior of Alaska. James and Blair document and argue for the benefits of incorporating Indigenous worldviews and rights at the foundation of planning for regional sustainability.

Chapter 12, the final chapter of this section, "Hupacasath First Nation: Roadmap to a Sustainable Economy" comes from Judith Kekinusuqs Sayers and Ana Maria Peredo. Sayers and Peredo examine the path that one First Nation community followed to build economic independence and self-governance. By means of a business partnership, Hupacasath became a model for clean energy development in the province of British Columbia, Canada. The chapter discusses the community processes behind the economic development and specifically explores two joint ventures.

Conclusion

We are optimistic that greater understanding of Indigenous perspectives on what constitutes a successful relationship between Indigenous peoples and business, and greater respect for and engagement with these perspectives, are key to realizing prosperity and wellbeing for all. Issues of cultural appropriation (Chapter 1 and Chapter 8), environmental disasters (Chapters 3 and 6), extractive industries (Chapters 4, 5, 6, and 9), forestry (Chapter 7), bio-trade (Chapter 8), legal and human rights (Chapters 3, 4, 5, 6, 7, and 8), Indigenous worldviews (highlighted throughout the book but most notably covered by Chapters 2, 4, 7, 8, 11, and 12), and engagement with Indigenous peoples (Chapters 7, 8, 9, 10, and 11) are but some of the areas in which there are opportunities for business to aim efforts at continuous improvement under the UN Global Compact, the BRG, and beyond that to recognizing and supporting Indigenous peoples' rights under the DRIP.

References

International Council of Thirteen Indigenous Grandmothers (n.d.) *Official Note of Clarification*. Retrieved from http://www.unprme.org/about-prme/history/index.php

Peredo, A.M. & McLean, M. (2013). Indigenous development and cultural captivity of entrepreneurship. *Business and Society*, 52(4), 592-620.

PRME Secretariat (2017a). About Us: History. Retrieved from http://www.unprme.org/about-prme/history/index.php

PRME Secretariat (2017b). Participants: Signatories. Retrieved from http://www.unprme.org/participants/index.php

Reading, J. (Ed.) (2015). *The State of the World's Indigenous Peoples: Indigenous Peoples' Access to Health Services* (Vol. 2). New York, NY: United Nations Secretariat of the Permanent Forum on Indigenous Issues. Retrieved from http://www.un.org/esa/socdev/unpfii/documents/2015/sowip2volume-ac.pdf

Schaefer, C. (2006). *Grandmothers Counsel the World: Women Elders Offer Their Vision for Our Planet*. Boston, MA: Trumpeter Books.

United Nations (2008). United Nations Declaration on the Rights of Indigenous Peoples. Retrieved from http://www.un.org/esa/socdev/unpfii/documents/DRIPS_en.pdf

United Nations Global Compact (2017a). Indigenous Peoples. Retrieved from https://www.unglobalcompact.org/what-is-gc/our-work/social/indigenous-people

United Nations Global Compact (2017b). Our participants. Retrieved from https://www.unglobalcompact.org/what-is-gc/participants

United Nations Human Rights (2016). Declaration on the rights of indigenous peoples. Retrieved from http://www.ohchr.org/EN/Issues/IPeoples/Pages/Declaration.aspx

Verbos, A.K., Gladstone, J., & Kennedy, D. (2011). Native American values and management education: Envisioning an inclusive virtuous circle. *Journal of Management Education*, 35, 10-26.

Verbos, A.K. & Humphries, M.T. (2014). A Native American relational ethic: An Indigenous perspective on teaching human responsibility. *Journal of Business Ethics*, 123(1), 1-9.

Verbos, A.K. & Humphries, M.T. (2015a). Amplifying a relational ethic: A contribution to PRME praxis. *Business and Society Review*, 120(1), 23-56.

Verbos, A.K. & Humphries, M.T. (2015b). Indigenous wisdom and the PRME: Inclusion or illusion? *Journal of Management Development* [Special Issue on the Unfulfilled Promise of the PRME], 34(1), 90-100.

Section I
Indigenous Perspectives on Failures

1

A business case examined through an Indigenous lens

Carma M. Claw
Doctoral Student, New Mexico State University; Diné Nation citizen

Deanna M. Kennedy, Ph.D.
Assistant Professor, University of Washington Bothell; Cherokee Nation of Oklahoma member

Deborah Pembleton, Ph.D.
Assistant Professor of Global Business Leadership, College of St. Benedict/St. John's University

We discuss the intersection between business decision-making and Indigenous perspectives that is central to the United Nations Declaration on the Rights of Indigenous Peoples. We acknowledge that currently there is a condition of invisibility about Indigenous perspectives and we want to help change this pattern. To address this need we will bring forward a recent business case that can serve as an example of the struggles Indigenous peoples have with business decisions by those outside of the Native culture. We consider the issues from the business side and the theory of corporate social responsibility; we also use an Indigenous lens to consider the case and the cultural appropriateness issues it invokes. Discussions that bring in both sides of the case can help the management of responsible futures.

Cultural appropriation, Native design, Business strategy

Introduction

In 2007 the United Nations Declaration on the Rights of Indigenous Peoples was adopted, and the 46 articles of the Declaration set forth individual and collective Indigenous rights (see p. 178, "Appendix"). However, the document was not easily applied to business practices involving Indigenous peoples. In 2010 a new project was initiated to promote better business engagement with Indigenous peoples. This culminated in the 2013 publication of the *Business Reference Guide to the UN Declaration on the Rights of Indigenous Peoples* (the "Guide"). The Guide offers advice and examples to develop and promote understanding, respect, and support of the rights of Indigenous peoples during business activities.

To help attune our future managers to Indigenous perspectives, we suggest including in business education issues that are particularly focused on Indigenous cultural issues. Moreover, we believe that business educators should be looking at local, national, and international Indigenous business stories as practical learning objects for business decision-makers. Herein we discuss a current business practice that has evolved over time and consider how decisions about the future implicitly create a paradox between the organization and its customer. Specifically, we discuss Pendleton's "Native American Inspired" line of products.

The Pendleton business case

Pendleton Woolen Mill started with Thomas Kay, a young English weaver, in 1863. His daughter and her husband, retail merchant, C.P. Bishop, further developed the company from operating as a wool-scouring plant to a dual textile-retail operation. The new business model continued with the three Bishop sons who, in 1893, started a separate wool scouring plant in Pendleton, Oregon. Due to market conditions and the increased shipping costs of wool, the plant became increasingly unprofitable. In 1895, the plant expanded and reestablished itself as a woolen mill producing blankets and robes for Native Americans. But, that venture also failed. However, in 1909, the Bishops created a new and improved facility that became the Pendleton Woolen Mills.[1]

Pendleton Woolen Mills continued its strategy as a trading company, producing blankets specifically to serve Native American customers. Indeed, during the early years, Pendleton's designer would conduct "market research" by visiting local Natives in northeastern Oregon to better understand the patterns that would be of interest. Later, the designer would visit Natives in the Southwest, including Navajo country, to gather information about the colors and patterns that those Native

---

1 "Company history." Pendleton. Retrieved from https://www.pendleton-usa.com/ custserv/custserv.jsp?pageName=CompanyHistory&parentName=Heritage

communities preferred. This led to many brilliantly colored blankets with detailed patterns that were very popular among a number of tribal members.[2]

At the time of writing, Pendleton is still a privately held company headquartered in Portland, Oregon with operations based in Pendleton, serving additional markets for woolen products. The Bishop family created this successful operation by working closely with tribes to create designs that would appeal to them.[3] From births, graduations, and wedding celebrations to ceremonies and memorial services, products from Pendleton's "Native American Inspired" line are highly prized and highly valued pieces given as indications of accomplishment, achievement, and recognition in Native American societies. Mandi Rae Henderson of the Blackfeet people wrote a poem about a sleeping baby girl, entitled "Dreams Wrapped in a Pendleton Blanket" (2005). It illustrates how truly infused Pendleton "products" are in Native American societies. Another example is that of the Diné[4] (Navajo) who wear gender-specific blankets in precise protocols to communicate specific ceremonial significance; for example, males wear a robe-style Pendleton blanket draped in a specific fashion while females wear blankets with fringes, again wrapped on the body in a specific manner. Before the arrival of Pendleton blankets, the Diné wove their own blankets and other textiles. The Diné believe that one of the Holy People, a deity of the Nation named Spider Woman, taught The People to weave. They "were weaving cloth from wild cotton" (Locke, 2001, p. 33) before the Spanish introduced sheep and wool for weaving in the 16th century. Such woven materials were used in conjunction with animal skins and furs. And, given that the origin story of weaving is associated with a deity, such work is imbued with philosophical and spiritual meanings (Locke, 2001). The market for blankets existed in Dinétah (Navajo territory), as well as other Indian nations, long before Pendleton offered its products to serve similar functions. Further evidence of such historical and cultural significance is clear, according to blanket collector, Friedman (2015, p. 2), who notes that antique blankets, "can sell for as much as $20,000 if they're in pristine condition and from before 1900" because Indians once owned them.

Diversifying and reaching other demographics

However, while Pendleton has a great history of serving its original Native American consumers, recently, there has been a change in marketing and growth strategies for the company. Collaborations with high-end retailers and development of projects which may distance this original customer base have emerged. The result of such developments is that Native American inspired products are now offered at exceedingly exorbitant prices, which many Native customers cannot afford.

2 "Indian trading blanket history." Pendleton. Retrieved from https://www.pendleton-usa.com/custserv/custserv.jsp?pageName=IndianTrading&parentName=Heritage

3 *Ibid.*

4 Diné is the term used by Navajos to identify themselves; it is translated to mean "The People." Diné and Navajo will be used interchangeably in this work.

Examples of such partnerships include those with Opening Ceremony, Nike, Urban Outfitters, and Hurley.[5] Each partner employs Pendleton's Native American inspired designs for its product lines. Additionally, Comme des Garçons is "a Japanese label that snips and sews patches of corduroy, canvas or leather onto Pendleton shirts that sell in Paris for $1,600" (Gunderson, 2009).

Questionable projects

A recent project that can be viewed as culturally questionable is that of using white buffalo hair blended with wool to produce "medicine blankets," as reported by *Indian Country Today* newspaper (ICMN Staff, 2010). White buffalo are revered as sacred entities by some nations like the Lakota Sioux (American Indian College Fund, 2012). "The white buffalo's presence is a prophesy of spiritual rebirth—an indicator of better times coming to tribal people," said Jim Stone, a Yankton-Yanktonai Sioux (Associated Press, 2014). According to ICMN, "[t]he first 11 special collectible blankets will run $5,250 each, featuring the name of one of the 11 white buffalo on them." There are 11 white buffalos on the ranch where the white hair will be obtained. Another example is using Geronimo as a marketing icon to sell the "Geronimo" blanket (Woolen Mill Store, 2011). According to Pendleton history, the Geronimo blanket is a tribute to him; the design of the Pendleton blanket was inspired by a blanket Geronimo wore in photos,[6] most likely after 1894 when he was a prisoner of war in the state of Oklahoma (Gaffney, 2008). Geronimo is widely perceived in American culture as the epitome of Native American "warriors." He sought revenge against Mexicans for the murder of his family and his tribe, the Chiricahua Apaches, and quarreled with non-Indian settlers for encroaching on their territory (Debo, 1979). He surrendered to the U.S. in 1886 after a long, hard fight (Gaffney, 2008). Geronimo attended Theodore Roosevelt's second inauguration ceremony in 1905 (Gaffney, 2008) for what may have been his final request, but he died as a prisoner at Fort Sill, Oklahoma. "He died of pneumonia on February 17, 1909" (Cavendish, 2009, p. 1) after many failed requests to return to his home in New Mexico. Pendleton has recently stopped making the Geronimo blanket;[7] therefore, the rarity of the blanket is likely to create a demand for it and increase the price of existing blankets.

Serving their original customers

The Pendleton company continues to work with Native American designers to create new products and designs, sometimes for specific Native organizations or events like the Adopt-A-Native-Elder program or the National Indian Education

---

5 Hurley by Pendleton. Retrieved from https://www.pendleton-usa.com/custserv/custserv.jsp?pageName=Hurley&parentName=AboutUs

6 Geronimo Blanket. Pendleton. Retrieved from https://www.pendleton-usa.com/product/GERONIMO-BLANKET/166756/fs/true.uts

7 *Ibid.*

Association (NIEA) and the UNITY (United National Indian Tribal Youth) commemorative event. Pendleton also provides a Legendary Series that invites selected artists to propose designs. For example, a Navajo story inspired artist Andrew Hobson to represent the buffalo creation story on a colorful Pendleton blanket. Other artists from the Navajo, Blackfeet, and Chickasaw Nations have also contributed and been selected for blankets designs with cultural inspirations over the years.

Pendleton attributes some designs to "the beliefs and traditions of their original and most valued customers".[8] The legacy of its heritage in Native American commerce is demonstrated by its contributions to organizations like the American Indian College Fund collection (Horwedel, 2015), and its partnership with Nike N7.[9]

While some may view Pendleton as acting honorably because it publically recognizes its strong Native American customer base and acknowledges its roots as an "Indian Trading Blanket" company, others are not convinced. For one Native commentator,

> ... seeing hipsters march down the street in Pendleton clothes, seeing these bloggers ooh and ahh over how "cute" these designs are, and seeing non-Native models all wrapped up in Pendleton blankets makes me upset. It's a complicated feeling, because I feel ownership over these designs as a Native person, but on a rational level I realize that they aren't necessarily ours to claim. To me, it just feels like one more thing non-Natives can take from us—like our land, our moccasins, our headdresses, our beading, our religions, our names, our *cultures* weren't enough? You gotta go and take Pendleton designs too? (Keene, 2011).

The business perspective and corporate social responsibility

We measure the social impact of the Pendleton case against the generally accepted definition of corporate social responsibility (CSR). For Blowfield CSR is:

> an umbrella term for a variety of theories and practices all of which recognize the following:
> a) that companies have a responsibility for their impact on society and the natural environment, sometimes beyond legal compliance and the liability of individuals;

8 "Indian trading blanket history." Pendleton. Retrieved from https://www.pendleton-usa.com/custserv/custserv.jsp?pageName=IndianTrading&parentName=Heritage
9 "Nike N7 is committed to inspiring and enabling participation in sport for Native American and Aboriginal populations in North America" (retrieved from http://www.pendleton-usa.com/catalog/search.cmd?form_state=searchForm&keyword=N7&keyword_entry=N7).

b) that companies have a responsibility for the behavior of others with whom they do business (e.g. within supply chains); and

c) that business needs to manage its relationship with wider society, whether for reasons of commercial viability or to add value to society (Blowfield, 2008, p. 503).

With this in mind we question what is the social responsibility of the Pendleton company to the Indigenous people impacted by its marketing strategy? We also question to what extent does the Pendleton company value the importance of the cultural legacies of the Indigenous peoples it purports to work closely with, particularly in relation to their profitability? Further, we ask whether this product strategy adds value to the lives of the Indigenous peoples, from whom the designs originated, and who may be culturally and spiritually affected by the appropriation and sale of such things as the white buffalo hair-blend or Geronimo blankets?

The Indigenous perspective and cultural appropriation

For American Indians, the concept of officially addressing cultural appropriation may have started when the National Congress of American Indians (NCAI) launched a campaign in 1968 to "address stereotypes of Native people in popular culture and media, as well as in sports" (NCAI, 2014). NCAI was created more than two decades before, in 1944, as one of the first encompassing Native organizations and is now the "largest and most representative American Indian and Alaska Native organization," serving tribal governments and communities.[10] However, the practice of purloining Indigenous knowledge and culture can be traced back to times long before 1944 and it continues to occur. Ziff and Rao's seminal book *Borrowed Power: Essays on Cultural Appropriation* defined cultural appropriation as "the taking—from a culture that is not one's own—of intellectual property, cultural expressions or artifacts, history and ways of knowledge" (1997, p. 1). A framework of cultural transmission used by Ziff and Rao (1997) puts the power structure of subordinate and dominant at the center of the phenomenon.

Figure 1 provides a parsimonious view of the cultural transmission model by Ziff and Rao (1997). The dichotomy of cultural assimilation (subordinate) *or* cultural appropriation (dominant) is illustrated with inputs from various sources of cultural capital including industrial, ideological, economic, political, institutional, and military (Ziff and Rao, 1997, p. 6). The dynamics is that if an entity is in a subordinate position, the cultural transmission of a foreign object is through assimilation, and vice versa; if dominant, it is through appropriation. Shanley's (1997) work specifically addresses such practices of absconding Native American objects, both tangible and intangible, resulting in an accelerated state of "… a people's being left

10 "Welcome to NCAI." Retrieved from: http://www.ncai.org/

'without' a specific history or language, and that such cultural appropriations inextricably belong to overall totalization efforts—the political and ideological domination of Indigenous American peoples by the mainstream culture" (Shanley, 1997, p. 675). Additionally, Riley and Carpenter (2016) coin the term **Indian appropriation** to situate the phenomenon in a legal context for American Indians as "the process by which the U.S. legal system has historically facilitated and normalized the taking of all things Indian for others' use, from lands to sacred objects, and from bodies to identities" (Riley and Carpenter, 2016, p. 3). The overarching essence of cultural appropriation is *mis*appropriation. The concept is imbued with colonial history and roots, and because of its many facets, like the innumerable sources of cultural capital, differing methods of how transfer occurs, and the context in which the thefts occur, as well as the definitions of the terms, culture and appropriation, it is a difficult and complex subject. The range of work of numerous scholars (Claw, 2016; Cuthbert, 1998; Deloria, 1969; Keeshig-Tobias, 1997; Polak, 2011; Barbour, 2015; Roemer, 2012; Tsosie, 2002) discussing the phenomenon is broad, ranging from elements including songs and stories to images, traditional knowledge and skills to textiles, and ceremonies and rituals to the identity of the peoples themselves. The phenomenon is pervasive and normative.

Figure 1.1 **Cultural transmission summarized from Ziff and Rao (1997)**

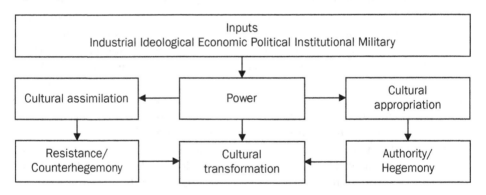

Applying the works of these, and copious other scholars, to the situation of the Pendleton case concludes that Pendleton is committing a form of cultural appropriation as they divert from the Indian blanket enterprise to new markets. Perhaps the distinction is its route through cooptation of property in that the original intent and purpose of the products seems to have changed from, designed by and for Native American consumers, to extending the products to an elite target market not easily accessible by the former. The tendency to consolidate Indigenous peoples into a larger group contributes to the misunderstandings of what "property" is and navigating the rules of what belongs to who, if they do at all. In Diné (Navajo)

many images, songs, and materials belong to the Diyin Dine'é (Holy People).[11] Roemer's (2012) title *It's Not a Poem. It's My Life* reveals the habitual fallacy that taking works out of context makes them *just* literature, art, song, etc. It does not. They are still connected to lives, albeit, in a fragmented way.

However, there is also an understanding within Indigenous communities that they do not exist in seclusion (Gladstone and Claw, 2016). Not only are Natives impacted by historical events of assimilation and thus continue to experience the imposed hegemony—that is behaving as an Indian is *expected* to (Deloria, 1969)— they are also very much still connected to and are an expression of their "old ways." This includes using items like Pendleton blankets for cultural purposes.

Further, innovation is not a new concept in Native societies, nor is interacting with others. Native societies have always found ways to adapt, advance, and exist with other tribal nations. There seems to be a perception that prosperity is incompatible with Native cultures, but Indigenous peoples *do* seek wealth. Wealth is essential to living a harmonious life. Native nations had self-sustaining economies long before the disruption of colonialism. For example, commerce existed between Pueblo Nations and the Navajo before the arrival of the Spanish (Locke, 2001). Additionally, remnants of "One of the greatest cities of the world, Cahokia was larger than London was in AD 1250," located in the state of Illinois, is evidence of trade and exchange activities in ancient Native cultures.[12] But, sometimes what is viewed and defined as wealth and prosperity in Native communities is also lost in translation, because wealth is not all that matters, but rather, is a part of a holistic Indigenous existence. In Diné philosophy, there is balance and moderation in all things to ensure harmony and the accumulation of wealth is not exempt from that idea. Wealth is not about an individual's amassing of materials, but about how much there is for the family (Locke, 2001). There is also the concept of family itself being the wealth and treasure of people. Ultimately, there *is* a way to negotiate and adapt to new circumstances because Native nations have done it from time immemorial.

Conclusion

In this chapter, we focused on a current business issue that has implications for business as well as native peoples. Our purpose is to show that a business case can have two sides to the story, one from the perspective of the business that accounts for its needs and goals, and the other from the perspective of the customer that has formed a relationship with the business. In the case of Pendleton blankets, the customer's perspective comes from the Indigenous peoples that have been an integral

---

11 The Diyin Dine'é, the Holy People, are the deities of the Diné (Navajo).
12 Cahokia Mounds State Historic Site. Retrieved from: http://cahokiamounds.org/

part of the business's success in the past. Whereas it is easy to focus only on the business perspective as our textbooks do, we hope to bring both mainstream business principles and Indigenous perspectives to the discussion. Moreover, the lack of attention to Indigenous perspectives when Indigenous culture is appropriated or affected is a failure on the part of corporate social responsibility; one that we hope companies reorganize, and address to rectify. By having a richer discussion, which will occur when both sides are represented, we can train the managers of the future to have better, more informed business and mutually beneficial engagement with Indigenous peoples.

References

American Indian College Fund (2012, May 9). The meaning of the sacred white buffalo. Retrieved from http://collegefund.org/blog/the-meaning-of-the-sacred-white-buffalo/

Associated Press (2014, Dec 08). Pendleton to make white buffalo hair blend blankets. *Native Times*. Retrieved from http://www.nativetimes.com/index.php?option=com_content&view=article&id=4714:pendleton-to-make-white-buffalo-hair-blend-blankets&catid=40&Itemid=16 3.

Barbour, C. (2015). When Captain America Was an Indian: Heroic Masculinity, National Identity, and Appropriation. *The Journal of Popular Culture*, 48(2), 269-284.

Cavendish, R. (2009, Feb). Death of Geronimo. *History Today*, 59(2). Retrieved from http://www.historytoday.com/richard-cavendish/death-geronimo

Claw, C.M. (2016, Aug 8). Without reservation: The commodification of Native Americans. Academy of Management Annual Conference. Anaheim, CA.

Cuthbert, D. (1998). Beg, borrow or steal: the politics of cultural appropriation. *Postcolonial Studies*, 1(2), 257-262. doi: 10.1080/13688799890174

Deloria, V. (1969). *Custer died for your sins: An Indian manifesto*. University Oklahoma Press.

Debo, A. (1976). Geronimo: The man, his time, his place. History.com. Retrieved from http://www.history.com/topics/native-american-history/geronimo

Friedman, B. (2015, June 1). Q&A: Something you might not know about Navajo Blankets. Retrieved from https://www.arizonahighways.com/blog/qa-something-you-might-not-know-about-navajo-blankets

Gaffney, D. (2008). *Geronimo: Beyond the name*. Antiques Road Show. PBS.org. Retrieved from http://www.pbs.org/wgbh/roadshow/fts/sanantonio_200703A47.html.

Gladstone, J.S. & Claw, C. (2016). Coyote drives a Rez truck: A commentary on theoretical diversity. Unpublished manuscript. Las Cruces, NM: New Mexico State University.

Gunderson, L. (2009, Dec 22). Pendleton Woolen Mills blanketing the runways. The Oregonian/OregonLive. Retrieved from http://www.oregonlive.com/business/index.ssf/2009/12/pendleton_takes_its_plaid_to_t.html

Henderson, M.R. (2005). Dreams wrapped in a Pendleton Blanket. *Tribal College Journal*, 17(1).

Horwedel, D. (2015, April 8). Pendleton adds two new blanket designs to benefit college fund. College Fund News. Retrieved from http://www.collegefund.org/press/detail/310

ICMN Staff (2010, Dec 14). Pendleton to sell white buffalo-hair blankets. *Indian Country Media Network*. Retrieved from https://indiancountrymedianetwork.com/news/pendleton-to-sell-white-buffalo-hair-blankets/

Keene, A. (2011). Let's talk about Pendleton. Native Appropriations Forum. Retrieved from http://nativeappropriations.com/2011/02/lets-talk-about-pendleton.html

Keeshig-Tobias, L. (1997). Stop stealing native stories. In Ziff and Roa (Eds.) *Borrowed Power: Essays on cultural appropriation.* (pp. 337). New Brunswick, NJ: Rutgers University Press.

Locke, R.F. (2001). *The Book of the Navajo.* New York, NY: Holloway House Publishing.

National Congress of American Indians (2014). *Ending the era of harmful "Indian" mascots.* [Video File]. Retrieved from http://www.ncai.org/proudtobe

Pendleton Woolen Mills (2015, Sept 4). *Pendleton Woolen Mills Partners with Disney and Lucasfilm on Exclusive Limited Edition and Hand-Numbered Star Wars Blankets.* Retrieved from http://finance.yahoo.com/news/pendleton-woolen-mills-partners-disney-130000270.html

Polak, I. (2011). The one about coyote going West: Mimesis and ethics in multicultural literary landscapes of Canada and Australia. *Brno Studies in English,* 37(1), 173-190.

Riley, A.R., & Carpenter, K.A. (2016). Owning red: A theory of Indian (cultural) appropriation. *Texas Law Review,* 94(5), 859-931.

Roemer, K. (2012). It's not a poem. It's my life. Navajo singing identities. *Studies in American Indian Literatures,* 24(2), 84-103.

Shanley, K.W. (1997). The Indians America loves to love and read: American Indian identity and cultural appropriation. *American Indian Quarterly,* 21(4), 675-702.

Tsosie, R. (2002). Reclaiming Native stories: An essay on cultural appropriation and cultural rights. *Arizona State Law Journal,* 299(34), 311-14.

Woolen Mill Store (2011, Dec 5). Own a piece of Pendleton history. Pendleton Woolen Mill Store. Retrieved from http://thewoolenmillstore.blogspot.com/2011/12/own-piece-of-pendleton-history.html

Ziff, B.H., & Rao, P.V. (1997). *Borrowed power: Essays on cultural appropriation.* New Brunswick, NJ: Rutgers University Press.

2

The dark side of responsible business management

Dennis Foley, Ph.D.

Professor, University of Canberra, Australia; First Nation Australian of the Gai-mariagal people

Indigenous small business creation is an important mechanism within Indigenous economic development. However, neo-liberal philosophy while purportedly promoting wealth creation via modern Indigenous enterprise creation can, in reality, be misguided in its attempts to rebuild commercial enterprise and wealth that pre-existed for Aboriginal Australians prior to invasion. The state, thus, finances their own industry that supports the symptoms and not the causation of colonial poverty. Governments may have good intentions but realistically they are blind in policy development, lacking empirical data and/or community interaction to understand the impact of modern enterprise creation. This chapter provides an insight into some of the stressors of Aboriginal enterprise activity, from the Indigenous perspective.

Aboriginal entrepreneurship, Self-determination, Indigenous small business, Racism in business, Aboriginal business practice

Introduction

This chapter is a reflection of both research and experience in the Indigenous small business space, written for those interested in understanding some of the stressors experienced by Indigenous Australian entrepreneurs. The author is an Aboriginal business scholar who has owned and operated several enterprises. If policy-makers and a wider audience are better informed about Indigenous peoples and business, perhaps they can show more ethical and responsible behavior with increased positive interaction when dealing with Indigenous enterprises.

It is undeniable that Indigenous small business creation is an important mechanism within Indigenous economic development. Policies driven both by the state and nongovernment organizations (NGOs) recognize this. However, a dichotomy exists in neo-liberal philosophy, with reduced funding for welfare, education, and social support, while purportedly promoting wealth creation through Indigenous enterprise. We must acknowledge and accept that the cause of Indigenous welfare dependency and poverty is a direct outcome of colonization. Modern Indigenous enterprise creation is often a misguided attempt by the colonizer to rebuild commercial enterprise and wealth that existed for Aboriginals prior to invasion. The state, thus, finances the symptoms and not the causation of poverty. The state may have good intentions, but their implementation and foresight is similar to that of "Mr. Magoo": blind to policy that is often lacking empirical data and/or community interaction.[1]

The Aboriginal people of Australia have experienced countless poorly funded federal and state-run programs. Indeed, the following recognizes governmental policies that fail to deliver on a regular basis. "Entrenched disadvantage is also a product of failed policy. Our Indigenous reform agenda seeks to redress decades of underinvestment, buck-passing, confused responsibilities within our Federal system, and piecemeal and poorly targeted investments" (Australian Government, 2009).

Yet the buck-passing, confused responsibilities and failed policies continue. For Indigenous people to explore responsible business management practice we need leadership from our government, yet it continually fails us. For example, the Northern Territory Government has repeatedly failed to use commonwealth funds for their intended purposes, for those most in need of it (Langton, 2008). Thus, for Aboriginal Australians,

> ... when people repeatedly experience unpleasant events over which they have no control, they will not only experience trauma, but will come to act as if they believe that it is not possible to exercise control over any situation and that whatever they do is largely futile. As a result, they will be passive even in the face of harmful or damaging circumstances which it is actually possible to change.
>
> Coming to accept that others control your life, and that nothing you can do will really make much difference is already a crippling combination of attitudes. Add to it the well-known effect of the "self-fulfilling prophecy" and you have a recipe for the social disorder evident in varying degrees in many Indigenous communities (Lawrence, 2008).

---

1 A statement attributed to former Prime Minister Paul Keating when referring to the Howard Government, "they have good intentions with all the foresight of Mr. Magoo," a near-blind cartoon character.

This is the space in which nascent Indigenous Australian entrepreneurs must operate, a negative space dominated by ineffective policy, creating or contributing to societal trauma, within a colonial environment (Anderson *et al.*, 2006; MacPherson and Ng, 2012).

In addition to the trauma and resultant depression that is the by-product of poor colonial policy, the dark side of responsible business and management can involve the cultural cost of being Indigenous, and conducting an enterprise in a non-indigenous business environment. These detrimental consequences of colonization directly influence Indigenous aspirations, impacting on their "rights" that exist in recognition of the specific experience as Indigenous peoples, which may vary widely from case to case (Attwood and Markus, 1999).

Based on extensive qualitative studies of Indigenous Australian entrepreneurs,[2] the concept of **responsible business management** is a tool for achieving the **physiological needs** of family and maintaining cultural survival (Klyver and Foley, 2012; Nagel and Snipp, 1993). Maslow (1943, 1954) defined basic **physiological needs** as food, water, warmth, and shelter. In view of Australia's long history of human rights abuse and violence towards Aboriginal peoples (Cooke *et al.*, 2007; Moses, 2004), these initial needs remain simple in the first few years of the business (Zubrick *et al.*, 2010); however, they do come at a cost to the entrepreneur's family. This may include long absences, working to establish the enterprise, together with negligible personal income, as wages are repaid into the bank to finance the business growth. Termed "bootstrapping,"[3] directors' drawings or salary are redeposited to finance the business, owing to the lack of financial capital.

Previous research has shown that there is a cultural cost to the entrepreneur, a cost which was not fully understood by the author when commencing this research two decades ago (Foley, 2000, 2005). Subsequent research has indicated that these cultural constraints, which either become stronger or evaporate, are based more on the fortitude of the individual than their social and cultural networks (Foley and O'Connor, 2015; Foley and Hunter, 2016; Klyver and Foley, 2012).

This chapter reviews a series of case study interviews, most of which were undertaken with Aboriginal entrepreneurs over the last 20 years.[4] The purpose behind these studies was to provide non-indigenous government, policy-makers, and researchers with a better understanding of the cost that Western business thinking, practice, and policies has on Indigenous entrepreneurs (Nakata, 2007), and allow the outsider a glimpse into the Indigenous business world (Brayboy and Deyhle, 2000; Dwyer and Buckle, 2009).

---

2 1,000 + qualitative case studies have been undertaken on Indigenous Australian entrepreneurs by the author.

3 "Bootstrapping" is one of the most effective and inexpensive ways to ensure positive cash flow in a business by reinvesting wages back into the small enterprise, which means less money has to be borrowed and associated interest costs are reduced.

4 Chosen from the author's bank of 1,000+ case studies.

Aboriginal cultural and business practice in Australia

In earlier work (Foley, 2000, 2005) examples of cultural values, based on the collective values and structure of Aboriginal society, were evident in Aboriginal business practice. However, those studies in retail industries identified problems for the business when extended family took stock under the tribal concept of "sharing wealth." Cultural reciprocity was often misunderstood in the urban area, as the "taker" did not provide any form of reciprocity, in cash or kind, often forcing business owners to stop credit (Foley, 2005). One retail outlet went out of business within a few months of opening when its cash flow dried-up, following continuous stock pilfering by extended family members who did not honor their obligations. This added to a negative stereotype that Aboriginal people cannot handle money, and indeed, in this case, the business owner failed to understand fixed costs and breakeven points in the operation (Foley, 2005). In urban, rural, and some remote districts I did witness cultural wealth sharing occur, by successful Aboriginal entrepreneurs, but they were unable to give back, or share with their community until their business was established and profitable (Foley, 2000, 2005).

In the 1990s and in the first decade of the new millennium, the majority of visible Aboriginal entrepreneurs operated in tourism and hospitality, which relied on commercializing and commodifying their culture for capital gain. Apart from these industry sectors, businesses rarely openly identified as Aboriginal, perhaps because of the negative, racist attitude of a sizeable proportion of the white Australian population. It is changing for the better slightly since the establishment of the Indigenous Chambers of Commerce and the Federal Government Supply Nation, which overtly support Aboriginal businesses through procurement policies within government and across corporate Australia. The values and cultural beliefs of Indigenous Australians remain juxtaposed against those of the dominant Western culture and business world. Thus, economic independence through self-employment for Aboriginal people can come at a price. This is the dark side for many Australian Aboriginal people engaging in entrepreneurial activity.

Methodology

This chapter reports on face-to-face, semi-structured interviews with 100 selected case studies,[5] chosen because of geography and industry spread. In revisiting the earlier fieldwork, the original qualitative methodology and inquiry process initially used was also applied with the 80 re-interviewed participants and the 20 new cases. The names and geographic locations of the participants remain confidential

---

5   80 from the author's research bank of 1,000 case studies; 20 new case studies chosen from the First Australians Chamber of Commerce & Industry (FACCI) membership lists.

to ensure privacy, with codes applied to participants, such as S3 or C13. Those selected were geographically representative, based on Aboriginal populations, with 56% from urban areas, 22% in regional communities, 8% in remote, and 14% in very remote areas (ABS, 2011).[6] The study also ensured that participants represented a broad cross-section of small businesses types, from retail and hospitality, including hotel owners and tour operators, manufacturing, construction, building supply wholesalers, builders, and other self-employed professionals.

The research methodology uses a multiple case study approach (Yin, 2002; Eisenhardt, 1989) alongside a systematic literature review (Tranfield *et al.*, 2003; Pittaway *et al.*, 2004) reviewing discourse on the dark side of entrepreneurship. To provide focus and unity, a thematic approach based on "the dark side" was constantly reviewed (Thorpe *et al.*, 2006).

The dark side of entrepreneurship

Based on the evidence, it was clear that the need for responsible business management, combined with owner's aspirations, together with the struggles of Aboriginal business for financial independence and control of their lives, places an intrinsic pressure on Indigenous Australian business people, reflected as "the dark side."

It is widely accepted from previous research that entrepreneurs are exposed to many factors known to generate high levels of stress (Jex and Beehr, 1991; Xie *et al.*, 2008). Recent research on non-indigenous entrepreneurs indicates they report relatively low levels of stress (Baron *et al.*, 2016), which is the opposite of the effects reported among Indigenous populations in this research. Baron *et al.*'s (2016) research obviously does not take into account the unique positioning of Indigenous entrepreneurs and the daily experiences of racism. Nor does it consider the erosion of positive psychological capital due to the lingering impact of colonization resulting in the historical diminution of confidence, hope, optimism, and resilience (Luthans *et al.*, 2004). When you add external influences such as the impacts of racism, be it covert or overt, exclusionary or physical, the dark side of Indigenous enterprise is evident.

Kets de Vries (1985) believes that personality traits and behaviors of entrepreneurs either allow or disallow them to succeed in business. These same traits often prove detrimental in their roles, as the energy necessary for achieving a business dream may consume the individual, thereby exacerbating business dysfunctionality. This stems from a need for control, creating suspicions regarding those in authority. Obsessive concern with detail can stifle decisions, inhibit managers, and prevent accountability. They can be poor collaborators and indeed many Aboriginal entrepreneurs distrust the world around them and fear being a victim (Foley,

6 The ABS 2011 data is the most recent, accurate, and accessible census information.

2005). Kets de Vries (1985) also wrote that entrepreneurs scan the environment anticipating the worst. Losing sight of the reality of situations may create an over-riding need for applause and recognition, which can affect their viability. I have yet to find a successful Indigenous business that seeks applause and recognition, as they search for diversification or new opportunities (Foley, 2000, 2005). Most of the Aboriginal entrepreneurs are intrinsically motivated by a deep-rooted, cultural positive attitude, the "fire in the belly" (Smilor, 1997). Indigenous Aboriginal entrepreneurs in general tend not to seek the limelight. Kramer *et al.* (2011) argue that the dark side of entrepreneurship is a triad of personality involving narcissism, Machiavellianism, and sub-clinical psychopathy, three undesirable personality traits that I have not witnessed in this or any previous studies concerned with Indigenous entrepreneurs.

The empirical evidence across the research, however, highlights the immediate family and wider family, and the related Aboriginal community, as key stakeholders (Foley, 2005; Foley and O'Connor, 2013; Klyver and Foley, 2012). This is especially important given the growing number of stakeholders involved in an Indigenous entrepreneurial ecosystem, not just the individual entrepreneur (Autio *et al.*, 2014; Henry, 2012; Harmsworth, 2005; Mead, 2003; Tinirau and Gillies, 2011). Included here are the institutions and other companies, including government-funded bodies in Australia, such as Supply Nation, and independent NGOs such as the Indigenous Chambers of Commerce. The dark side of this is the unacceptable failure rate of Aboriginal start-up ventures including social entrepreneurship ventures that traditionally are funded based on community benefit projections rather than commercial profitability (Foley, 2005).

The activities of Indigenous entrepreneurs may also appear unproductive or dysfunctional (Baumol, 1986), with a large percentage of their time taken up with work that makes a limited contribution to the business thereby producing poor economic outcomes (Shane, 2009). These may include family matters or cultural activities, for example, NAIDOC (Aust.),[7] Waitangi Day (NZ), Prince Jonah Kuhio Kalanianaole Day, King Kamehameha I Day and 1st birthday achievements (Hawaii). Outsiders might interpret these cultural commitments as a dark side of Indigenous enterprise as they are not income generating; this points to a failure to understand the importance of cultural capital and strengthening of cultural networks that these events produce.

Some might argue that entrepreneurship takes individuals away from their community and social obligations, as they are now busy in their business; therefore entrepreneurship is "un-aboriginal." This is arguably false (Foley, 2015), and within a modern society, Aboriginal people cannot remain as spectators in the economy; they must be active participants to ensure their social position is strengthened. The work of Foley and Hunter (2016) measured social capital and entrepreneurial

---

7 NAIDOC (National Aborigines and Islanders Day Observance Committee) celebrations are held each July to celebrate the history, culture, and achievements of Aboriginal and Torres Strait Islander peoples.

impact on the Aboriginal community. Indigenous entrepreneurs can be self-made role models who have a positive impact on the wider Indigenous community. The dark side underestimates the beneficial impact of enterprise and entrepreneurship on Indigenous communities and its importance in developing self-esteem and financial independence, which is effectively self-determination. In practice, this is the developing positive psychological capital, which is established in the business life cycle as the Indigenous entrepreneurs' human and social capital reserves improve (Luthans *et al.*, 2004).

Discussion

Stress was a common issue that affected many of the participants in their business and private lives. Further probing revealed that financial stressors influenced personal relationships and were related to dysfunction around mental and emotional wellbeing, and additional domestic stress. In some instances this also produced increased levels of alcohol, cigarette, and coffee consumption. Two interviewees acknowledged, with shame, that stress had been so extreme it had led to acts of domestic violence, as their tempers flared towards partners over money issues. For both, fortunately, these were isolated events that galvanized serious self-reflection. Recent research undertaken in eastern India also showed those engaging in farming or small business were significantly associated with physical violence, though spouses (women) with a higher level of education were less likely to experience this physical violence (Babu and Kar, 2010).

Prior to and during the research period, 15 of the original 100 participants passed away, due predominantly to cardiovascular failure, brought on by high blood pressure and/or compounded by diabetes, with one suicide directly related to business pressure. In the owners' absence their spouses, siblings, and children continued to assist with the research. Of the remaining 85 participants, the majority reported that they suffered from depression; only 35% believed they exhibited similar symptoms prior to entering business. Looking at possible causes, most referred to the constant stress, "to not fail," believing the "white" world expected them to fail, which played on their mind. One noted that their non-indigenous accountant expressed surprise that he was still trading profitably after 5 years: "he thought I would have gone walkabout by now" (S13, 2015). Another participant who owns a large construction company felt that both non-indigenous and Koori[8] people are waiting for him to go into liquidation. "People have trouble accepting that a blackfella can be successful in construction" (S2, 2015). Others believed that it was

---

8 Koori is an Indigenous word from the Sydney region used by some Aborigines to refer to themselves.

normal stress associated with business, but also felt, "this is my chance to be successful, to provide for my family, I cannot afford to fail" (C1, 2015).

As previously mentioned, 15 entrepreneurs died during this research. A common characteristic is that they had suffered extreme highs and lows. The spouses and offspring of the deceased referred to the ways that they felt the deceased had been "ripped off" by accountants, solicitors, property owners, and even in one case by ATSIC staff.[9] These stressors entailed overcharging, theft, embezzlement, sudden increases in rentals, and cancelling of leases on business premises, thereby forcing them to move at short notice. After lengthy discussion with their partners and their children, it was found that some traumatic event, financial or otherwise, created additional strain that preceded their premature deaths.

When asked whether they regretted their partners going into business, "no" was the most common response. They felt that their partners never loved life more than when they had established their business and were trading successfully, providing for their children and taking control of their lives. Twelve businesses continue, driven by the spouse or children, three ceased immediately and the enterprises were liquidated.

The following lists the hurdles they faced in establishing and operating their businesses, listed in the order of importance they recorded in the interviews:

1. Racism (overt or covert; physical or exclusionary)

2. Lack of business and working capital finance

3. Stress, increased blood pressure, increased coffee and cigarette intake

4. Lack of business expertise, naivety coupled with poor business planning

5. Lack of business training

6. The inability to get after-hours industry assistance with business problems

7. Inability to recruit qualified, trained staff prepared to work for minimal wages

8. Time away from families in the start-up phase of the business, especially time away from the children in their formative years when 60–80 hours a week are spent in the business

9. Loss of cultural capital due to the lack of time spent with children and or wider community and family

---

9 The Aboriginal and Torres Strait Islander Commission (ATSIC) (1990–2005) was the Australian Government body through which Aboriginal Australians and Torres Strait Islanders were formally involved in the processes of government representation. It is alleged that ATSIC staff copied the entrepreneur's business plan and a person closely related to the ATSIC staff member commenced a copycat business in the same tourist strip funded by ATSIC in direct opposition to the entrepreneur.

10. In the early stages of the business the financial constraints limit what you can do

Once the business was established, points 6–10 were no longer applicable as they could afford to employ staff and enjoy more time with their families.

Conclusion

This chapter provides an Indigenous viewpoint regarding business practices and Indigenous aspirations, whether successful or unsuccessful. It falls within a broad umbrella of responsible business management practice presenting ongoing unresolved issues and calls for respect, cooperation, and collaboration. The chapter's purpose is to address and illustrate the need to understand how modern commercial business practice intersects with Australian Indigenous peoples, from the Indigenous standpoint; especially the impact of racism, poverty and unsustainable government policy. This is research on Indigenous entrepreneurs by an Indigenous researcher for the betterment directly or indirectly of these same participants, similar to a Kaupapa Māori[10] approach. There is much to be learned from this insider perspective in order to fulfill the promise of the PRME (Principles for Responsible Management Education) and the United Nations Global Compact, vis-à-vis making a positive impact on the aspirations and rights of Indigenous peoples.

My aim was to provide a background of my research on Aboriginal Australia to highlight the prevalence of Indigenous values in business, then to study 100 Aboriginal Australian entrepreneurs to get an update on their beliefs and values. To my shock, the impact of stress and widespread coronary disease among my peers has taken 15 from our community. Has entrepreneurial activity been to blame or can we simply shrug off the statistics based on a widened gap between life expectancies? This results in the death of Aboriginal Australian men some 15 years younger on average than our non-indigenous counterparts with the gap for women of 8 to 9 years younger. Based on continuing discussions with Aboriginal entrepreneurs, it is my belief that the current business climate in Australia—with the continual angst of racism; lack of specialist business, finance and working capital facilities; and the constantly changing governmental business programs, combined with numerous uncoordinated ineffective training and education facilities—increases stress, which in turn is a major facilitator of depression. This is the true dark side of Aboriginal business, which responsible business management needs to address.

---

10 Kaupapa Māori research seeks to identify and uphold Māori views, solutions, and ways of knowing. It is about empowering Māori people, voice, processes, and knowledge.

References

Anderson, R.B., Dana, L.P., & Dana, T.E. (2006). Indigenous land rights, entrepreneurship, and economic development in Canada: "Opting-in" to the global economy. *Journal of World Business*, 41(1), pp. 45-55.

Attwood, B., & Markus, A. (1999). *The Struggle for Aboriginal Rights.* Sydney: Allen & Unwin.

Australian Bureau of Statistics (ABS) (2011). Estimates of Aboriginal and Torres Strait Islander Australians, June. Retrieved from http://www.abs.gov.au/ausstats/abs@.nsf/mf/3238.0.55.001

Australian Government (2009). The Policy Challenge, Budget Speech 2009-2010. http://www.budget.gov.au/2009-10/content/ministerial_statements/indigenous/html/ms_indigenous-02.htm

Autio, E., Kenney, M., Mustar, P., Siegel, D., & Wright, M. (2014). Entrepreneurial innovation ecosystems and context. *Research Policy*, 43, pp. 1097-108.

Babu, B.V., & Kar, S.K. (2010). Domestic violence in Eastern India: factors associated with victimization and perpetration. *Public Health,* 124(3), pp. 136-148.

Baron, R.A., Franklin, R.J., & Hmieleski, K.M. (2016). Why entrepreneurs often experience low, not high, levels of stress: The joint effects of selection and psychological capital. *Journal of Management*, 42(3), pp. 742-768.

Baumol, W.J. (1986). Entrepreneurship: Productive, unproductive, and destructive. *Journal of Business Venturing*, 11, pp. 3-22.

Brayboy, B.M., & Deyhle, D. (2000). Insider-outsider: researchers in American Indian communities. *Theory into Practice*, 39(3), pp. 163-169.

Cooke, M., Mitrou, F., Lawrence, D., Guimond, E., & Beavon, D. (2007). Indigenous well-being in four countries: an application of the UNDP's human development index to Indigenous peoples in Australia, Canada, New Zealand, and the United States. *BMC International Health and Human Rights*, 7(1), p. 1.

Davidsson, P., Steffens, P., & Fitzsimmons, J. (2009). Growing profitable or growing from profits: Putting the horse in front of the cart? *Journal of Business Venturing*, 24, pp. 388-406.

Dwyer, S.C. & Buckle, J.L. (2009). The space between: On being an insider-outsider in qualitative research. *International Journal of Qualitative Methods*, 8(1), pp. 54-63.

Eisenhardt, K. (1989). Building theories from case study research. *The Academy of Management Review*, 14(4), pp. 532-550.

Foley, D. (2000). Successful Indigenous Australian entrepreneurs: A case study analysis. *Aboriginal and Torres Strait Islander Studies Unit Research Report Series*, 4, Brisbane: Merino Lithographics.

Foley, D. (2005). *Understanding Indigenous Entrepreneurs: A Case Study Analysis.* Unpublished PhD Thesis, School of Management, The University of Queensland. http://espace.library.uq.edu.au/view/UQ:179923

Foley, D. (2006) Indigenous standpoint theory: An acceptable academic research process for Indigenous academics. *The International Journal of Humanities*, 3(8), pp. 3-15.

Foley, D. (2015). Enterprise and entrepreneurial thinking: It's a black thing! In Kaye Price (Ed.), *In Knowledge of Life: Aboriginal &Torres Strait Islander Australia* (pp.118-140).Cambridge University Press, Port Melbourne, Vic.

Foley, D., & Hunter, B. (2016). Indigenous entrepreneurship: Some theory and evidence. In Clark, D.N., Mazzarol, T., McKeown, T., Kotey, B., & Battisti, M. (eds.), *Rhetoric and Reality: Building Vibrant and Sustainable Entrepreneurial Ecosystems* (Chapter 11). Tilde University Press: Prahran, Vic.

Foley, D. & O'Connor, A. (2013). Social capital and the networking practices of minority entrepreneurs. *Journal of Small Business Management*, 55(3), pp. 276-296.

Fryges, H. & Wright, M. (2014). The origin of spin-offs: A typology of corporate and academic spinoffs. *Small Business Economics*, 43, pp. 245-59.

Harmsworth, G. (2005). Report on the incorporation of traditional values/tikanga into contemporary Māori business organisation and process. *Landcare Research Contract Report LC.*

Henry, E. (2012). *Te wairua auaha: emancipatory Māori entrepreneurship in screen production.* Unpublished PhD thesis-exegesis, Auckland University of Technology, in AUT Scholarly Commons. Retrieved from http://hdl.handle.net/10292/4085

Hunter, B. (2014). *Indigenous Employment and Businesses: Whose Business is it to Employ Indigenous Workers?* Working Paper No. 95/2014, Centre for Aboriginal Economic Policy Research, Australian National University, Canberra.

Jex, S. & Beehr, T. (1991). Emerging theoretical and methodological issues in the study of work-related stress. *Research in Personnel and Human Resource Management,* 9, pp. 311-365.

Kets de Vries, M. (1985). The dark side of entrepreneurship. *Harvard Business Review,* 63(6), pp. 160-167.

Klyver, K. & Foley, D. (2012). Networking and culture for minority entrepreneurship. *Journal of Entrepreneurship & Regional Development,* 24(7), pp. 1-28.

Kramer, M., Cesinger, B., Schwarzinger, D. & Gelleri, P. (2011). *The Dark Side of Entrepreneurial Personality: Effects of Narcissism, Machiavellianism and Psychopathy on Entrepreneurial Intention and Performance.* British Academy of Management Conference, Birmingham, UK.

Langton, M. (2008). Trapped in the Aboriginal reality show. *Griffith Review,* 19, February 8, 2008. Also extracted in *The Australian,* Jan 26-27, 2008.

Lawrence, C. (2008). *Us and Them: Breaking Down the Barriers.* Paper presented at Fulbright Conference: Healthy People Prosperous Country, July 11.

Luthans, F., Luthans, K. & Luthans, B. (2004). Positive psychological capital: Beyond human and social capital. *Business Horizons,* 47(1), pp. 45-50.

MacPherson, S. & Ng, D.F. (2012). Education and sustainability learning across the diaspora, Indigenous, and minority divide. *Diaspora, Indigenous, and Minority Education,* 6(4), pp. 258-260.

Maslow, A.H. (1943). A theory of human motivation. *Psychological Review,* 50(4), p. 370.

Maslow, A. (1954). *Motivation and Personality.* New York, NY: Harper.

Mead, H.M. (2003). *Tikanga Māori: Living by Māori Values.* Wellington, Aotearoa: Huia Publishers.

Moses, A.D. (2004). *Genocide and settler society: Frontier violence and stolen indigenous children in Australian history,* Vol. 6. Berghahn Books.

Nagel, J. & Snipp, C.M. (1993). Ethnic reorganization: American Indian social, economic, political, and cultural strategies for survival. *Ethnic and Racial Studies,* 16(2), pp. 203-235.

Nakata, M. (2007). The cultural interface. *The Australian Journal of Indigenous Education,* 36(S1), pp. 7-14.

Nicholls, A. (2009). We do good things, don't we? "Blended value accounting" in social entrepreneurship. *Accounting, Organizations and Society,* 34, pp. 755-69.

Pittaway, L., Robertson, M., Munir, K., Denyer, D. & Neeley, A. (2004). Networking and Innovation: a systematic review of the evidence. *International Journal of Management Reviews,* 5/6(3/4), pp. 137-168.

Shane, S. (2009). Why encouraging more people to become entrepreneurs is bad public policy. *Small Business Economics,* 33, pp. 141-149.

Smilor, R. (1997). Entrepreneurship: Reflections on a subversive activity. *Journal of Business Venturing,* 12(5), pp. 341-346.

Thorpe, R., Holt, R., Pittaway, A. & Macpherson, L. (2006). Using knowledge within small and medium-sized firms: A systematic review of the evidence. *International Journal of Management Reviews,* 7(4), pp. 257-281.

Tinirau, R. & Gillies, A. (2011). Utilising Māori research methodologies in Māori business contexts. ANZAM Conference, Wellington NZ, December 7-9. http://www.anzam.org/wp-content/uploads/pdf-manager/645_ANZAM2011-480.PDF Accessed 1 July, 2016.

Tranfield, D.R., Denver, D. & Smart, P. (2003). Towards a methodology for developing evidence-informed management knowledge by means of systematic review. *British Journal of Management,* 14, pp. 207-222.

Webb, J.W., Tihanyi, L., Ireland, R.D. & Sirmon, D. (2009). You say illegal, I say legitimate: Entrepreneurship in the informal economy. *Academy of Management Review,* 34, pp. 492-510.

Wright, M. & Stigliani, I. (2013). Entrepreneurship and growth. *International Small Business Journal,* 31, pp. 3-22.

Wright, M. & Zahra, S. (2011). The other side of paradise: Examining the dark side of entrepreneurship. *Entrepreneurship Research Journal,* 1(3).

Xie, J., Schaubroeck, J. & Lam, S. (2008). Theories of job stress and the role of traditional values: A longitudinal study of China. *Journal of Applied Psychology,* 93, pp. 831-848.

Yin, R.K. (2002). *Case Study Research, Design and Methods.* Newbury Park: Sage Publication, 3rd edition.

Zahra, S.A. & Wright, M. (2015). Understanding the social role of entrepreneurship. *Journal of Management Studies,* 53(4), pp. 610-629.

Zubrick, S.R., Dudgeon, P., Gee, G., Glaskin, B., Kelly, K., Paradies, Y., Scrine, C. & Walker, R. (2010). Social determinants of Aboriginal and Torres Strait Islander social and emotional wellbeing. *Working together: Aboriginal and Torres Strait Islander mental health and wellbeing principles and practice,* pp. 75-90.

3

Environmental crisis in New Zealand

Tribal, government, and business responses to the sinking of the MV *Rena*

Ella Henry, Ph.D.
Senior Lecturer, Auckland University of Technology; Māori citizen

Hugh Sayers, M.B.A.
Project Manager, Motiti Rohe Moana Trust; Pākehā citizen of New Zealand

The sinking of the MV *Rena* on the Astrolabe Reef in 2011 has been described as "New Zealand's worst maritime environmental disaster." The Astrolabe Reef is located near to Motiti Island, occupied by Māori in the Bay of Plenty. Since it occurred, the sinking and its consequences have pitted local tribes against government and the corporation that owns the vessel. This chapter provides an Indigenous perspective, from one of the Iwi (tribes) of Motiti Island, on how the sinking has affected the Iwi, their maritime environment, and their relationship with government, business, and neighboring tribes. It draws on articles from the Declaration on the Rights of Indigenous Peoples (DRIP) and the UN Global Compact to analyze the events, and responses from government and business. It explores the implications of such events on Indigenous peoples, and the ways that institutions that are signatories to the Principles for Responsible

Management Education (PRME) might utilize this case to inform responsible management education, and to learn from such failures.

New Zealand, MV *Rena*, Environmental disaster, Tribal response, Māori, Waitangi Tribunal

Introduction

This chapter explores the grounding of the MV *Rena* in the Bay of Plenty in 2011. It focuses on impacts on, and views from, one Māori community from Motiti, the island closest to the Astrolabe Reef, upon which the *Rena* floundered. It is co-authored by a Māori/Indigenous academic and a non-Māori, community activist with close links to these Māori communities. The case draws on the Declaration on the Rights of Indigenous Peoples, and the UN Global Compact to inform analysis of the events, and responses from government and business. Further, it informs the Principles for Responsible Management Education (PRME) by providing an Indigenous perspective on an event with local, national, and global implications.

The case

Māori are the Indigenous people of New Zealand, having settled the islands as part of the Polynesian diaspora across the South Pacific over the last 3,000 years. For centuries, Polynesian peoples lived in isolation, settling and commuting between the islands, until the arrival of Europeans from the 17th century. Thereafter followed the intensive exploration of, among others, James Cook in 1769, resulting in the identification of New Zealand as separate from Australia (King, 2003). In the ensuing decades, increasing numbers of Europeans (Pākehā) visited New Zealand, and in the early decades of contact Māori embraced Europeans, developing a thriving trade by the 1830s (Petrie, 2006).

Relations between Māori and Pākehā were generally cordial. This growing relationship underpinned a formal agreement between Māori and the British Crown, the Treaty of Waitangi, signed on 6 February 1840. It did not prove to be the mutually beneficial accord envisaged by Māori. It is not the purpose of this chapter to relitigate that Treaty of Waitangi. However, colonization, the New Zealand Wars of the 19th century (stimulated by the settler government desire for more land for settlers), plus the arrival of unknown diseases decimated Māori society, and unraveled the Māori economy over the 19th and early 20th centuries (Orange, 2015; Kawharu, 1989; Durie, 1998; Belich, 2015, King, 2003).

Extensive migration, post-World War II, saw Māori even further disenfranchised from traditional roots, but out of this has emerged what is now termed the Māori Renaissance. Since the 1960s, Māori entered universities, professions, and politics in unprecedented numbers, driving social and legislative changes resulting in revitalization of language, culture, and identity (Walker, 1990; Smith, 1999). Important among these was the creation of the Waitangi Tribunal to address breaches of the Treaty. In 1985, the Tribunal was given the power to look retrospectively to 1840, and since then, thousands of claims have been lodged (Ward, 2015). Dozens of Treaty Claims have been settled and many millions of dollars in cash and land returned to Māori, albeit small recompense for that which was lost (Te Aho, 2010). For Lashley (2000, p. 1), "Despite more than twenty years of landmark Treaty policy providing indigenous New Zealanders social justice and economic redress, the majority of Maori households still have incomes well below the national and subgroup medians." Thus, Māori have suffered the loss of land, language, and identity since the first arrival of Europeans, exacerbated by the brutal treatment of successive governments. Though some of these worst impacts have been ameliorated by legislation and social change in recent decades, forged by a revitalized and empowered Māori community, many Māori continue to languish. It was into this realm that the MV *Rena* sailed on October 5, 2011, grounding on Otaiti or Astrolabe Reef, situated immediately north of Motiti Island.

Motiti Island

Motiti is only 7.2 km², hosting 36 Pā sites (fortified villages), with fresh water from 27 natural springs. It lies approximately 21 km northeast of Tauranga, the largest center in the Bay of Plenty. When Cook first encountered Motiti in November 1769, "he reported the most extensive complex of fortified villages he had yet seen" (Te Ara, 1966). It is one of the few places in the region with contiguous Māori ownership and occupation, and continuous use of the foreshore and seabed. There is no wharf, but it has three private airstrips. The island has 68 houses but little infrastructure, and no electricity, water supply, or sewerage system. There is a weekly mail plane, and between 45 and 60 people live there permanently, almost all of whom are Māori.

Through the centuries, Motiti has been occupied by members of more than one of the voyaging *waka* (canoes) which first settled the region, originally settled by Ngātōroirangi, navigator of Te Arawa *waka*. Later, people from the Mataatua *waka* settled there, and over time, these communities melded into a tribal entity known as Ngāi Te Hapū. In 1865, as a consequence of the New Zealand Wars, Governor Grey confiscated the Tauranga Land District, out to sea, including Motiti. In 1867 Hori Tupaea, of Ngāi Te Rangi (a tribe from Tauranga) made an application to the Māori Land Court for ownership of Motiti. He applied from Katikati (a settlement on the mainland) because he had earlier been told by Māori locals to leave the island and never return. Judge Fenton also received a claim from Te Patuwai, a confederation of Ngāi Te Hapu tribes living on Motiti at the time, plus others from Pukehina and Whakatāne (on the mainland). They all opposed the claim from Tupaea. Fenton found in favor of both sets of applicants in 1868, dividing the island in two. Motiti South was awarded to Tupaea in trust for the Tauwhao sub-tribe of Papaunahi. Though no one from the Tauwhao tribe has lived there since, they retain ownership interests and have sold some of the land to Europeans. Motiti North was awarded to the Karanga Hapū (sub-tribe) of Ngāi Te Hapū. In between these two communities, the "ditch of disputation" was dug to enshrine the boundary. Despite a history of division and antipathy, the community has come together to fight for common causes and struggles over the years.

Motiti Rohe Moana Trust

The Department of Internal Affairs prepared the Motiti Island Environmental Management Plan District Plan in 2009. Under the Resource Management Act (RMA), Iwi are to be consulted or involved in the preparation of such plans, but this did not occur to the satisfaction of those on the island, which precipitated formation of a special interest group. Furthermore, Motiti is not specifically included in the Treaty settlements for the Bay of Plenty, and the Office of Treaty Settlements (OTS) has yet to resolve all those with interests in the waters around Motiti, which are presently awarded to mainland tribes. Thus, the Motiti Rohe Moana Trust was established in 2009, to address surrounding waters, fisheries, and resource management issues on behalf of the community with genealogical links to the island. The trustees are tribal elders born and raised on Motiti.

In October 2009, the Trust filed a Treaty Claim relating to the aforementioned District Plan, followed by a historical Treaty Claim in March 2010, to clarify tribal connections to the island. This Claim is currently adjourned, pending the outcome of the OTS Kinship Review to establish the identity of Motiti descendants, and whether or not the Motiti historical claims were settled with the Ngāti Awa Claim Settlement of 2005, which those living on the island contest. The Trust continues to represent the island community, though even those relationships have been strained in the aftermath of the *Rena* grounding. It receives no government funding for projects, except legal aid for litigation, which is "negative funding," setting the Trust in continual opposition to the Crown. The story of the relationship between Motiti and the Crown is a litany of unresolved conflicts.

Since its inception, the Trust has been actively engaged in developing a planning framework for Motiti Island and the surrounding seas. It has participated in Environment Court litigation over the Motiti District Plan, secured consent orders for the Bay of Plenty Regional Policy Statement, and is a submitter on the Bay of

Plenty's Proposed Regional Coastal Plan. The Trust has also been heavily involved in dealing with the aftermath of the MV *Rena* disaster and the resulting Treaty Claims.

Grounding of the MV *Rena*

The MV Rena went aground on Otaiti in the middle of the night, October 5, 2011, and over the coming weeks it broke apart. The grounding has been described as "New Zealand's worst maritime environmental disaster" (Fa'aui and Morgan, 2014, p. 4). The Transport Accident Commission Report concluded that the *Rena* grounding was entirely attributable to the crew (TAIC, 2014). According to Fa'aui and Morgan, "The grounding of the MV *Rena* had significant environmental impacts that were experienced in anthropocentric terms as impacts upon social, economic and cultural well-being" (2014, p. 3).

When the oil slick hit Papamoa and Mt Maunganui, popular tourist beaches on the mainland, the seriousness of the environmental damage was evident. Maritime NZ and its parent, the Ministry of Transport, led the *Rena* response. The Ministry for the Environment initiated the *Rena* Long-Term Environment Recovery Plan in partnership with the Bay of Plenty Regional Council, who established the Plan. This included a governance group, which appointed mainland Iwi (tribal) leaders to represent Māori interests, but excluded Motiti, perhaps as a consequence of long-standing tensions between those tribal communities and local government. That exclusion continues to rankle among Māori on the island. When the clean-up became too big for Maritime NZ and the Regional Council to handle, a "whole of government" approach was adopted.

In October 2012, the New Zealand Government entered into three deeds with the *Rena* owners (Daina Shipping Company, a subsidiary of Greek company Costamare) to settle claims for environmental damage and clean-up. It had cost the Crown NZ$47 million in the initial response, and, in the settlement with the *Rena* owners, the insurers paid NZ$27.5 million, plus another NZ$10.4 million that would have been paid as part of the Wreck Removal Deed (WRD). It continues to mystify as to why the Crown would settle for less than the costs incurred for the clean-up, but cynics might suggest complicity between government and business, or even that government officials were unnecessarily impressed by the opulence of the wealthy European representatives of the company. Nonetheless, the WRD "provided the Crown with an opportunity for an additional payment of $10.4 million for public purposes if it supported a resource consent application by the owners to leave part or the whole of the wreck on the reef" (Waitangi Tribunal, 2013, p. 1).

The WRD was considered so contentious by the people of Motiti that they submitted claims to the Waitangi Tribunal. One was lodged by the Ngāi Te Hapū.

Incorporated Society, and another by the Motiti Rohe Moana Trust with the Mataatua District Māori Council. It took the claimants six months of wrangling with Crown Law and *Rena* legal counsel, through the Waitangi Tribunal, to obtain limited, confidential disclosure of these Deeds. The Trust had sought Official Information Act disclosure about the agreement in 2012, which was refused, as it was supposedly commercially sensitive. What exasperated the Trust was a whole year of trying to engage with Crown agencies, which refused to recognize the people of Motiti or their interest in these matters. Their Treaty Claims were lodged under urgency, as the claimants alleged the Crown's actions, in entering these agreements constituted,

> A breach of the principles of the Treaty of Waitangi. They submit that the Crown has failed to act honourably and in good faith, and has failed to fulfil its duty of active protection, in particular by failing to consult with Māori prior to signing the WRD (Waitangi Tribunal Report, 2014, p. 1).

The report further stated that, "Both claims relate to alleged Crown conduct in relation to the removal of the *Rena* from Otaiti. Both claims state that complete removal of the wreck is necessary to restore the mauri (spiritual wellbeing) of the reef" (Waitangi Tribunal, 2014, p. 62).

Meanwhile the *Rena* owners continued to seek Resource Management consent to leave the remainder of the wreck on the Astrolabe Reef. Their application was proposed by the Astrolabe Community Trust, which was setup in May 2014 by Daina Shipping to achieve charitable, educational, and environmental purposes (Astrolabe Community Trust Deed, 2014). Daina also commissioned highly reputable companies to conduct reports on their behalf (Beca, 2014). Other advisers included esteemed Māori cultural experts. One of these, Kahotea, prepared a "cultural values assessment" on behalf of the owners, then another for the resource consent hearing, in which he outlined the different groups and their relationships with Motiti. His report affirmed the strongest relationships were those who maintained continuous occupation on Motiti (Kahotea, 2015).

The Tribunal expressed concern at the repeated recalcitrance of the Crown to disclose information to Māori, stopping short of accusations of collusion between government and business. Further, the Tribunal found that the Crown did not act in a Treaty-compliant manner, and that both the reef and the Motiti Tribunal claimants "were in a damaged and vulnerable state." These events were also acknowledged in the 2014 report, which found,

> The Crown's consultation process with Māori in preparation for deciding its position on the *Rena* owners' resource consent application to leave the wreck on Otaiti had breached the principles of good faith and partnership. We have therefore found that the Crown's conduct in entering the WRD without having consulted Māori breached the principle of partnership (Waitangi Tribunal Report, 2014, pp. viii-ix).

It is apparent from these two reports that the New Zealand Government had breached the principles of the Treaty, had not acted in good faith, and had given preference to the needs of business before Māori.

By July 2015, two of the mainland tribes agreed to a settlement with the owners (*Bay of Plenty Times*, 2015) in return for rescinding their opposition to the application, which caused acrimony within and among the Māori tribal communities in the region. The *Rena* grounding, consequent pollution, clean-up efforts, and the necessity to submit a Treaty claim just for the grounding, all contributed to ongoing pain for the people of the island, which some see as a form of "cultural genocide". The scramble for resources, pitting communities against each other, has also been detrimental. The economic power of the *Rena* owners and influence of those they have brought in to support their cause, have disrupted Māori dynamics in the region, and impacted negatively on the health and wellbeing of the people of the island.

For one member of the community,

> It is fundamental that we get our heads around identity, leadership and facilitating the identity of our culture; the sad reality is, within the Māori world we are ingrained to distrust, a division that is connected to our whenua, that binds us, but is now divided—a disconnect for our people, that has made us essentially ghosts on our lands, and in our country, suicide, despair, drugs, are symptoms of lost identity, and other social ailments.[1]

Another, who was born on Motiti, and is now an elder (*kaumātua*) and trustee, stated that "the grounding of the *Rena* has brought the [Motiti] community together, the drive is to gain recognition from the Crown for the Iwi and the *whenua* (land), then everything else will flow from that".[2] Thus, despite tensions between Motiti and some mainland Māori groups, there appears to be more cohesion among those on the Island.

In February 2016, the RMA Panel reported on the application from the Astrolabe Community Trust for resource consent to abandon the remains of the MV *Rena*, its equipment and cargo, and associated debris on Otaiti/Astrolabe Reef. Giving evidence, John Owen from the Swedish Club Insurers recorded that NZ$429.7 million had been spent on the recovery, with NZ$220 million of that spent since they announced they would seek consent to abandon the wreck. The Commissioners noted that, of the 151 submissions, 48 were from Māori and 46 of those opposed the application. However, after consideration, the Panel granted consent on the following conditions:

- That structural components of the ship may remain, but any further debris must be removed

---

1 Interview with Te Atarangi Sayers, Iwi Resource Manager, Papamoa, April 22, 2016.
2 Interview with U. Matehaere, Papamoa, April 19, 2016.

- That relationships with Māori be recognized and provided for, through establishment of a Kaitiakitanga (stewardship) Reference Group (KRG), to oversee cultural monitoring and a Shoreline Debris Management Plan, the Wreck Condition and Debris Monitoring Plan and the setup of an Independent Technical Advisory Group

- That restoration and mitigation funds be provided by the applicant

- Recognition of the significant relationship between Otaiti Reef and Motiti Island, therefore giving additional weight to the evidence from hapū of Motiti

- Acknowledgement that the Applicant engaged in respectful and dignified consultation with Māori (which included a number of visits and *Hui* (meetings) between local tribes and the Executive Director of Costmare, who states in his evidence that he developed a huge respect for Maori traditions and world viewpoint; Zacharatos, 2014, p. 2)

- Section 5 specifically addressed Māori values that must be considered, in particular:
  - Taonga: recognition that Otaiti is a highly prized treasure
  - Wāhi Tapu: recognition that it is also a sacred site
  - Mauri: ensuring the spiritual life-force of Otaiti is monitored and protected
  - Kaitiakitanga: maintaining and enabling Māori guardianship responsibilities
  - Mana: protecting the status of the reef, including the food resources
  - Manaakitanga: ensuring obligations of reciprocity and hospitality can be maintained through food gathering by Māori
  - Mahinga Kai: protecting the food-basket that is Otaiti
  - Ara Wairua: protecting the role of reef, as a stepping stone to the spiritual world after death, for Māori in the region

These provisions clearly acknowledge Māori values and culture, yet the overall decision is in conflict with the aspirations of Māori on Motiti, despite their being the most negatively affected. Therefore, the people of Motiti remain deeply cynical about the outcomes of this litigation and consent process, but they do not have adequate resources to further monitor the activities of government and the company. Furthermore, they continue their litigation with the Crown to protect their status as *tangata whenua* of Motiti, and to ensure they receive fair benefits of the Treaty settlements in the region. They are a small tribal group, whose community leaders are vocal, strategic, and driven to support their aspirations. The effects of the grounding of the *Rena* are ongoing, but so too is the fortitude of this small, but staunch community of Māori in one of the most isolated places in the country.

Discussion

This case study, albeit brief, lays the foundations for analysis of ways that government, business, and tribal entities have interacted, and to which we can apply articles and principles of the initiatives created to enhance the rights and further the aspirations of Indigenous peoples.

Declaration on the Rights of Indigenous Peoples (DRIP)

The following sections of DRIP are useful in that they highlight what the New Zealand Government has, or has not, done adequately to protect the rights of the people of Motiti:

- Section 8 is particularly relevant to this case, as it enshrines the right of Indigenous peoples to not be subjected to the destruction of their culture and calls on states to provide effective mechanisms for prevention of, or redress for, actions which deprive them of such.

- *Article 11 calls on states to provide redress through effective mechanisms, which may include restitution, developed in conjunction with indigenous peoples, with respect to their cultural, intellectual, religious and spiritual property taken without their free, prior and informed consent or in violation of their laws, traditions and customs.* The Waitangi Tribunal has limited legislative power, but great moral weight to ensure protection of these rights, but even this body is frustrated by the machinations of other arms of government, in this case, the Ministry for the Environment and the Regional Council have been found wanting in their dealings with Māori.

- *Article 19 calls on states to consult and cooperate in good faith before adopting and implementing legislative or administrative measures that may affect them.* This clearly did not happen in the Crown's dealing with the people of Motiti over the grounding of the *Rena*.

- *Article 25 asserts the right of Indigenous peoples to maintain and strengthen their distinctive spiritual relationship with their traditionally owned or otherwise occupied and used lands, territories, waters and coastal seas and other resources and to uphold their responsibilities to future generations in this regard.* The UN Rapporteur visited New Zealand in 2010. He acknowledges improvements since the 2005 visit and report, in particular New Zealand's support for DRIP in 2010. His report emphasizes the need for the principles enshrined in the Treaty of Waitangi to be protected within the domestic legal system of New Zealand. Also, he recommends the Marine and Coastal Area Act, adopted on March 31, 2011, be implemented to ensure the rights of Māori to traditional lands and resources. He notes, "efforts to secure Māori political participation at the national level should be strengthened, and the State should focus special attention on increasing Māori participation in local governance" (Anaya, 2015, p. 2).

The UN Global Compact

The United Nations Global Compact is a call to companies to align their strategies and operations with universal principles on human rights, labor, environment, and anti-corruption, and to take actions that advance those societal goals. The following two principles have the most applicability to this case, because this case clearly relates to the human rights of the people of Motiti, and the grounding has had profound impacts on the environment.

- **Human Rights, Principle 1.** Businesses should support and respect the protection of internationally proclaimed human rights, such as those articulated in the DRIP (see the comments above).

- **Environment, Principle 8.** Businesses should undertake initiatives to promote greater environmental responsibility: One could argue the *Rena* owners have engaged in consultation with Māori, thereby protecting Indigenous human rights. They have invested in salvage and restoration, ostensibly to protect the environment. However, those most affected by the grounding would disagree that their rights have been protected, or that Costamare has been as environmentally responsible as it should have been.

Thus, organizations adhering to these principles have a moral obligation to ensure that they fully engage with the most affected parties in Indigenous communities that are impacted by their business decisions, and that mutually agreed resolutions are achieved.

Business Reference Guide (BRG)

The Business Reference Guide has been designed to help businesses understand, respect, and support the rights of Indigenous peoples. Applying the Business Reference Guide principles to this case yields the following points (see United Nations Global Compact, 2013, p. 13).

> 1. Adopt and implement a formal policy (whether on a stand-alone basis or within a broader human rights policy) addressing indigenous peoples' rights and committing the business to respect indigenous peoples' rights.

Daina Shipping, originally, did not feel the need to engage with local tribes, having negotiated a Wreck Removal Deed with the New Zealand Government. However, once local tribes lodged claims with the Waitangi Tribunal, and the government retracted its commitment to the WRD, the company initiated an engagement process, for which they received due praise. However, the receipt of financial redress by some tribes, and not others, has driven a further wedge between some communities in the region. This may act in the interests of business, when local communities engage in struggles with each other, rather than against the business. However, the whole purpose of the BRG is to avoid such outcomes.

> 2. Conduct human rights due diligence to assess actual or potential adverse impacts on indigenous peoples' rights, integrate findings and take action, track and communicate externally on performance.

The *Rena* owners commissioned Cultural Assessment and other Reports from Māori experts, as well as engaging in direct negotiations with local tribes. While they settled claims and gave funding to two mainland tribes, those who lodged claims with the Waitangi Tribunal remained strenuously opposed to leaving the wreck on the reef and refused funding from the company. Further research and consultation by the company and their representatives might have ameliorated this tribal division, if that was their real objective.

> 3. Consult in good faith with Indigenous peoples in relation to all matters that may affect them or their rights.

The response to this Principle depends on which tribe one discusses this matter with. Those who have settled believe they have made a just decision for their people, while other tribes have a contrary view. The latter argue that they are closest to the reef, and they seek spiritual and cultural, rather than financial restoration, and it is their views that are the basis of this case study.

> 4. Commit to obtain (and maintain) the free, prior and informed consent of indigenous peoples for projects that affect their rights, in line with the spirit of the UN Declaration.
> 5. Establish or cooperate through legitimate processes to remediate any adverse impacts on indigenous peoples' rights.
> 6. Establish or cooperate with an effective and culturally appropriate grievance mechanism.

Daina Shipping would argue that they have addressed each of the above, though the people of Motiti Island may not agree with that view. The company has invested significant amounts of time and money in consultation with various government agencies and tribal communities, in preparation for the Resource Consent. They have guaranteed funding for ongoing reparations and community initiatives. They no doubt believe they have done everything in their power to be a responsible and responsive business. However, the people of Motiti, closest to the impacts, do not feel they have been heard, or respected, or valued throughout the processes and government machinations in the last five years. They have greater concerns about the role that government has played, isolating their interests, and appearing to collude with business.

Time will tell what the long-term effects of the grounding will be on the *mauri* (spiritual wellbeing) of the reef and its guardians. For the people of Motiti, there is optimism around a current proposal initiated by Te Atarangi Sayers for Rāhui, designated as a no-take, marine protected area around Otaiti, to be instituted by government. This would go further to ensure the long-term sustainability and well-being of the marine and cultural environment, thereby protecting it for all New Zealanders.

Ultimately, this case highlights the ongoing need for vigilance on the part of Indigenous peoples to protect their rights and resources. It also focuses on the need for governments to adhere to international agreements to which they are party. Finally, it invokes businesses to deal with Indigenous peoples in a respectful way, as a pathway to mutually beneficial outcomes, regardless of opportunities provided by governments to diminish the role and rights of Indigenous peoples.

References

Anaya, S.J. (2015). Report of the special rapporteur on the rights of indigenous peoples on the situation of Māori people in New Zealand. *Arizona Journal of International and Comparative Law*, 32(1), pp. 2-26.

Bay of Plenty Times. (2015). Another iwi accepts Rena offer, June 24. Retrieved from http://www.nzherald.co.nz/bay-of-plenty-times/news/article.cfm?c_id=1503343&objectid=11470310

Beca (2014). Social Impact Assessment: Proposal to leave the remains of the MV Rena on Astrolabe Reef. Beca Carter Hollings & Ferner Ltd, Wellington.

Cheung, M. (2008). The reductionist-holistic worldview dilemma. *MAI Review*, 3(5), pp. 1-7.

Durie, M. (1998). *Politics of Māori self-determination*. Oxford University Press, USA.

Environment Court. (2016). Decision of Panel on MV Rena Resource Consent Applications, February 26th. Bay of Plenty Regional Council. Retrieved from http://www.renaresource-consent.org.nz

Fa'aui, T.N. & Morgan, T.K.K.B. (2014). Restoring the Mauri to the pre-MV Rena state. *MAI Journal*, 3(1), pp. 3-17.

Henry, E. (2012). *Te Wairua Auaha: emancipatory Māori entrepreneurship in screen production*. (Doctoral thesis). Auckland University of Technology, Auckland, New Zealand. Retrieved from http://hdl.handle.net/10292/4085

Kahotea, D. (2015). Cultural Assessment. Evidence for the Bay of Plenty Regional Council resource consent. Retrieved from http://www.renaresourceconsent.org.nz/wp-content/uploads/2015/09/Hearing-Statement-Des-Kahotea.pdf

Kawharu, I.H. (1989). *Waitangi: Māori & Pākehā Perspectives of the Treaty of Waitangi*. Oxford University Press, Oxford.

King, M. (2003). *Penguin History of New Zealand*. Penguin Books, New Zealand.

Lashley, M.E. (2000). Implementing treaty settlements via indigenous institutions: Social justice and detribalization in New Zealand. *The Contemporary Pacific*, 12(1), pp. 1-55.

Orange, C. (2015). *The Treaty of Waitangi*. Bridget Williams Books, New Zealand.

Salmond, A. (1997). *Between worlds: early exchanges between Māori and Europeans, 1773-1815*. Chronicle Books, New Zealand.

Smith, L.T. (1999). *Decolonizing methodologies: Research and indigenous peoples*. Zed Books, New Zealand.

TAIC (2014). Marine Inquiry 11-204, Container ship MV Rena grounding on Astrolabe Reef. Transport Accident Investigation Commission, Wellington. Retrieved from http://www.taic.org.nz/ReportsandSafetyRecs/MarineReports/tabid/87/ctl/Detail/mid/484/InvNumber/2011-204/language/en-US/Default.aspx?SkinSrc=%5BG%5Dskins%2Ftaic Marine%2Fskin_marine

Te Aho, L. (2010). Indigenous challenges to enhance freshwater governance and management in Aotearoa New Zealand: The Waikato river settlement. *The Journal of Water Law*, 20(5), pp. 285-292.

Te Ara. (1966). Motiti Island. A.H. McClintock (ed.), *An Encyclopedia of New Zealand*. Wellington: Government Printer.

United Nations Global Compact (2013). *A Business Reference Guide: United Nations Declaration on the Rights of Indigenous Peoples*. Retrieved from https://www.unglobalcompact.org/docs/issues_doc/human_rights/IndigenousPeoples/BusinessGuide.pdf

Waitangi Tribunal. (2013). The final report on the MV Rena and Motiti Island Claims. Wellington: Waitangi Tribunal. Retrieved from: http://www.teara.govt.nz/en/1966/Motiti-island

Waitangi Tribunal (2014). Final Report on the MV Rena and Motiti Island Claims, WAI 2391, 2393 Report (Nov. 28, 2014). Wellington.

Walker, R. (1990). *Ka Whaiwhai Tonu Matau*. Penguin Books: Auckland, NZ.

Ward, A. (2015). *An Unsettled History: Treaty Claims in New Zealand Today*. Bridget Williams Books: Wellington, New Zealand.

Zacharatos, K. (2014). Konstantinos Zacharatos on Behalf of Applicant. Rena Resource Consent, Environment Court. Retrieved from http://www.renaresourceconsent.org.nz/wp-content/uploads/2015/06/Evidence-of-Konstantinos-Zacharatos.pdf

4

The Chinese, political CSR, and a nickel mine in Papua New Guinea

Benedict Y. Imbun, Ph.D.

Senior Lecturer, Western Sydney University; Papua New Guinea citizen

This chapter's conceptual framework builds on Scherer and Palazzo's work on political corporate social responsibility (PCSR) which acknowledges the greater political role played by corporations in countries characterized by a weak state. In a globalized political economy, corporations seek new ways to maintain legitimacy beyond the stable framework of law and moral custom. I utilize the PCSR framework to investigate whether "deliberative democracy" is a factor in planning and implementing community development (CD) programs in Papua New Guinea's Chinese-operated Ramu nickel mine (RNM). I investigate pressures and challenges by local indigenous communities for tangible development benefits from the mine and RNM's strategies and responses. Although RNM is receptive to taking on the CD challenges, it has inherent constraints. RNM would have to consolidate its fledging PCSR role to successfully operate the nickel mine over time.

Political corporate social responsibility, Community development, Papua New Guinea, Ramu nickel mine, Local communities

Introduction

Scholars of extractive industry investment in developing countries concede, generally, that the adoption of corporate social responsibility (CSR) by business corporations is pivotal to the successful operations of their projects (see Hilson, 2012). From the perspective of extractive companies, one reason for this is that implementation of CSR programs (i.e. community development (CD) projects) in areas of impact on local communities allows the company to gain a "social license to operate"—at the same time that it successfully achieves its core business goals. Scherer and Palazzo (2011, p. 907) postulate that in a globalized political economy corporations seek new ways to maintain their legitimacy beyond "the stable framework of law and moral custom." They (2011, p. 910) described it as "political CSR" (PCSR)—that is "a movement of the corporation into the political sphere in order to respond to environmental and social challenges such as human rights, global warming and deforestation."

With these reflections in mind, the purpose of the chapter is to investigate the utilization of PCSR in the process of planning and implementing CD programs in Ramu Nickel Mine (RNM), project operated by a Chinese company in Papua New Guinea (PNG). The chapter analyzes how RNM has approached and implemented CD projects, and how these have impacted on local communities around its mining and processing activities.

Specifically, it is argued that the implementation of CD projects could be improved if CSR is embraced and supported by well-thought-through strategies and adequate human resources that fully engage stakeholders, particularly local communities who are affected by the implementation of the mining project. This is premised on the fact that reactionary and ad hoc CSR strategies do not effectively take into consideration the CD needs and thus marginalize local communities that are affected by the company's operations.

The chapter is structured as follows. The next section provides a brief review of literature on deliberative democracy in the context of PCSR involving commercial enterprises. The subsequent section contextualizes the research through a brief overview on PNG, and the unique issues and challenges that besieged the country. This is followed by a discussion on the socioeconomic and political factors that have affected RNM during and after construction of the project. Next, the methodological foundations of the study are explained, followed by an analysis of the fieldwork findings of RNM's CD activities in Madang province of PNG. The conclusion recaps some of the key themes of the chapter.

The term CD is used in this chapter to mean tangible developments (improvements) in economic, social, and cultural conditions that host local communities have received as a result of the pressures exerted on these international organizations, particularly mining companies.

PCSR: the literature

The conceptual framework for the chapter draws on the work of Scherer and Palazzo (2011) on PCSR, which acknowledges the increasingly political role played by corporations in countries characterized by a weak state. In these contexts, corporations have become increasingly active in the delivery of services traditionally provided by the government, including CD programs to address issues such as poverty, HIV/AIDS, and infrastructure (Strongman, 1998). Scherer and Palazzo (2011, p. 918) offer an alternative perspective of PCSR which includes, inter alia, a **deliberative model of democracy**. Deliberative democracy is a form of political engagement that involves "the argumentative involvement of citizens in decision making processes" (Scherer and Palazzo, 2011, p. 919). Another relevant feature of Scherer and Palazzo's perspective is an alleged shift from the traditional notion of pragmatic legitimacy toward moral legitimacy. According to them, this will endow corporations with an "enlarged understanding of responsibility," thus making them better positioned to solve problems "in cooperation with state actors and civil society actors" (Scherer and Palazzo, 2011, p. 919).

Scherer and Palazzo's PCSR framework is suitable for the analysis in this chapter because it takes into account the complex patterns of relationships between corporations and communities. As noted by Banks *et al.* (2013), the scenario is in fact more nuanced and complex, involving shifting degrees of cooperation, conflict and accommodation. Scherer and Palazzo's PCSR framework also rejects simplistic depictions of host communities as powerless and dependent on company operations for hand-outs (Strongman, 1998). The deliberative democracy concept assumes that local communities are actively engaged agents, able to influence decisions about the design and delivery of CD programs. The theoretical framework therefore enables a better understanding of the nature of CD partnerships in PNG, and the deliberative strategies used by the key stakeholders to negotiate initiatives and grievances.

PNG country context

Since political independence from Australia in 1975, PNG's economy has been dominated by the extractive industry, which accounts for nearly two-thirds of export earnings (Filer *et al.*, 2016). The industry is likely to expand even further in 2018 through the development of a second liquefied natural gas (LNG) project run by TOTAL, the French LNG giant. This is by far the largest investment project in PNG's history, and can potentially double GDP in the medium term and triple PNG's export earnings (Jubilee Australia, 2012).

However, the sizeable proceeds of PNG's extractive industry have not significantly benefited populations in the rural areas, who continue to live in poverty

(Lea, 2004). Failure of development projects in rural PNG has been attributed to factors such as poor governance, deteriorating infrastructure, failing institutions, entrenched inequalities, and law and order issues (ADB, 2008). Reflecting broader trends in the global context, a rapid decline in government assistance since the 1980s has been a pressing problem in rural PNG (Dinnen, 2009). As a result, extractive companies have "stepped in" to become increasingly involved in the provision of social and economic services to their host communities (Imbun, 2006; Callan, 2012). It has been argued that initiatives to meet the needs of host communities contribute to ensuring the companies' legitimacy, as the recipients of CSR programs tend to be more inclined to grant them a social license to operate (Scherer and Palazzo, 2011).

The Bougainville and Ok Tedi mine cases significantly influenced how community-based development programs are delivered in PNG by the extractive industry (Kepore and Imbun, 2010). The post-Bougainville-Ok Tedi period in PNG is characterized, not by open antagonism between communities and company, but by a more deliberative model of partnerships based on legal requirements for compensation, equity, and inclusion. Imbun (2013) has found, for example, that the post-Bougainville period saw the establishment of formal land use agreements between company and land owners, specifying the nature and scope of extractive projects, and expected socio-environmental impacts. This is becoming the norm in PNG, with some benefits for communities. For example, partnership arrangements in Porgera, Lihir, Ok Tedi, Kutubu, and Hidden Valley mines have provided employment opportunities, business spin-offs, infrastructure developments, health services, and other benefits for local landowners and other community stakeholders (Imbun, 2013; Filer *et al.* 2016).

The RNM

The RNM is one of PNG's recent mines. Like all other extractive projects in rural hinterlands, it is located in an underdeveloped backwater of coastal Madang province. With 85% equity, Metallurgical Corporation of China (MCC) is the majority shareholder followed by Australian company Highlands Gold, claiming 5.56% equity. The remaining 5.94% and 3.5% shares are, respectively, owned by PNG Government and customary landowners of the Special Mining Lease (SML) area. Depressed nickel prices on the world market over the last four decades had deterred investors despite the discovery of the ore deposit in the 1960s. That changed in 2002 when then Prime Minister, Michael Somare, promised the people of Madang in a national election speech that, should his party be returned to power, he would find a developer for the Ramu nickel (Matbob, 2014).

The return of Somare's National Alliance Party to power in 2003 saw an invitation to the Chinese Government to develop the Ramu project, which was assessed in 2003, and the two governments finalized an agreement in 2005 (Matbob, 2014). As an incentive for investing in the country, the MCC was given a 10-year tax holiday, a first for any foreign company in PNG. The agreement signaled one of China's largest overseas investments (US$2.1 billion), particularly in the South Pacific. Commissioning commenced in 2012 and by 2013 was at 50% capacity, with a target of 70% in 2014, and 100% by 2015 (Highlands Pacific, 2014).

Figure 4.1 **Location of RNM and associated slurry pipeline and processing plant facilities**

Source: Highlands Pacific, 2014.

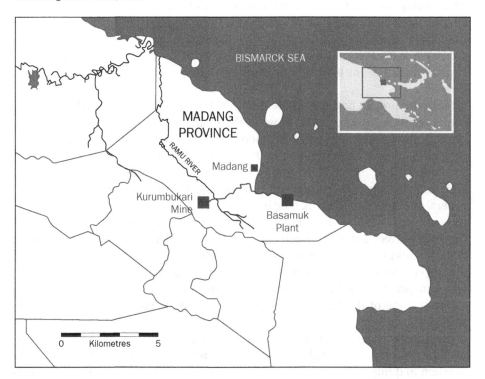

The RNM is connected by a 135 km slurry pipeline from the Kurumbukari plateau to the Basamuk processing plant which is 75 km east of the provincial capital of Madang, along the Rai Coast of the Vitiaz Basin. The majority of the pipeline has been buried and has road access for ease of maintenance. With a mine life in excess of 20 years, annual production at design capacity is 31,150 tonnes of nickel and 3,300 tonnes of cobalt contained in a mixed nickel cobalt hydroxide intermediate product. Based on advice from international experts and permitted stages it was decided to dispose of the tailings into the 1,500 meter-deep sea canyons as this represented the most appropriate and safe method of disposal (Highlands Pacific, 2014). This spread of the mining and processing operations over sparsely populated local communities in underdeveloped regions of the Madang province has become a nightmare for RNM management responding to CD demands.

Political imperatives, controversies, and civil discontent

As much as the Chinese Government was eager to invest in PNG, equally the PNG Government viewed the engagement as an economic imperative to make up for its declining income from its extractive sector. The declining output from PNG's long established mining projects, such as Ok Tedi, Porgera, and Lihir, was a major catalyst for the Somare Government's engagement with the Chinese (Matbob, 2014). While the PNG and Chinese politicians worked together in the background, Papua New Guineans and their institutions were oblivious that this bonding had occurred.

Since the project began in 2005, the RNM has been fraught with disputes and controversies (Matbob, 2014). Most of the disputes and controversies were the result of the government-to-government agreement that paved the way for Chinese development and operation of the Ramu nickel project. The issues spanned a wide spectrum and involved multiple stakeholders including PNG Government departments, company employees, provincial government, landowners, and the general population of Madang. The influx of Chinese workers to the mining project, most of them unable to speak English or *Pigin*, which is a condition for a PNG work visa, was waived, despite staunch criticism from the Department of Labour. Other departments and state agencies also voiced similar concerns about visa breaches, the project's substandard occupational health and safety practices, and the lack of adequate protocols at the provincial level (Interview, December 15, 2014).[1]

The rushing of the Ramu project meant that landowner issues pertaining to assessing ownership of the SML were also not effectively settled. This included inadequate compensation, which exacerbated in-fighting between landowners over the proceeds from royalties. The most controversial issue has been the RNM's decision to dump tailings into the sea at Basamuk Bay, via the "Deep Sea Tailings Pipeline" (DSTP). This decision was challenged in the courts by seaside villagers on countless occasions. Eventually, the Somare Government used its dominance in Parliament, and in 2010 amended the Environment Act to ensure the DSTP disposal could take place as intended. However, this and other issues such as employment relations, training, and "respect for local culture and communities" consumed the best part of eight years of the project. Production finally rolled out in 2010 (Matbob, 2014).

---

1 Interviews were conducted by Imbun, with stakeholders of RNM, in Madang and Port Moresby, between December 14 and December 20, 2014.

Methodology

This chapter draws on the case study technique, which helps to investigate a contemporary phenomenon within its real-life context when the boundaries between the phenomenon and context are not clearly evident and in which multiple sources of evidence are used (Yin, 2003).

The importance of the analysis is linked to the perception that RNM's CSR policy of CD engagement and programs is ad hoc and not fully fledged, partly compounded by its lack of experience and inability to seek advice (Interview, December 16, 2014). Thus, in order to explain and describe how the company engages and implements its CSR policies, the chapter utilizes a qualitative methodology (Yin, 2003). The qualitative paradigm allowed the researcher to collect data "in the form of impressions, nuances, words, photos, symbols and so forth" (Neuman, 2007, p. 85), for analysis.

The major benefit in using the case study technique is that it allows the researchers to closely examine data within its real-life, natural context in order to achieve detailed understanding of the issues under study (Crowe *et al.*, 2011). Five groups of stakeholders associated with RNM's CSR CD programs were selected and interviewed for the study, individually and in focus groups: Kurumbukari customary landowners, Basamuk villagers, Madang Provincial Government, PNG National Government Agencies, and RNM management. The purposive sampling technique was applied in selecting respondents for interview (Neuman, 2004).

Insights from research

Most of the views and opinions expressed from the stakeholder interviews reflected several main themes relating to RNM management of their CSR programs, both in the vicinity of their operations, and in Madang province as a whole. The four main themes that emerged included the key perceptions of the informants, defined as "Appreciate the investment but RNM must live up to the game." The other three relate to the participants' perceptions of the RNM CD strategies, including "Learning the new ropes of CSR," "Action speaks louder than words—the Chinese way," and "One RNM, one community." Broadly, CD activities spearheaded by the company were implemented with much fanfare and publicity. The slogans and affirmations were purposely designed and presented to make them stand out, and in the process attempt to elicit the attention of the local community. However, the response from the community has not been universally positive.

"Appreciate the investment but RNM must live up to the game"

While Papua New Guinea in general, and local communities in particular, welcomed and appreciated the anticipated economic and social benefits the RNM has brought them, they would like the project to "up its ante" in terms of CSR. Aided by the country's long mining history and familiarity with what companies can do to develop infrastructure, economic and social activities in programs in impacted communities and beyond (Filer and Imbun, 2009), there is a view that RNM has to invest more in projects that will have a tangible and positive impact in their communities. Two articulate Kurumbukari villagers echoed the sentiments of the focus group, stating, "We are aware of what big rich mining companies provide to impacted local communities in the country," and, "We want to know what they can do in terms of projects" (Interview, December 15, 2014). The expectations of some local and international non-governmental organization (NGO) representatives are that they "appreciate the investment but RNM must live up to the game" and "come good, particularly on the environment side" (Interview, December 15, 2014).

For RNM, its CSR role has been clearly articulated in the Memorandum of Agreement (MoA) signed in 2002 with four project-impacted communities. The recipients have included landowner associations comprising Kurumbukari villagers near the mine site, villagers around the inland pipeline, other villages along the coastal pipeline, and villagers by the Basamuk refinery. The development benefits contained in the MoA reflected benefits other local communities of mining areas enjoy which emanate from the stipulations outlined in the PNG benefit sharing policy framework. Those included local communities receiving preferential treatment in terms of: employment opportunities, education and training scholarships and apprenticeships, and business development assistance. But the respective local communities have criticized the degree of implementation and emphasis placed on each of the supposed benefits. For example, although the project employs a significant number of Papua New Guineans (90% of the near 2000 workforce), the proportion of local community members has been marginal, which is contrary to the MoA stipulations. The company, in an effort to achieve efficiencies, has opted to employ a highly skilled workforce from outside the area, which has infuriated the local communities.

The pressure for more employment opportunities for locals had been brewing since commencement of the project and locals were not shy of showing their frustrations. This culminated in a spate of violent attacks on the project and its properties at the Kurumbukari and Basamuk sites. The worst attack came from a group of Kurumbukari youth who burned mine equipment at the site in September 2014. The damage cost the company US$4 million (Middleton, 2014). The incident was triggered when mine management overlooked local people for operator jobs, instead hiring skilled workers from Madang.

An aggrieved old man at the mine site, whose eldest son and six others were recently arrested as suspects in the incident, said, "I'll tell my second son to do the same thing (again), because the Chinese are not fulfilling the MoA" (Interview, December 16, 2014). Similar sentiments alleging the company is not fulfilling most of the provisions in the MoA were echoed by interviewees along the pipeline and in

Basamuk. The company, however, spurred by the violent attacks has promised to continue the rollout of the promises made in the MoA (Middleton, 2014).

"Learning the new ropes of CSR"

It was apparent from the sentiments expressed by the various interviewees that as much as Chinese management was eager to forge and consolidate political patronage, particularly at the national level, its support for CSR at community level seemed superficial and rudimentary. The strategic importance of CSR was yet to be incorporated by executive and line management. One of the RNM community relations officers (CRO) confirmed that "we (the mine management) are learning the new ropes of CSR" as the "Chinese are unfamiliar with this concept and struggling at the moment" (Interview, December 15, 2014). This was of little surprise as the Community Relations Office has only expanded from two to ten staff members between 2000 and 2013. These ten full-time CROs are responsible for overseeing the entire mining operations, affecting 60,000 villagers and overlapping two political districts. There were also other officers who handled public relations, agriculture, and health matters. Likewise, the public relations officers carried out the important task of keeping the media up to date with the implementation of projects, and cultivating and strengthening political contacts. The government officers of relevant agencies such as Labour and the Mineral Resources Authority (MRA) were surprised about the minimal staff covering such a sensitive function for the mine in contrast to other established PNG mines. "We'll wait and see," one MRA officer mentioned, "as there is a lot on their plate and they have to listen to the villagers fast or things will blow up in their face" (Interview, December 19, 2014).

For RNM, the country's advanced policies and controls related to mining, coupled with assertive and politically savvy local communities, caught them by surprise. They were not adequately prepared for the barrage of expectations from the people as the president of the company acknowledged in a company statement, "We have experience in 33 countries outside China, but to date working with local communities in PNG is trying and complex ... It will take some time to understand but we'll overcome" (RNM, 2006–2008). Generally, Chinese companies have been heavily criticized for giving scant regard to their CSR obligations, particularly relating to allegations of maltreatment of labor, poor pay, environmental degradation, substandard structures, and the flaunting of laws and processes in African, Asian, and Latin American countries (Smith, 2013). With the RNM, there seems to be no escape as the local communities are watchful of every move that RNM makes in terms of its community development.

"Action speaks louder than words"—the Chinese way

If RNM was learning the means and ways of dealing with local communities, this was not apparent, as the company indulged in its Chinese motto of "Action speaks louder than words" as a response to the scrutiny of government, NGOs, and civil society. The minimalist approach to communicating with the civil community on all aspects of its operations (most critically on its impacts) is viewed by stakeholders, particularly environmental NGOs, as intolerable and self-serving.

This strategy is not only confined to the PNG project but is widely practiced among Chinese companies particularly in Africa where they are criticized for not engaging in broader partnerships and corporate citizenship equivalent to the outputs produced (Cheng and Liang, 2011). Persistent local community, worker and NGO activism, particularly concerning its DSTP waste disposal system, have convinced RNM to concentrate on "actions" rather than words (Interview, December 17, 2014). A local academic commented that as long as the PNG politicians and government were in the "pockets of the company," critics and commentators were viewed by RNM as not important to their long-term success (Interview, December 17, 2014).

In all fairness, the company seemed to have taken on CD assignments as quickly as it could in its initial phase of investment in the project (RNM, 2014). However, opinions and views from the recipients of these projects vary according to their respective impacts on local communities. The degree of impacts and resultant anticipation of compensation from local communities are obvious in the sentiments expressed. For example, the Kurumbukari villagers were adamant that whatever RNM was providing in terms of projects was not adequate compensation for the hardships they experienced.

> We hear, Ok Tedi, Porgera and other mining companies look after their local communities ... electricity, roads, employment of SML landowners. There is an influx of other people seeking employment here and we are the victims of exaggerated compensation and bride price demands from our neighbours (Interview, December 17, 2014).

While the inland and costal pipeline communities experienced the least adverse impacts, they feel much of the anticipated benefits from local CD projects developed by RNM and the PNG Government were not enhancing their communities. "Yeah, for us, this so-called 'Action' which the Chinese are saying happening in our communities is hardly taking place" (Interview, December 18, 2014). They are generally bitter about the limited CD benefits coming to them. To them, the pipeline route is as essential as the ore pit or DSTP areas. However, the Basamuk villagers also fear the disposal of tailings. This environmental issue has besieged the project since its construction in the mid-2000s and has seen countless court filings backed by local and international environmental NGO organizations such as Basamuk Ramu Group and Mining Watch Canada. But, the company has the support of the government, through the amendment of the Environment Act (2010), which allows it to dispose of the waste with impunity, therefore barring individuals and local communities from mounting legal challenges.

"One RNM, One Community"

If "Action speaks louder" is the catchcry of RNM's strategy for implementing CD programs, certainly its motto of "One RNM, One Community" is the overarching community relations strategy, with the intended objective of having significant and positive impacts on the local communities and beyond. Much akin to China's recently successful slogans of "One World, One Dream" (2008 Beijing Olympic theme) and "Better City, Better Life" (2010 Shanghai World Trade Expo), "One RNM, One Community" is applied to forge political and social bonding between China and PNG, particularly the communities impacted by the project (Yakai, 2009). The message implicit in the slogan also means "learning about the local people and establishing trust and communication with landowners" which the company views as central to its achievement of sustainability goals (Lai and Liu, 2012). The slogan has been the guide for the community relations office as well as a publicity strategy for RNM in its attempt to appease media tensions and community negativism.

The "One RNM, One Community" strategy has culminated in the rollout of cultural and political initiatives aimed at displaying Chinese educational, cultural, and technological expertise to Papua New Guineans. Between 2006 and 2012 the RNM has sent local PNG mine engineers for more technical training and also for Chinese language and cultural training. That has been coupled with sponsorship of select national and provincial leaders associated with the project to travel to China on "fact finding" missions and bringing Chinese development, health, and cultural teams back to Madang. Raine (2009) has termed this an example of "soft power" by the Chinese and he refers to similar strategies in African countries. One might assume there is a political hegemony attached to these CSR activities. According to Raine (2009, p. 8) "Chinese authorities are responding here as they have in Africa, and elsewhere in increasing development aid, under this 'developing world' banner, and it is important to remember the broader context in which China is developing its relations". Whether through "hard" or "soft" politics, what is obvious is that RNM is increasing its political and cultural agenda, intertwined with CD projects, in an attempt to make itself more acceptable to the critical masses in local and national communities, while promoting Chinese language, culture, and business practice.

Conclusion

This chapter discussed PCSR in the context of RNM in its development and operations in the Madang province of PNG. There are and have been from the outset a multitude of complex issues besieging the company. RNM management recognize the growing criticisms of its operations and expectations of greater benefits for the local communities. They have wielded political corporate social responsibility as a corporate strategy to satisfy government and appease local communities. Members of those communities believe that RNM has a moral obligation to contribute as much energy to their economic and social development needs as it does to exploiting the local communities for its mining endeavors. Notwithstanding that, the company has started implementing developments for the local communities in the midst of some of the stoutest criticism, from government bureaucrats and NGO representatives. The various PCSR strategies that RNM has embraced include, "Learning new ropes," "Action speaks louder," and "One RNM, One Community," which are supposed to enhance their community development initiatives, but which have also been criticized by locals.

However, this obvious and growing scrutiny by civil society is driving RNM to make a real commitment to its PCSR obligations. Politically savvy local communities, government agencies, and NGOs are having an impact. It is also obvious that this Chinese mining company is receptive to taking on the CD challenges. What this means is RNM will have to build and consolidate its fledging PCSR strategies if it truly wishes to thrive in Papua New Guinea, and build sustainable and mutually beneficial relationships with the country and its local communities.

References

Asian Development Bank. (2008). *Public-Private Partnership Handbook*. Manila: ADB.

Banks, G., Kuir-Ayius, D., Kombako, D. & Sagir, B. (2013). Conceptualizing mining impacts, livelihoods and corporate community development in Melanesia. *Community Development Journal*, 48(3), pp. 484-500.

Callan, M. (2012). *What do we know about the private sector's contribution to development? Development Policy Centre, Discussion Paper 11*. Canberra: ANU.

Cheng, S., & Liang, G. (2011). Social responsibility of Chinese investment in Africa: What does it mean for EU-China Cooperation on development policy towards Africa? *Trade Negotiations sights*. Retrieved from http://www.ictsd.org/bridges-news/trade-negotiations-sights/news/social-responsibility-of-chinese-investment-in-africa.

Crowe, S., Cresswell, K., Robertson, A., Huby, G., Avery, A. & Sheikh, A. (2011). The case study approach, *Medical Research Methodology*. Retrieved from http://www.biomedcentral.com/1471-2288/11/100

Dinnen, S. (2009). Thirty Years of Law and Order Policy and Practice: Trying To Do "Too Much, Too Badly, With Too Little"? In R.J. May (Ed.), *Policy Making and Implementation: Studies from Papua New Guinea* (pp. 233-260). Canberra: ANU ePress.

Filer, C. & Imbun, B.Y. (2009). A Short History of Mineral Development Policies in Papua New Guinea, 1972-2002. In R.J. May (Ed.), *Policy Making and Implementation: Studies from Papua New Guinea* (pp. 75-116). Canberra: ANU ePress.

Filer, C., Andrew, M., Carr, P., Imbun, B.Y. & Sagir, B. (2016). Jobs, Poverty, and Resources. In G. Betcherman & M. Rama (Eds.), *Jobs for Development: Challenges and Solutions in Different Country Settings* (in press). London: Oxford University Press.

Highlands Pacific. (2014). Ramu Nickel. Retrieved from http://www.highlandspacific.com/current-projects/ramu-nickel

Hilson, G. (2012). Corporate Social Responsibility in the extractive industries: Experiences from developing countries. *Resource Policy*, 37(2), pp. 131-137.

Imbun, B.Y. (2006). Cannot Manage without the "Significant Other": Mining, Corporate Social Responsibility and Local Communities in PNG. *Journal of Business Ethics*, 3(2), pp. 177-192.

Imbun, B.Y. (2013). Maintaining land use agreement in Papua New Guinea mining: "business as usual"? *Resource Policy*, 38(3), pp. 310-319.

Imbun, B.Y. (2014). "Look North policy," Asian investment, and Papua New Guineans: A trinity formed for development, In P. D'Arcy, P. Matbob, & L. Crowl (Eds.), *Pacific-Asia Partnerships in Resource Development* (pp. 22-35) Madang: Divine Word University Press.

Jublie Australia. (2012). Pipe Dreams: The PNG LNG Project and Futures of a Nation. Retrieved from http://www.Jubilee+Australia_PIPE+DREAMS+Report_April2013_Web. pdfJublie

Kepore, K. & Imbun, B.Y. (2011). Mining and Stakeholder Discourse in a PNG mine. *Corporate Social Responsibly & Environmental Management*, 18, pp. 220-223.

Lea, D. (2004) Can democratic reform enhance Papua New Guinea's economic performance? *Pacific Economic Bulletin*, 19(1), pp. 23-29.

Matbob, P. (2014). We are not anti-Asian-just victims of poor governance: A media perspective. In P. D'Arcy, P. Matbob, & L. Crowl (Eds.), *Pacific-Asia Partnerships in Resource Development* (pp. 59-71). Madang: Divine Word University Press.

Middleton, A. (2014). Ramu, landowners heal with contracts. PNG Industry News Net. Retrieved from http://www.pngindustrynews.net/storyview.asp?storyid=824242392&sectionsource=s0

Neuman, W.L. (2007). *Basics of social research: Qualitative and quantitative approaches.* Boston: Pearson.

Raine, S. (2009). *China's African Challenges.* London: Routledge.

RNM. (2006–2008). RNM 2006-2008 Sustainability Report. Retrieved from http://www.ramunico.com/download/updater/Sustainability%20Report%202006-2008%20Full%20Version.pdf

RNM. (2014). RNM impress Media workshop. *Ramu Garamut*, 37(May-June). Retrieved from http://www.ramunico.com/plus/list.php?tid=176

Scherer, A.G. and Palazzo, G. (2011). The new political role of business in a globalized world: A review of a new perspective on CSR and its implications for the firm, governance, and democracy. *Journal of Management Studies,* 48(4), pp. 899-916.

Smith, G. (2013). Nupela Masta? Local and Expatriate Labour in a Chinese-Run Nickel Mine in Papua New Guinea. *Asia Studies Review*, 37(2), pp. 178-195.

Strongman, J. (1998). *Mining and the community - From enclave to sustainable development.* Paper presented at the Mining and the Community for Asian and Pacific Nations Conference, Madang, July 26–28, 1998.

Yakai, M. (2009). "One RNM, One Community Aims for Prosperity," Asia Pacific Perspective–China. Retrieved from http://mathewyakai.blogspot.com.au/2009/05/one-ramu-nico-one-community-aims-for.html.

Yin, R.K. (2003). *Case study research: Design and methods.* Beverly Hills: SAGE.

Section II

Business and Ongoing Challenges to Indigenous Aspirations and Rights

5

Indigenous rights capital
The basis for sustainable enterprise creation

Bob Kayseas, Ph.D.
Professor of Business and Academic Associate Vice President, First Nations University of Canada; Fishing Lake First Nation member

Bettina Schneider, Ph.D.
Assistant Professor, School of Business and Public Administration, First Nations University of Canada

Raquel Pasap
Masters of Public Administration candidate, First Nations University of Canada; Assiniboine First Nation member

Moses Gordon
Masters of Public Policy candidate, First Nations University of Canada; George Gordon First Nation member

Bob Anderson, Ph.D.
Professor, University of Regina, Canada

This chapter asks two key questions. First, what is the nature of the Indigenous rights being recognized? Second, what role can these increased rights have in the development activities of Indigenous people? To explore these questions, we will focus on the recognition of Indigenous Rights in Canada through international doctrines, the Constitution, the courts, and treaties. We further explore how First Nations people in Canada have expanded their rights and land through specific and comprehensive land claims and how they have also been challenged by the restrictions imposed by reserves and the Indian Act. In particular, we share a brief case study of the Fishing Lake First Nation, and their efforts to assert their inherent land rights for economic gain.

First Nations, Treaty rights, Fishing Lake First Nation

Introduction

According to the 2011 National Household Survey, there were 1,400,685 Canadians who claimed Aboriginal identity, representing 4.3% of the total Canadian population (Statistics Canada, 2013). As we mention later in the chapter, the Canadian Constitution recognizes three Indigenous groups as being "Aboriginal," the Indian, Métis, and Inuit (Government of Canada, 2016). Those who were originally referred to as "Indians" now prefer to be called First Nations. Those First Nations people on the official Indian Register in Canada are referred to as "status Indians" or "status First Nations"; however, there are many First Nations people who are considered "non-status" for a number of reasons and therefore are not subject to the Indian Act and don't have access to the same programs and services under the Indian Act as status First Nations (Brown *et al.*, 2016). The term Métis refers to those of "mixed First Nations and European heritage, typically of the prairies, who developed a unique culture and language (Michif) during the North American fur trade" (Brown *et al.*, 2016, p. iv). Aboriginal peoples who have traditionally lived in the Arctic, having similar cultures, are referred to as "Inuit." Métis and Inuit people, like non-status First Nations, are not subject to the Indian Act, legislation we will address later in the chapter (Brown *et al.*, 2016). Throughout this chapter, we regularly use Indigenous peoples and Aboriginal peoples interchangeably.

As recently stated by Canadian Prime Minister Justin Trudeau, "Reconciliation starts with recognizing and respecting Aboriginal title and rights, including Treaty rights," which he acknowledges as not only constitutional obligations, but also obligations under the UN Declaration on the Rights of Indigenous Peoples (Trudeau, 2016). These words were spoken at the Assembly of First Nations 36th Annual General Assembly and a month after the release of the Truth and Reconciliation Commission summary report and findings. Trudeau went on to further emphasize the need for a

> ... renewed, nation-to-nation relationship with Aboriginal communities. A relationship based on recognition, rights, respect, co-operation and partnership. One that is rooted in the principles of the United Nations Declaration on the Rights of Indigenous Peoples. One that is guided by the spirit and intent of the original Treaty relationship, and one that respects the decisions of our courts. One that takes us beyond our formal agreements and speaks to how we ought to treat each other—person to person and spirit to spirit. One that remembers that when we conduct ourselves with dignity, we manifest our respect for the Creator, and for Creation (Trudeau, 2016).

In Canada and globally, there has been a strong movement in recent decades to recognize the rights of Indigenous people to have access to and control over their traditional lands and resources. In this chapter, we address two key questions. First, what is the nature of the Indigenous rights being recognized? Second, what role can these increased rights have in the development activities of Indigenous people? To explore these questions, we will focus on the recognition of Indigenous Rights in Canada through international doctrines, the Constitution, the courts, and treaties. We further explore how First Nations people in Canada have expanded their rights and land through specific and comprehensive land claims and how they have also been challenged by the restrictions imposed by reserves and the Indian Act. In particular, we share a brief case study of the Fishing Lake First Nation, and their efforts to assert their inherent land rights for economic gain.

Indigenous rights in Canada

What are Indigenous rights? Indigenous rights in Canada are a complex issue to understand for a number of reasons. There is no definitive list that outlines what specifically are the rights of Indigenous Canadians just as there is no homogeneous Indigenous community or cultural group. There are a number of legal distinctions made when referring to Indigenous Canadians that add to the complexity. For example, the Canadian Constitution recognizes three Indigenous groups as being "Aboriginal," the Indian, Métis, and Inuit (Government of Canada, 2016). Indians typically use the term First Nation to refer to themselves and their communities. A report based on the 2011 National Household Survey (NHS) reported 1,400,685 Aboriginal people in Canada with 851,560 First Nations (60.8% of all Aboriginal people), 451,795 (32.2%) people identified as Métis, and 59,445 (4.2%) Inuit (Statistics Canada, 2013).

The First Nations population is further divided into status Indians and non-status Indians. Status Indians are registered under the Indian Act and are thus eligible for a wide range of programs and services offered by federal agencies and provincial governments that other Aboriginal people, including non-status Indians, are not (Indigenous and Northern Affairs Canada, 2016). There are also treaty Indians and non-treaty Indians—treaty Indians are status Indians that belong to a First Nation community that has signed a treaty with the Crown.

Indigenous Canadians have asserted inherent rights to land and self-governance. The term "inherent" means that the right is not derived from the Constitution of Canada or from a delegation of powers from either the federal or provincial government. Indigenous Canadians believe they have the right to govern themselves because they did so for hundreds of years before contact with European settlers as established in several Supreme Court of Canada proceedings. A number of Supreme Court of Canada rulings have agreed to the concept of Indigenous peoples as original inhabitants—which accords a special status and rights that are still not clearly defined. For example, in *R. v. Van der Peet*, the Supreme Court of Canada (SCC) ruled:

> In my view, the doctrine of aboriginal rights exists, and is recognized and affirmed by s. 35(1), because of one simple fact: when Europeans arrived

in North America, aboriginal peoples were already here, living in communities on the land, and participating in distinctive cultures, as they had done for centuries. It is this fact, and this fact above all others, which separates aboriginal peoples from all other minority groups in Canadian society and which mandates their special legal, and now constitutional, status (Hopkins and Peeling, 2004, p. 5).

Section 35(1) of the Constitution Act, 1982, provides recognition of Aboriginal people's rights and affirms their interests in traditional lands (Wright and White, 2012). The Constitution Act states that "The existing Aboriginal and treaty rights of the Aboriginal Peoples of Canada are hereby recognized and affirmed" (Constitution Act, 1982). Although the Constitution Act (1982) secures Aboriginal rights over common law, federal legislation, or provincial legislation, according to Wright and White (2012), "it does not create them; Aboriginal rights are inherent, collective rights based on their original occupancy of the land" (p. 2). In his review of the 1970 first edition of *Indigenous Rights in Canada*, author Thomas R. Berger wrote, "the rights of Indigenous people in Canada are founded upon Aboriginal title ... treaties, reserves, hunting and fishing rights that all spring from Aboriginal title" (Berger, 1972). Inherent Indigenous rights based on Aboriginal title exist "independently of any form of legislation or executive recognition" and are based on notions of joint rights and jurisdictional-based legal concepts and ideas that existed before colonial contact (Berger, 1972). They are collective rights based on Indigenous peoples' original occupation of territory lands and pre-existing institutions of private property and Indigenous rights (Alcantara, 2003).

The uncertainty over the nature of the "existing Aboriginal and treaty rights" gave rise to efforts by Aboriginal people to define and assert these rights through legal challenges both before and after the repatriation of the Canadian Constitution.

Since the occupation and settlement of non-treaty territories, constituting what Thomas Berger describes as, "expropriation without compensation," the concept of Indigenous rights and Indigenous access to land and resources has both evolved and continued to create practical difficulties and legal uncertainty in Canada. This has resulted in judicial consideration of Indigenous rights claims, which have fundamentally altered the legal status and potential scope of Indigenous claims to rights, land, and resources. The recognition and affirmation of Indigenous rights in Section 35 of the Constitution Act of Canada acted as a "catalyst for the reconceptualization" of Indigenous rights in economic, legal, and political discourses (Asch and Bell, 2002).

In order to illustrate, this section references seven relevant Supreme Court cases (see Appendix) that demonstrate the evolution of Indigenous rights within the last 50 years. The first six cases all address issues arising in regions where there are no historic treaties in effect. These areas include almost all of British Columbia, portions of the provinces of Newfoundland and Labrador, Ontario, Quebec, and the territories of the Yukon, Northwest Territories, and Nunavut. These decisions and the circumstances they reflect gave rise to the Modern Treaty process (Comprehensive Claims) which in turn has given rise to the recognition of 60 million hectares of Indigenous-owned lands and over 600 million hectares of lands over which Indigenous people exercise significant control (Anderson, 2015). The final case, Grassy Narrows, related to rights in an area covered by Historic Treaties.

Some areas where rights have been defined in much greater detail are found with the various historical treaties signed between Indigenous peoples and the burgeoning Canadian state.

Treaty rights

According to Alfred (1999), treaties "never gave consent to European ownership of territory or the establishment of European ownership over them. Treaties did not do this, according to both historic Native understandings and contemporary legal analysis" (p. 59). Rather, treaties guaranteed First Nations certain rights in return for allowing the settlement of the Europeans into their territories and provided a way in which the land and its resources could be shared by First Nation peoples and settlers in Canada (Alfred, 1999; Anderson *et al.*, 2004). As stated by Robert Anderson *et al.* (2004), "Aboriginal people in Canada did not view the land and its resources as something they owned, so they did not see the treaties as a transfer of ownership" (p. 638).

There is a long history of Treaties that were signed between First Nations and European colonizing countries, particularly Great Britain, and then with Canada following Confederation in 1867. Both the British and Canadian Treaties are grounded in British Common Law Concepts. There are seven groups of Historic Treaties stretching from 1701 to 1921 (see Treaty maps; Indigenous and Northern Affairs, 2013). The terms of these various agreements are thoroughly described on this website.

The most important fact about the Treaties described is that with the exception of the first two, European settlers viewed the treaties as an acknowledgement by the Indigenous peoples involved that they had ceded all claims to ownership of traditional lands in exchange for specific benefits. It is clear that the Crown's (Britain and then Canada) purpose was to extinguish Indigenous people's broad land title for specific smaller areas of land (reserves) and other benefits. The Royal Commission on Aboriginal Peoples (1996) stated that the "treaties constitute promises, and the importance of keeping promises is deeply ingrained in all of us and indeed is common to all cultures and legal systems" (Dussault and Erasmus, 1996, Vol. 2, p. 9). The Commission briefly covered a number of written provisions that contribute to ensuring a continued livelihood for treaty beneficiaries—these provisions are outlined in the text of the treaties and are summarized as:

- Education
- Medical care

- Tax exemption

- Provisions for land

- Treaty annuities

- Hunting, fishing, trapping

- Materials included in various treaties, for example twine, fish hooks and nets, ammunition, agricultural equipment, and seeds (Dussault and Erasmus, 1996, pp. 70-74)

While subject to disagreement about details, the land regime associated with the area of Canada covered by Historic Treaties remained largely unchanged from the signing of the last Numbered Treaty the 1970s.

In total, there are more than 3.5 million hectares of lands associated with Historic Treaties and Additions. Just over 3 million hectares are Reserve Lands set aside under Historic Treaties. Since 2006, about 350,000 hectares have been added to reserves under the federal Additions to Reserves/New Reserves Policy primarily from the settlement of land claims (Indigenous and Northern Affairs Canada, 2015b).

The reality of Indigenous First Nations groups today is one full of contradictions. While First Nations continue to achieve success within the Canadian court systems, and thus increased power especially regarding approval and participation (if so desired) in resource development projects, concurrently they have many authority and control challenges within their own communities because of the Indian Act. The Indian Act is a "controversial and intrusive" piece of legislation that has governed almost all aspects of life of status Indians, especially those that live on any of the 617 reserves. The Indian Act was passed into law in 1876. It was created to manage the affairs of "Indians" and the reserve lands set aside for their use. The Act places unique rules on "Indians" that do not apply to anyone else in Canada. The laws impact governance, land tenure, and land use as well as placing limits or restrictions on economic activity. For example,

- Many common legal rules that apply to land do not apply to reserve land because "reserve" land cannot be bought or sold. Ownership is vested with the Crown. The band council can allocate land for use to its members but those members cannot sell, lease, or mortgage it (Shulze, 2008, p.14).

- Real property cannot be seized. Section 89 does not allow creditors to seize the real property of "Indians" (Imai, 2017, p. 150).

The next section provides a glimpse into a First Nation that exists within the legislative framework described here, but also recognizes their rights as Indigenous peoples and the associated power those rights confer on them.

Fishing Lake First Nation: rights to traditional territories

Fishing Lake First Nation (FLFN) is an independent[1] Saulteaux First Nation located in southern Saskatchewan. Fishing Lake First Nation's "reserve"[2] originated at the signing of an adhesion to Treaty #4 in 1876. FLFN's lands consist of approximately 3,970 hectares located southeast of Wadena, Saskatchewan and three other parcels purchased for economic or cultural purposes that are not yet reserve status. FLFN has a population of 1,739 members, with 495 members living on reserve (Statistics Canada, 2015). FLFN's socioeconomic indicators in relation to Saskatchewan as a whole offer a statistical representation of the disparity between these two populations. For example, earnings as percentage of total income were significantly lower at FLFN in 2011 at 55% compared with the provincial figure of 76%. Workforce characteristics also show considerable disparity. The labor participation rate was almost 30% lower in Fishing Lake First Nation at 40% compared with 69.2% for Saskatchewan. FLFN's reported employment rate was 30%, considerably lower than Saskatchewan's rate of 65.1%. And, finally, the Saskatchewan unemployment rate in 2011 was 5.9% compared with 25% in FLFN. These figures cannot convey a clear understanding of life within FLFN. The community has few jobs—almost all employment is through government funded administration and programs. The Chief and Council and administration rely on government transfers, and the school consists of five modular buildings attached by a deck; it is unlike any other school off reserve in Canada.

This community, like many other Canadian First Nations, has been impacted by the various initiatives undertaken by the federal government as they sought to assimilate Indigenous peoples into mainstream society. Residential schools, illegal land surrenders, Indian Act policies that restricted the sale of agricultural products by "Indians," and many other policies led First Nations communities to exist outside of the mainstream economy with many on non-productive lands. Chief Yellow Quill together with two headmen, Kenistin and Ne-Pin-Awa, signed an adhesion to Treaty #4 in 1876 on behalf of three separate First Nation bands recognized today as Yellow Quill First Nation, Kinistin First Nation, and Fishing Lake First Nation. Fishing Lake First Nation's "reserve" originated at the signing of this numbered treaty, together with the separate reserve lands of these other two First Nations. Originally considered part of the overall Yellow Quill First Nation, in 1907, the Canadian Federal Government recognized the distinct status of the three First Nations by separating the bands into the three First Nations that can be seen today (Indian Claims Commission, 1997).

1 Many First Nations belong to Tribal Councils, regional organizations responsible for providing programs and services to their member First Nation communities—some First Nations are independent of these.
2 Reserve is a legal term for the Crown land designated for use by Indigenous communities. The term is outlined in the 1876 Indian Act.

This separation was primarily undertaken with one motivation in mind: FLFN was situated on highly productive arable land suitable for agricultural development. In 1901, the Canadian Northern Railway Company was granted a right to construct a railroad through the Fishing Lake reserve. Recognizing the agricultural potential of the surrounding land, the company afterwards petitioned that the northern portion of the reserve be opened for settlement (Indian Claims Commission, 1997). After a number of days of intense negotiations, the band members of the FLFN agreed to the surrender, which took place in 1907. The surrendered land—numbering 5,330 hectares—was then sold mostly in public auctions between 1909 and 1910 (Indian Claims Commission, 1997). This historical context would provide a background of contention, ultimately leading to the 1997 submission of a specific land claim on the part of the FLFN to the federal government. The band argued that the process of the historic land surrender violated contemporary governmental policy as enshrined within the Indian Act, and had furthermore been obtained under duress and undue influence (Nicholat, 2002).

The current Chief of the Fishing Lake First Nation believes that there is an opportunity to change the economic and social challenges that exist within FLFN by taking advantage of the rights they have as Indigenous peoples and as a legally recognized "band." Chief Derek Sunshine states they are moving forward with a variety of projects concerning lands, governance, administration, and economic development:

> The way I see it is having these small steps, these small increments, are good. A lot of people think you have to be 100 percent ownership in business ... the more you have a small piece in something; the better off it is for the community ... these small steps make our community much better and stronger (Derek Sunshine, personal communication, 2016).

The growth that the current leadership hopes to achieve is being pursued in a manner that takes advantage of their rights as an Indigenous nation, inherent rights to their land, and Treaty rights gained by their ancestors signing a treaty from the nation-to-nation perspective. A land claim settlement provided the FLFN with almost $35 million to compensate for damages and losses suffered because of the land surrender that occurred in 1907. The surrender involved almost 60 percent of the best agricultural land of the First Nation at that time (Windspeaker, 2001). Today, the FLFN is pursuing land purchases that are focused on providing opportunity for cultural and traditional hunting and gathering practices, agriculture, expansion of the land base near the main reserve, and economic pursuits wherever possible within the province of Saskatchewan. Councillor Steve Sunshine stated,

> We had a specific land claim settlement in 2001 for the expropriation of 13,190 acres [5,340 hectares] of land ... We as First Nations [people] are educated enough to know what is best and to know what works well ... We use our community purchases to put us in a better economic and social position (personal communication, 2016).

Opportunities in First Nations traditional territory

Recent Supreme Court challenges have led to an increased responsibility of the Crown, represented by the federal government and provincial governments, regarding the duty to consult with First Nations that are potentially impacted by large-scale development projects. The Supreme Court of Canada, in *Haida Nation v. British Columbia* and *Mikisew v. Canada*, ruled that the Crown has a duty to consult with First Nations if there is a potential impact on the rights of Indigenous communities. In *Mikisew v. Canada*, which dealt specifically with a Treaty First Nation, the Court determined that the following minimum standards must be met when accommodating the interests of Indigenous communities:

- The Crown must provide notice of the proposed infringement and engage directly with the treaty nation in question.

- The Crown has a duty to disclose relevant information in its possession regarding the proposed development or decision.

- The Crown is under an obligation to inform itself of the impact of a proposed project on the treaty nation in question.

- The Crown must communicate its findings to the affected treaty nation.

- The Crown must, in good faith, attempt to substantially address the concerns of the treaty nation.

- The Crown cannot act unilaterally.

- Administrative inconvenience does not excuse a lack of meaningful consultation.

- The Crown must solicit and listen carefully to the expressed concerns and attempt to minimize the adverse impact on the treaty interests.

- The concerns of the treaty nation must be seriously considered by the Crown and "whenever possible, demonstrably integrated into the proposed plan of action" (Morellato, 2008, p. 41).

BHP Billiton, an international mining company with $44.6 billion in revenues in 2015 (BHP, 2016, p. 8), submitted an application to the province of Saskatchewan that was approved on June 28, 2011. The proposal involved the development of an estimated $12 billion greenfield potash mine that would eventually be the "biggest potash mine on the planet" (Briere, 2012). In its approval, the Province of Saskatchewan's Ministry of Environment stated it:

> considers there to be no potential impact to Treaty and/or Aboriginal rights and/or traditional use due to the project occurring on privately held land and having no expected off-site impacts. No notification is required beyond what is typically provided to the public as required by legislation (Province of Saskatchewan, 2011, p. 4).

Chief Darin Poorman of the Kawacatoose First Nation did not agree with the province. He stated the following in an Indigenous-owned newspaper in 2011,

> It is inconceivable that one of the largest potash mines in the world would not have an impact on the First Nations who continue to exercise Aboriginal and Treaty rights in the area ... Our community is just 55 km from the mine site. Of course it's going to have an impact on Kawacatoose (*First Nations Drum*, 2011).

BHP Billiton did engage the local First Nations communities by pursuing the signing of "opportunities agreements" with five local First Nations, including Fishing Lake First Nation. BHP reported the signing of two separate agreements in November 2013 with Kawacatoose First Nation, Day Star First Nation, and Muskowekwan First Nation and in October 2014 with the Fishing Lake First Nation and Beardys & Okemasis First Nations (BHP, 2013, 2014).

The agreement provides opportunities for training and community development projects to be funded, but it also offers the First Nations leverage when negotiating joint venture agreements with industry seeking to provide services to the mining giant. For example, companies seeking contracts at the Jansen site must attempt to include First Nations as co-owners of bidding ventures. This agreement, as is the case for almost all impact benefit agreements in Canada, is governed by a non-disclosure agreement and thus the details of the arrangement must remain confidential.

To date, FLFN has two joint ventures with one contracted in the catering and housekeeping area and the other pre-qualified for construction and maintenance services and there are three other ventures in the negotiation stage. The FLFN hopes to change the lives of its current and future members incrementally, without taking on all the risks involved in large-scale projects, and by taking advantage of the resources and assets that industry partners bring to projects.

Conclusion: Indigenous rights

Nearly 400 years of sustained contact has left Canada's relationship with Aboriginal peoples in a state of denial, disarray, and despair. Aboriginal peoples were ruthlessly stripped of land, culture, livelihood, and leadership with devastating impacts in terms of poverty, powerlessness, and marginality. Unemployment is a major cause of Aboriginal distress that leads directly to poor housing, illness, a sense of powerlessness, and cycles of poverty. Access to land and resources remains a key problem.

What are Indigenous rights? Section 35 of the Constitution Act 1982 recognizes and affirms existing "Aboriginal" and Treaty rights but does little to define them. Youngblood Henderson (2007) states that the Constitutional recognition and affirmation of rights related to First Nations living on the land within their distinctive societies, with their own legal orders, practices, traditions, and cultures creates a constitutional protection.

> Aboriginal rights arise from prior social organization, laws, and distinctive cultures of First Nations peoples. Aboriginal rights include a sub-category of Aboriginal title which deals with a sui generis First Nations proprietary tenure existing in pre-contact North America. Aboriginal rights include other component rights—such as First Nations right to hunt, fish, or trap—as well as other matters not related to land such as trade, education and health that have generated their distinctive Aboriginal culture (p. 13).

Historic and Modern treaties in Canada have resulted in a considerable amount of land under Indigenous ownership or partial management, almost 60 million hectares of the former and almost 340 million hectares of the latter. Treaty negotiations continue and quantities of both categories of lands will increase.

Indigenous land ownership and/or management rights are having a considerable impact in Canada in two respects in particular. First, they are giving Indigenous people a real voice in major resource development projects central to the country's long-term development strategy. Two very recent examples are the Northern Gateway Pipeline project and the Petronas LNG projects. In both instances, Indigenous groups are opposing major projects on their lands. In response, proponents of the projects are offering concessions and development opportunities to communities.

More generally, Indigenous people are pursuing development opportunities associated with their lands and resources. In their pursuit of greater protection and control over their lands and resources, Aboriginal people want to be different and to have their difference recognized as a basis for engagement and entitlement; they want a minimization of bureaucratic interference in their lives; they want collective access to power and resources; they want to maintain meaningful involvement over issues of immediate concern. Aboriginal people don't necessarily want to separate from Canada, but want enough of their own territory to allow institutional sovereignty. Aboriginal people want to live in a just and equal society where their cultural lifestyles and languages are protected from assimilationist pressures and where they can select relevant elements of the past and incorporate them into the present for advance into the future (Maaka and Fleras, 2005, p. 325).

References

Alcantara, C. (2003). Individual Property Rights on Canadian Indian Reserves: The Historical Emergence and Jurisprudence of Certificates of Possession. *Wilfred Laurier University Political Science Faculty Publications.* Paper 6.

Alfred, T. (1999). *Peace, power, righteousness: an indigenous manifesto.* Don Mills, Ont.: Oxford University Press.

Amnesty International. (2013, Nov 20). *Indigenous land rights in Canada: Landmark case points the way to true reconciliation.* Retrieved from http://www.amnesty.ca/news/public-statements/indigenous-land-rights-in-canada-landmark-case-points-the-way-to-true-reconci

Anderson, R.B., Kayseas, B., Dana, L.P. & Hindle, K. (2004). Indigenous land claims and economic development: The Canadian experience. *American Indian Quarterly,* 28 (3/4), pp. 634-648.

Anderson, R. (2015). *Tracking the Statutory Tenure Rights of Indigenous Peoples and Local Communities in Canada.* Unpublished report.

Berger, T. (1972). Indigenous Rights in Canada. *The University of Toronto Law Journal,* 22(4), pp. 305-308.

BHP Billiton (2013). *BHP Billiton Potash cements ties with three First Nations.* Retrieved from http://www.bhpbilliton.com/society/communitynews/bhp-billiton-potash-cements-ties-with-three-first-nations

BHP Billiton (2014). *BHP Billiton and First Nations Sign Jansen Project Opportunities Agreement.* Retrieved from http://www.bhpbilliton.com/society/communitynews/bhp-billiton-and-first-nations-sign-jansen-project-opportunities-agreement

BHP Billiton (2016). *2015 Annual Report.* Retrieved from http://www.bhpbilliton.com/~/media/bhp/documents/investors/annual-reports/2015/bhpbillitonannualreport2015.pdf

Briere, K. (2012, April 20). When potash comes to town: Giant potash mines come with benefits, responsibilities. *The Western Producer.* Retrieved from http://www.producer.com/2012/04/when-potash-comes-to-town%E2%80%A9/

Brown, K., Doucette, M. & Tulk, J. (Eds.). (2016). *Indigenous Business in Canada: Principles and Practices.* Sydney, Nova Scotia: Cape Breton University Press.

Dussault, R. & Erasmus, G. (1996). *Report of the Royal Commission on Aboriginal Peoples.* Ottawa, Ontario: Indian and Northern Affairs Canada.

First Nations Drum (2011, July 28). Kawacatoose First Nation demands consultation on BHP's Jansen potash mine. *First Nations Drum.* Retrieved from http://www.firstnationsdrum.com/2011/07/kawacatoose-first-nation-demands-consultation-on-bhps-jansen-potash-mine/

Government of Canada. (2016). *Constitution Acts, 1867 to 1982.* Retrieved from http://laws-lois.justice.gc.ca/eng/const/page-16.html#h-52

Henderson, J.Y. (2007). *Treaty rights in the Constitution of Canada.* Toronto: Thomson Carswell.

Hill Notes (2016, May 25). *The United Nations Declaration on the Rights of Indigenous Peoples.* Retrieved from https://hillnotes.wordpress.com/2016/05/25/the-united-nations-declaration-on-the-rights-of-indigenous-peoples-moving-forward/

Hopkins, J. & Peeling, A. (2004). *Aboriginal Judicial Appointments to the Supreme Court of Canada.* Retrieved from http://www.indigenousbar.ca/pdf/Aboriginal%20Appointment%20to%20the%20Supreme%20Court%20Final.pdf

Indian Claims Commission. (1997). *Inquiry into the 1907 surrender claim of the Fishing Lake First Nation.* Retrieved from http://publications.gc.ca/collections/collection_2009/indianclaims/RC31-58-1997E.pdf

Indian Claims Commission. (2002). *Report on the Mediation of the Fishing Lake First Nation 1907 Surrender Claim.* Retrieved from http://publications.gc.ca/collections/Collection/RC31-13-2002E.pdf

Indigenous and Northern Affairs Canada. (2013). *Summary of pre-1975 Treaties.* Retrieved from http://www.aadnc-aandc.gc.ca/eng/1100100028574/1100100028578, http://www.aadnc-aandc.gc.ca/eng/1370362690208/1370362747827

Indigenous and Northern Affairs Canada. (2015a). *First Nations Profiles.* Retrieved from http://fnp-ppn.aandc-aadnc.gc.ca/fnp/Main/Index.aspx?lasng=eng

Indigenous and Northern Affairs Canada. (2015b). *Land Base Statistics*. Retrieved from https://www.aadnc-aandc.gc.ca/eng/1359993855530/1359993914323

Indigenous and Northern Affairs Canada. (2016). *Indian Status*. Retrieved from https://www.aadnc-aandc.gc.ca/eng/1100100032374/1100100032378

Maaka, R. & Fleras, A. (2005). *The politics of Indigeneity: Challenging the state in Canada and Aotearoa New Zealand*. Dunedin, New Zealand: Otago University Press.

Nicholat, C.L. (2002). *Exploring a shared history: Indian-White relations between Fishing Lake First Nation and Wadena, 1882-2002* (Master's Thesis, University of Saskatchewan, Saskatoon, Canada). Retrieved from https://ecommons.usask.ca/handle/10388/etd-06262007-080136

Province of Saskatchewan, (2011) Reasons for Decision: Ministerial Approval Pursuant to Section 15(1)(a) The Environmental Assessment Act. *BHP Billiton Canada Inc. Jansen Project Potash Mine*. Retrieved from http://www.environment.gov.sk.ca/2008-102ReasonForDecision

Statistics Canada. (2013). Aboriginal Peoples in Canada: First Nations Peoples, Métis and Inuit (99-011-X2011001). Ottawa: Statistics Canada. Retrieved from http://www12.statcan.gc.ca/nhs-enm/2011/as-sa/99-011-x/99-011-x2011001-eng.pdf

Statistics Canada. (2015). *Fishing Lake First Nation, Indian Band Area, Saskatchewan*. Retrieved from https://www12.statcan.gc.ca/nhs-enm/2011/dp-pd/aprof/details/page.cfm?Lang=E&Geo1=BAND&Code1=630390&Data=Count&SearchText=Fishing%20Lake%20First%20Nation&SearchType=Begins&SearchPR=01&A1=All&B1=All&GeoLevel=PR&GeoCode=630390&TABID=1

Trudeau, J. (2016). *Remarks by Justin Trudeau at the Assembly of First Nations 36th Annual General Assembly*. Retrieved from https://www.liberal.ca/realchange/justin-trudeau-at-the-assembly-of-first-nations-36th-annual-general-assembly/

White, J. & Wright, L. (2012). Developing oil and gas resources on or near Indigenous lands in Canada: An overview of laws, treaties, regulations and agreements. *The International Indigenous Policy Journal, 3*(2). Retrieved from http://ir.lib.uwo.ca/cgi/viewcontent.cgi?article=1089&context=iipj

Appendix

Supreme Court of Canada Decisions: confirmation of rights

Calder v. British Columbia (1973)	Legally confirmed that Aboriginal title as a right derived from traditional occupation and use of tribal lands
R. v. Van der Peet decision (1996)	Established a structured test around the cultures and practices of Aboriginal peoples in the pre-colonial period to use in establishing current rights
R. v. Gladstone decision (1997)	Structured a more flexible test for constitutionally permitted limits to Aboriginal rights
Delgamuukw v. British Columbia (1996)	Established the basic characteristics of Aboriginal title: 1) the inalienability of title, except to the Crown in right of Canada; 2) the origin of that interest originating from prior occupation; and 3) the collective, not individual, Aboriginal interest in land
Haida Nation v. British Columbia (2004)	Defined the legal duty to consult when there existed a contemplated Crown conduct and a possible adverse impact on a potential or established Aboriginal or treaty right
Tsilhqot'in Nation v. British Columbia (2014)	Found that Aboriginal title confers a right to 1) possess the land, 2) the economic benefits of the land, and 3) use and manage the land
Grassy Narrows First Nation v. Ontario (2014)	Found that while provinces have the exclusive power to manage natural resources on Crown lands, this right is subject to the prior duty to consult the Aboriginal group concerned and accommodate its interests

6

Indigenous human rights perils as an ongoing challenge

Amy Klemm Verbos, J.D., Ph.D.
Assistant Professor of Business Law, University of Wisconsin-Whitewater; Pokagon Band of Potawatomi enrolled citizen

Across the globe, Indigenous peoples' human rights are imperiled by businesses operating within their traditional territories. The global murder epidemic of environmental and land defenders is exemplified by the death of Berta Cáceres in Honduras in March 2016. Indigenous struggles for judicial remedies for environmental disasters are highlighted by Texaco/Chevron maneuvering in the lawsuits relative to toxic waste dumping in the Ecuadorian Amazon. Each represents an unfinished story and an Indigenous human rights challenge. These ongoing crises require substantive legal changes to further the cause of justice. There is also a vital role for the UN Global Compact to highlight, educate, and increase corporate responsibility and accountability for Indigenous rights under the UN Declaration on the Rights of Indigenous Peoples.

Indigenous peoples, UN Global Compact, Human rights, Alien Tort Claims Act, UN Declaration on the Rights of Indigenous Peoples

Introduction

At around midnight on 2 March 2016, gunmen broke down the door of the house where Berta Cáceres was staying in La Esperanza, Honduras, and shot and killed her. Berta was a high-profile environmental campaigner and activist on indigenous land rights (Global Witness, 2016).

Berta Cáceres co-founded the Council of Indigenous and Popular Organizations of Honduras (COPINH) in 1993 and was its General Commissioner at the time of her murder (COPINH, 2016). Her story is emblematic of a global human rights crisis for Indigenous peoples that cries out for justice and significant change. Every day, across the globe, Indigenous peoples face murder and other human rights perils associated with business within Indigenous territories, reservations, and traditional lands. Burger (2014) writes,

> Human rights abuses associated with the exploration and exploitation of non-renewable resources include, among others, violation of the right to life, forced displacement and destruction of the environment on which indigenous peoples depend. Extractive industries have had impacts on the health and well-being of indigenous peoples and destroyed sacred sites thereby affecting the right to religion of the peoples concerned. The consequences of such projects have violated the right to an adequate standard of living and the right to food, water and subsistence (p. 5).

It is not just that human rights abuses occur. The victims of these abuses, including many Indigenous people, are also denied justice or redress. This chapter touches upon these rather complex concerns in the context of what might be done under the United Nations Global Compact and its Business Reference Guide to the Declaration on the Rights of Indigenous Peoples (BRG). This is not to suggest that these initiatives are a perfect solution. However, it is important for businesspeople to understand what Indigenous peoples' rights are and what is happening, why the remedies Indigenous peoples possess are inadequate, what the responsibility of business is vis-à-vis these rights, and how responsible business and management may contribute to a way forward for Indigenous peoples.

Indigenous rights to life and land

Life is a basic and essential human right under international law (International Covenant on Civic and Political Rights, Article 6). This right has been recently incorporated into Article 1 of the United Nations Declaration on the Rights of Indigenous Peoples, adopted by the UN General Assembly on September 13, 2007 (UNDRIP):

> Indigenous peoples have the right to the full enjoyment, as a collective or as individuals, of all human rights and fundamental freedoms as recognized in the Charter of the United Nations, the Universal Declaration of Human Rights and international human rights law (United Nations, 2008).

Please see the Appendix to this book for the full Articles.

It is especially important to understand that most of the rights enumerated in UNDRIP already existed and were restated and better enumerated in UNDRIP. The right to life and to live free of violence or intimidation is reiterated in UNDRIP Article 7 (United Nations, 2008).

Nevertheless, according to Global Witness, a UK-based, non-governmental organization (NGO) which documents the murders of environmental and land defenders, Indigenous people constitute 40% of the 185 such murders across 16 countries in 2015 (Global Witness, 2016). It was the deadliest year Global Witness has recorded since it began in 2002. Indigenous rights to land are under attack worldwide, with murder as a tool to intimidate, silence, and extinguish these rights. UNDRIP recognizes and protects Indigenous land rights, rights to subsist, rights to sacred sites, and environmental protection rights, including the specific provisions contained in Articles 10, 20, 25, 26, 27, 28, and 32 (United Nations, 2008). These rights are so important to Indigenous peoples because:

> For Indigenous peoples who live on the land, habitat is human rights. It provides the resources that sustain life and much more. It is also a space, a territory and living environment through which, and in which, Indigenous peoples can realize their cultural, social, economic, and political rights. In other words, it is a space where Indigenous peoples can exercise genuine self-determination ... And without it, they cannot survive (Kimerling, 2016, p. 449).

The UN makes clear that corporate responsibility pursuant to UNDRIP includes consultation with Indigenous people *and* the free, prior, and informed consent for projects that impact Indigenous rights (see, e.g., Casten Centre *et al.*, 2008; United Nations, 2008; United Nations Global Compact, 2013). "The UN Special Rapporteur on the Rights of Indigenous Peoples clarified that consultation and consent together are a special requirement safeguarding substantive human rights firmly enshrined in international law, including the right to self-determination" (United Nations Global Compact, 2013, p. 25). Businesses may find that certain financiers and others require compliance with these rights and that a business choosing to ignore Indigenous rights may be subjected to legal action or reputation risk (United Nations Global Compact, 2013). Some businesses choose to ignore these rights and related corporate responsibilities. Consider Berta Cáceres' murder on March 2, 2016.

Berta Cáceres

Berta Cáceres, a mother of four and member of the Lenca people, brought global attention to the Rio Blanco Lenca people's fight against the Agua Zarca Dam project on the Gualcarque River in Honduras, being built by Desarrollos Energéticos SA, a Honduran company (DESA) (Goldman Environmental Foundation, 2016). These efforts began in 2006 when COPINH, and Cáceres in particular, began working with the Lenca people of Rio Blanco to oppose the project, which they learned about only when they saw heavy equipment being moved in (Bird, 2013; Goldman Environmental Foundation, 2016). The Gualcarque River is sacred to them, allows for sustainable living, and the dam would cut off water, food, and medicine for hundreds of Lenca people (Bird, 2013; Goldman Environmental Foundation, 2016).

The government and businesses involved in the dam project ignored these rights, protected by the UNDRIP, and prior international human rights law. In response to peaceful protests and other actions to block the project, Cáceres and other activists received threats and at least one activist was murdered. In a 2013 interview, recounted by Nina Lakhani of *The Guardian*, a British newspaper, Cáceres said:

> I cannot freely walk on my territory or swim in the sacred river and I am separated from my children because of the threats. I cannot live in peace, I am always thinking about being killed or kidnapped. But I refuse to go into exile. I am a human rights fighter and I will not give up this fight ... I want to live, there are many things I still want to do in this world. I take precautions, but in the end, in this country where there is total impunity I am vulnerable. When they want to kill me, they will do it (Lakhani, 2016a).

In 2015, Cáceres eloquently accepted the 2015 Goldman Environmental Prize for her grassroots efforts to thwart the dam (Goldman Environmental Foundation, 2016). In Spanish, she first describes the responsibility of the Lenca people as guardians of the river, then presciently states that in giving one's life to protect the river, one is giving one's life to protect humanity and the Earth. Cáceres calls on humankind to wake up, that we are out of time, it is time to break free from "the rapacious capitalism, racism, and patriarchy" that will ensure our self-destruction (Goldman Environmental Foundation, 2016). Cáceres is but one martyr of many in Honduras, the most dangerous place for environmental and land defenders per capita, with more than 100 murders between 2010 and 2015 (Agren, 2016; Global Witness, 2016). Her legacy is the continuing struggle for recognition and support of Indigenous human rights.

Perhaps Cáceres' global profile will result in some measure of justice against her killers. Time will tell. *The Guardian* reported on May 3, 2016 that Honduran officials detained four people in connection with her death, including a current and a former employee of Honduran dam-builder DESA (Lakhani, 2016b; Voith, 2016). A later article reports five arrests, including the two associated with DESA and an active-duty major in the Honduran army (Agren, 2016); this has risen to eight arrests as of January 16, 2017 (Hunter, 2017). Corporate and government murderers allegedly worked in concert in this case, possibly following a military hit list (Lakhani, 2016c). Justice is not ensured, as Global Witness (2016) states that most of these murders go completely unpunished. Perhaps that is the reason that murders continue unabated.

Nelson Garcia, a second activist from COPINH, the group co-founded by Cáceres, was murdered just 12 days after Cáceres. According to Oxfam International (2016), "Nelson García was supporting Lenca people who were being evicted from their land when he was shot and killed." And in early July 2016, Lesbia Janeth Urquía, a 49-year-old mother of three and an environmental activist associated with COPINH, was found murdered (Agren, 2016). The government alleges robbery as the motive in her murder, but COPINH disputes this (Agren, 2016).

What, then, is the multinational business role in this? There are financiers, suppliers, and DESA, the dam builder. Sinohydro Projects Group, a Chinese state-owned dam builder, was involved in earlier stages of the project. According to its response to a Business & Human Rights Resource Centre query about its involvement in Agua Zarca, Sinohydro placed blame for human rights abuses squarely on DESA, but it describes its withdrawal from the project and termination of the contract as due to "serious interest conflicts between the Employer of the Project, i.e. DESA, and the local communities, which were treated as unpredictable and uncontrollable to the Contractor" (Sinohydro Group Limited, 2013), rather than because DESA violated international human rights law.

Rights Action, a non-profit organization based in Toronto, Canada with offices in Washington, D.C., supports the COPINH campaign against the Agua Zarca Dam project. On the Rights Action website, COPINH condemns financing and construction participants in the Agua Zarca dam project in no uncertain terms as "violators of the historic collective and individual rights of the Lenca People," including Netherland's Development Fund FMO; FINNFUND of Finland; Siemens AG and its joint venture partner Voith GmbH in Voith Siemens Hydro Power Generation GmbH & Co KG ("Voith Hydro"); a number of Honduran companies; and the USAID-MARKETS Projects (Rights Action, 2016).

Following Cáceres and Garcia's murders, Dutch development bank FMO and Finnish FINNFUND, two European funders of the Agua Zarca Dam project suspended their support (Bosshard, 2016), but notably did not withdraw from participation in the project. Nevertheless, following the arrests of DESA employees, FMO (2016) and FINNFUND (2016) express the clear desire to withdraw:

> FMO is deeply concerned by the fact that charges have been brought against an employee of the Honduran company DESA (the developer of the Agua Zarca project). FMO will withdraw from the project if a credible connection between one of our clients and an act of murder were to be established. FMO stands for respect for human rights and condemns all kinds of violence and does not tolerate illegal conduct.
>
> FMO is seeking official confirmation and additional information from the Honduran authorities about the arrests and the course of judicial proceedings. We have confirmed to our client DESA that this implies that the suspension of disbursements will continue and, while keeping in mind that charges are not convictions, there is a need for FMO to seek a responsible and legal exit from the project.
>
> We are preparing a mission of independent experts to travel to Honduras to make a thorough assessment of the situation and draw lessons learned for FMO. The mission will consider the interests of the local communities and analyze how an exit could take place responsibly (FMO, 2016).

FINNFUND (2016) echoed this statement. While this would be welcome news to COPINH, Rights Action, Oxfam, and others, one may question why FMO and FINNFUND financed it in the first place when the Lenca people were not consulted about the dam project, and this is not the first human rights incident associated with the project, it is merely the most prominent.

The UN Global Compact and the Business Reference Guide to the Declaration on the Rights of Indigenous Peoples (the BRG) explicitly address Indigenous human rights. Specifically, UN Global Compact Principles 1 and 2 call upon businesses to support and respect internationally recognized human rights and not to be complicit in human rights abuses. This reiterates the UN position that business enterprises' responsibility to respect human rights

> refers to internationally recognized human rights—understood, at a minimum, as those expressed in the International Bill of Human Rights and the principles concerning fundamental rights set out in the International Labour Organization's Declaration on Fundamental Principles and Rights at Work (United Nations, 2011).

The BRG asks Global Compact participants to "commit to obtain (and maintain) the free, prior and informed consent of indigenous peoples for projects that affect their rights, in line with the spirit of the UN Declaration" (United Nations, 2013). This is difficult when governments do not support Indigenous people's challenges to businesses which negatively impact their rights and aspirations.

Although the Agua Zarca case began before the BRG was issued, the international human rights at issue, and Indigenous peoples' rights have been long recognized (United Nations, 2011). Yet, FINNFUND (2016) states that this project was "prepared in accordance with international best practice for responsible investment" and that it has financed such projects in Honduras for 10 years without similar problems. In contrast, Global Witness (2016) reports that there have been 100 murders of land and environmental defenders in Honduras from 2010 to 2015, suggesting that problems in that country are systemic rather than isolated to the Agua Zarca dam project.

Voith Hydro suspended deliveries to DESA in response to DESA's possible involvement in Cáceres' murder, according to a press release (Voith, 2016). Again, this was a suspension, not a withdrawal. Oxfam International (2016), a global NGO, continued its call for the financiers and Voith Hydro to pull out and the project itself to be cancelled as a part of its Land Rights Now campaign. Suspension of support and even justice against murderers will not address the underlying problem, a systematic campaign to silence Indigenous people and extinguish their human rights, including land rights and environmental rights.

DESA, the Honduran dam builder, is not a participant in the UN Global Compact, nor would its record in this matter support involvement. The UN Global Compact requires that voluntary participants comply with its Principles, whereas this case illustrates that DESA has not. The European or Honduran financiers and companies named by Rights Action are not participants, nor is Sinohydro. Thus, many of the players on the world stage associated with Indigenous human rights abuses have not even agreed to abide by the UN Global Compact Principles, and by extension, the BRG. In contrast, Siemens AG, a joint venture partner in Voith Hydro, is a UN Global Compact participant. One might then question why Voith

Hydro is involved at all, in that the Lenca people clearly did not give free, prior, and informed consent to the Agua Zarca dam. Siemens' most recent report on progress documents merely mention a commitment to human rights and improvement in respecting employees' human rights and not using child labor (Siemens AG, 2015). The word "indigenous" does not appear in the documents. There is clearly room for Siemens to apply the UN Global Compact standard for continuous improvement as it relates to Indigenous peoples and responsible business practices.

A murder epidemic

In *On Dangerous Ground*, Global Witness (2016) reports that there have been 1,176 *documented* murders of environmental and land defenders since 2002, with 185 murders in 2015 alone, up 59% from 2014. It shocks the conscience that there is a global murder epidemic against environmental and land defenders, with 2015 marking the deadliest year since Global Witness (2016) began documenting such murders in 2002. The report alleges that many more murders likely occurred in remote areas and are not recorded in public records. Corporations seeking to illegally grab Indigenous lands, mine, expand agri-business, build hydro-electric projects, or otherwise compromise water rights, illegally log, or engage in other "development" are, at a minimum, benefiting from murder, at times, complicit in murder, and, in some instances as is alleged in the Berta Cáceres murder, actively engaged in these atrocities. Global Witness (2016) alleges rampant collusion between governments and corporate interests where perpetrators go unpunished, while activism is increasingly being criminalized. In the Cáceres case, Rights Action (2016) published a statement by COPINH, including: "We fervently reject the dirty defamation campaign that tries to discredit the historic struggle of COPINH, and criminalize our organization." This use of legal process against the human rights abuse victims suggests that they might look elsewhere for justice.

Obstacles to remedies against multinational companies in U.S. courts

Kiobel v. Royal Dutch Petroleum

Since the late 1970s, human rights abuse victims sought redress in U.S. Courts relying on the 1789 Alien Tort Claims Act[1] (ATCA) (Austin and Mahmud, 2014; Skinner, 2014, 2015). ATCA simply states: "The district courts shall have original jurisdiction of any civil action by an alien for a tort only, committed in violation of the law of

---

1 28 U.S.C. §1350.

nations or a treaty of the United States."[2] For most such claims, the courthouse door closed due to a unanimous 2013 U.S. Supreme Court decision, *Kiobel v. Royal Dutch Petroleum Co*,[3] in which the Court ruled that United States federal courts do not have jurisdiction under ATCA for civil cases against multinational corporations by victims of corporate human rights abuses that occur on foreign soil. Although Justice Roberts, in writing the opinion of the Court, relied on a presumption that extraterritoriality does not apply to actions under the ATCA, Justice Breyer's concurring opinion, joined by Justices Ginsburg, Sotomayer, and Kagan, states:

> Unlike the Court, I would not invoke the presumption against extraterritoriality. Rather, guided in part by principles and practices of foreign relations law, I would find jurisdiction under this statute where (1) the alleged tort occurs on American soil, (2) the defendant is an American national, or (3) the defendant's conduct substantially and adversely affects an important American national interest, and that includes a distinct interest in preventing the United States from becoming a safe harbor (free of civil as well as criminal liability) for a torturer or other common enemy of mankind.[4]

Nevertheless, unless the parties bringing suit allege such facts, the *Kiobel* decision effectively closed U.S. Courts to many human rights abuse victims (Skinner, 2014, 2015). And, *Kiobel* is not the only impediment to human rights abuse victims seeking redress in the United States.

The Texaco/Chevron cases

In 1993, over 25,000 Ecuadorian and Peruvian Indigenous people filed class action cases in U.S. federal district court against Texaco for environmental damages and personal injuries due to what Kenney (2009) describes as "the worst oil-related disaster in recorded history" (p. 857), its alleged intentional dumping of more than 18 billion gallons of toxic waste into a region of the Ecuadorian Amazon. In cases that took twists and turns too numerous to document here (see, e.g. Business & Human Rights Resource Centre, 2016; Kenny, 2009; Skinner, 2014, 2015), in 2002, the Second Circuit Court of Appeals dismissed the actions in favor of justice in Ecuador and Peru, when Texaco consented to jurisdiction.[5] Chevron acquired Texaco, so it became the defendant. According to the Business & Human Rights Resource Centre (2016), in 2013, the Ecuador Supreme Court affirmed lower court decisions holding Chevron liable, but reduced damages to from $18 billion to $9.51 billion. All along, Chevron attempted additional appeals, action in international courts, and political maneuvers to try to block the decision and its enforcement (Business & Human Rights Centre, 2016; Kenney, 2009; Skinner, 2014). Chevron also resorted

---

2 *Ibid.*
3 133 S. Ct. 1659 (2013).
4 *Ibid.*, at 1671.
5 *Aguinda v. Texaco, Inc.*, 303 F.3d at 470 (2nd Cir. 2002).

to U.S. Courts to block the plaintiffs and keep them from enforcing the judgment (Business & Human Rights Resource Centre, 2016; Kenney, 2009; Skinner, 2014), which is ironic when you consider that it sent the action to Ecuadorian courts. Chevron also sued the plaintiffs' lawyers in U.S. courts, alleging racketeering and fraud. While the New York state fraud charges were dismissed,[6] on August 8, 2016, the Second Circuit upheld a racketeering finding and equitable relief to block the Ecuadorian plaintiffs from recovery anywhere in the world other than Ecuador.[7] Notably, Chevron Corporation is not a participant in the UN Global Compact. Its 2015 Corporate Responsibility Report states that Chevron puts its values into practice, stating:

> Our values are integrity, trust, diversity, ingenuity, partnership, *protecting people and the environment*, and high performance (Chevron Corporation, 2016, p. 2, italics added).

These values and its stated commitment to the UN Sustainable Development Goals (Chevron Corporation, 2016) stand in stark contrast to its battle to avoid responsibility to clean up its legacy in Ecuador and Peru, and the extent to which it used legal processes and U.S. courts to postpone and, as of this point, completely avoid corporate responsibility outside of Ecuador.

Skinner (2014, 2015) calls for substantive law changes to hold corporations accountable and enable the United States to fulfill its obligation to support human rights. She highlights several key issues: 1) developing nations hosting multinational businesses or their affiliates are dependent on foreign direct investment and neither regulate nor hold accountable bad corporate actors; 2) not only is regulation lax, but many judicial systems are woefully inadequate, witnesses are killed or intimidated, and corruption is rampant; 3) industries adopt codes of conduct, supply chain certifications and the like, but these do little; 4) parent corporations profit from and then hide behind limits on their liability for atrocities and environmental disasters caused by foreign subsidiaries (Skinner, 2014, 2015). Her recommendations to expand victims' access to courts in order to sue U.S. corporations and multinational corporations with a substantial presence in the U.S. are not likely to find friends in the present Republican majority in the U.S. Congress.

The UN Global Compact, as a voluntary initiative, may fall into Skinner's valid concern over voluntary initiatives, as critics contend that it is toothless and provides cover for unscrupulous businesses wishing to appear responsible (see, for example, Sethi and Schepers, 2014). Yet absent sweeping changes to U.S. law that corporate lobbyists would vociferously challenge, there is a vitally important role for the UN Global Compact and businesses which seek to lead in best practices relative to Indigenous human rights (for a rejoinder and more general defense of the UN Global Compact, see, for example Rasche and Waddock, 2014). I believe that this role is to 1) draw attention to how businesses negatively impact Indigenous

---

6 *Chevron Corp. v. Donziger*, 871 F. Supp. 2d 229 (S.D.N.Y. 2012).
7 *Chevron Corp. v. Donziger*, 833 F.3d 74 (2nd Cir. 2016).

human rights issues around the globe; 2) support Indigenous peoples' efforts to bring their rights under UNDRIP and aspirations to the attention of corporate managers worldwide; 3) assist corporate managers to adopt appropriate policies and procedures to enforce Indigenous peoples' rights under UNDRIP; 4) disseminate best practices in dealing with Indigenous peoples; and 5) create a forum for dialogues and greater understanding in the corporate community about Indigenous peoples' rights and struggles for their very survival as Indigenous peoples. Moreover, this work must expand through the Principles for Responsible Management Education to involve researchers and teachers who train the next generation of managers about these vitally important issues.

Conclusion

Indigenous human rights have been too often overlooked, even by "responsible" companies. There are urgent Indigenous human rights crises involving businesses unfolding across the globe. Berta Cáceres is but one murder victim in a global murder epidemic linked to business in Indigenous territories, reservations, and traditional lands. Financiers, suppliers, construction, extractive, agribusiness, and other corporate entities must become part of the solution and not the problem. Moreover, corporations use legal process to stall, foreclose, and stymie human rights victims' attempts to seek legal remedies in the U.S. and elsewhere. It is time for these urgent issues to be given greater attention in the UN Global Compact initiative, PRME participant business schools, and in the court of public opinion to force real and significant change.

References

Agren, D. (2016, July 7). Honduras confirms murder of another member of Berta Cáceres's activist group; Four months after the assassination of award-winning environmentalist Berta Cáceres, an indigenous activist and member of her organization has been killed. *The Guardian*. Retrieved from www.lexisnexis.com/hottopics/lnacademic

Aldana, R.E. & Abate, R.S. (2016). Banning metal mining in Guatemala. *Vermont Law Review*, 40, pp. 597-671.

Austin, W.C. & Mahmud, A. (2014). Human rights take a back seat: The Supreme Court hands out a pass to multinationals and other would be violators of the law of nations. *Denver Journal of International Law and Policy*, 42, pp. 373-388.

Bird, A. (2013). *The Agua Zarca Dam and Lenca Communities in Honduras: Transnational Investment Leads to Violence against and Criminalization of Indigenous Communities.* Washington, D.C.: Rights Action. Retrieved from http://rightsaction.org/sites/default/files//Rpt_131001_RioBlanco_Final.pdf

Bosshard, P. (2016, March 16). European Funders Suspend Support for Agua Zarca Dam. [Blog] *The Huffington Post*. Retrieved from http://www.huffingtonpost.com/peter-bosshard/european-funder-suspend-s_b_9479642.html

Burger, J. (2014). *Indigenous peoples, Extractive Industries and Human Rights*. EU Directorate-General for External Policies of the Union. Retrieved from http://www.enip.eu/web/wp-content/uploads/2014/11/Julian-Burger-EU-report-on-extractives.pdf.

Business & Human Rights Resource Centre (2016). Texaco/Chevron lawsuits (re Ecuador). Retrieved from https://business-humanrights.org/en/texacochevron-lawsuits-re-ecuador#c9332

Castan Centre for Human Rights Law, International Business Leaders Forum, and Office of the United Nations High Commissioner for Human Rights, United Nations Global Compact. (2008). *Human Rights Translated: A Business Reference Guide*. Melbourne, AU, London, UK, Geneva, CH, and New York, NY: Authors. Retrieved from http://www2.ohchr.org/english/issues/globalization/business/docs/Human_Rights_Translated_web.pdf

Chevron Corporation (2016). *2015 Corporate responsibility report*. Retrieved from https://www.chevron.com/-/media/chevron/shared/documents/2015-corporate-responsibility-report.pdf

FINNFUND (2016, May 9). FINNFUND seeks to exit Agua Zarca. Retrieved from http://www.finnfund.fi/ajankohtaista/uutiset16/en_GB/agua_zarca_honduras/

FMO (2016, May 9). FMO seeks to exit Agua Zarca. Retrieved from https://www.fmo.nl/k/n1771/news/view/28688/20819/fmo-seeks-to-exit-agua-zarca.html

Global Witness (2016). *On Dangerous Ground*. London, UK: Global Witness. Retrieved from https://www.globalwitness.org/en/reports/dangerous-ground/

Goldman Environmental Foundation. (2016). *Berta Cáceres: 2015 Goldman Prize Recipient South and Central America*. Retrieved from http://www.goldmanprize.org/recipient/berta-caceres/

Hunter, S. (2017, January 16). Eighth arrest made in hunt for killer of environmentalist Berta Cáceres. *El País*. Retrieved from http://elpais.com/elpais/2017/01/16/inenglish/1484565802_632640.html

Kimerling, J. (2016). Habitat as human rights: Indigenous Huaorani in the Amazon rainforest, oil, and Ome Yasuni. *Vermont Law Review*, 40, pp. 445-524.

Lakhani, N. (March 3, 2016a). Remembering Berta Cáceres: "I'm a human rights fighter and I won't give up"; Nina Lakhani recounts an interview in 2013 with the Honduran human rights activist at her home in La Esperanza, where she was murdered early Thursday. *The Guardian*, Retrieved from www.lexisnexis.com/hottopics/lnacademic

Lakhani, N. (May 3, 2016b), Berta Cáceres murder: four men arrested over Honduran activist's death; Honduras officials report arrests of two people linked to company building hydroelectric dam which Cáceres had fought. *The Guardian*. Retrieved from www.lexisnexis.com/hottopics/lnacademic

Lakhani, N. (June 21, 2016c) Berta Cáceres's name was on Honduran military hitlist, says former soldier; A unit trained by U.S. special forces was ordered to kill the environmental activist who was slain in March, according to an ex-member who now fears for his life. *The Guardian*. Retrieved from www.lexisnexis.com/hottopics/lnacademic

Oxfam International (2016, May 10). End the violence, stop the Agua Zarca dam. Oxford, UK: Oxfam International. Retrieved from https://act.oxfam.org/international/end-the-violence

Rasche, A. & Waddock, S. (2014). Global sustainability governance and the UN global compact: A rejoinder to critics. *Journal of Business Ethics*, 122, pp. 209-216.

Rights Action (2016, February 23). COPINH denounces: "DESA Agua Zarca" relaunches illegal hydroelectric project that violates rights & life of Lenca people & territories (Translated by L. Berenson). Retrieved from http://us9.campaign-archive2.com/?u=ea011209a243050dfb66dff59&id=d67d425588

Sethi, S.P. & Schepers, D.H. (2014). United Nations Global Compact: The promise-performance gap, 122, pp. 193-208.

Siemens AG (2015). *Additional sustainability information to the Siemens annual report 2014.* https://www.unglobalcompact.org/system/attachments/cop_2015/158621/original/siemens_ar2014_sustainability_information.pdf?1431080607

Sinohydro Group Limited (2013, November 25). Sinohydro Group response to report by Rights Action about alleged violence & intimidation against Lenca indigenous communities related to the constructions of Agua Zarca dam, Honduras. Retrieved from https://business-humanrights.org/en/honduras-agua-zarca-dam-construction-leads-to-violence-intimidation-against-lenca-indigenous-communities-ngo-says#c77673

Skinner, G.L. (2014). Beyond *Kiobel*: Providing access to judicial remedies for violations of international human rights norms by transnational business in a new (post-*Kiobel*) world. *Columbia Human Rights Law Review*, 46, pp. 158-265.

Skinner, G.L. (2015). Rethinking limited liability of parent corporations for foreign subsidiaries' violations of international human rights law. *Washington & Lee Law Review*, 72, pp. 1769-1864.

United Nations (2008). *United Nations Declaration on the Rights of Indigenous Peoples.* New York, NY: UN. Retrieved from http://www.un.org/esa/socdev/unpfii/documents/DRIPS_en.pdf.

United Nations (2011). *Implementing the United Nations "protect, respect, and remedy" framework.* New York, NY and Geneva, CH: United Nations Publications. Available at http://www.ohchr.org/Documents/Publications/GuidingPrinciplesBusinessHR_EN.pdf.

United Nations Global Compact (2013). *Business Reference Guide to the UN Declaration on the Rights of Indigenous Peoples.* New York, NY: UNGC. Retrieved from https://www.unglobalcompact.org/docs/issues_doc/human_rights/IndigenousPeoples/BusinessGuide.pdf.

Voith (2016, May 4). Voith suspends deliveries for Agua Zarca. Retrieved from http://voith.com/en/press/press-releases-99_69778.html

7

Reclaiming pluriverse in CSR
Brazilian Indigenous peoples and the Finnish forest cluster

Susanna Myllylä
Independent Researcher and Lecturer, Finland

This chapter introduces how the Finnish forest industry cluster has fulfilled its corporate responsibility on Brazil's Atlantic coast with regard to three Indian communities: the Tupinikim, Guaraní, and Pataxó. The chapter starts by addressing Indigenous aspects of development in Latin America. Hence, rather than relying on the usual top-down perspective, this chapter is based on a study focusing on what the Indigenous peoples considered significant in corporate responsibility in terms of the business impact on community development. The performance of Finnish companies was also assessed through the prism of the national and international human rights and Indigenous rights systems. Research results are summarized as a "Concentric Corporate–Community Responsibility Roadmap Model", which is meant for analyzing and guiding interaction between firms and Indigenous communities.

Agribusiness, Corporate social responsibility, Indigenous peoples, CSR model

Indigenous development alternatives

This chapter presents the Brazilian Indigenous peoples' perspective on agribusiness and what they consider significant in the corporate responsibility of the

Finnish forest industry cluster operating on the Atlantic coast. Owing to the Brazilian Government's inefficiency, the Finnish companies are entangled to various degrees in land struggles, since the firms took advantage of delays in registering Indigenous Territories in their entirety. I introduce here the results of my long-term ethnographic research in Brazil (see Myllylä, 2015). Collecting the Indians' microhistories, "rays from the past," offers an alternative narrative on the Finnish firms' success stories in South America. I conducted interviews among three Indigenous groups: the Tupinikim, the Guaraní, and the Pataxó Indians. In order to shift away from the Northern ethos in corporate responsibility discourses, I developed a **corporate–community responsibility** (CCR) framework to enrich and specify corporate responsibility discourse in an Indigenous context.

In Brazil today, 817,963 individuals are identified as Indigenous, and the country has 243 Indigenous ethnic groups or tribes (Instituto Brasileiro de Geografia e Estatística, 2010). Indigenous peoples suffer severe consequences as corporations extract natural resources at an increasing rate across South America. Brazil, with over 200 million people, favors state-led extractive and infrastructure development mega-projects. Many projects are situated in Indigenous territories (ITs) and nature reserves. Brazil's development strategy enables national and foreign investors to grab land and create new business spaces (Clements and Fernandes, 2012). Brazilian and international law broadly protects Indigenous peoples' cultures, lands, and livelihoods. Hence, Indigenous people possess specific and extensive land rights. However, the Brazilian state does not fulfill its obligations to Indigenous people, since ITs are often without official status. But even legal status does not protect ITs from invading outsiders.

When I compiled a socio-environmental conflict map marking Indigenous struggles in South America, the broader picture started to evolve (see Myllylä, 2015, pp. 32, 33, 34): the Indians have fought to defend their territorial land rights vis-à-vis diverse local-, national-, and global-level actors. Regionally, what has happened before in the industrialized and urbanized Atlantic coast—a massive socio-environmental change—is currently taking place in the frontier regions, namely Amazonia. Observed from a distance, the Amazon appears to be a huge, single forest unit. But when one zooms in on Google satellite images, the situation is alarming: brown and gray patches can be observed, indicating traces of human influence that are growing over time (see Myllylä, 2015, pp. 9, 31, 32). South America faces an accelerating decline in ITs, due to the spread of extractive industries, highways, hydroelectric projects, monocultures, cattle ranching, small-scale logging, forest conservation areas, tourism, and drug trafficking, among others.

Contemporary South American post-neoliberal development thinking is largely based on Indigenous conceptions and belief systems; that is, the *cosmovisions* related to specific societal contexts and social movements reacting to the dominant development model's negative societal impact. Gudynas (2011) has considered the main South American trends in the discourse around *Buen vivir*, a Spanish concept that means "living well" or "good living", describing alternative development in a broad sense (see Myllylä, 2015, pp. 79-83). However, it is not a question of juxtaposing different models but rather, analyzing how diverse lifeworlds encounter each other, as Escobar (2015) has described: *"Pluriverse* is what needs to be sustained—a world where many worlds fit." Negotiations and struggles among diverse worlds are important encounters with economic and cultural transitions towards the pluriverse (Escobar, 2015). Socio-environmental conflicts also entail a positive phenomenon since these struggles are the "avant-garde of the search for post-capitalist sustainable models of life" (Escobar, 2011, 2015).

The aim of this study was to move from merely introducing corporate dominance and asymmetrical power relations in land struggles to "grassroots meaning-making with subaltern communities, to decipher and strengthen alternative systems of organizing, which re-define 'corporate responsibility'" (Mitra, 2011). By presenting an alternative Indigenous development vision for the "one truth"; that is, the *universe*, referring to the Western modernization narrative and its corporate dominance in corporate social responsibility (CSR) discourses, this research also contributes to the idea of the *pluriverse*, and points the way toward finding other alternative conceptualizations for corporate stakeholder research in the global South contexts.

One of the major tasks of Indigenous protests or resistance movements against corporations is to develop Indigenous knowledge systems, and to use alternative ways to produce and justify knowledge—in other words, to challenge Western scientific knowledge. It is a question of power to define the Indigenous group and its needs, including the entire development process: survival, progress, identity, health, nutrition, time/space, and the human–nature relationship (Parajuli, 1991; Myllylä, 2010).

Case studies and the regulatory context

The study examined various agribusiness impacts on three Indigenous groups, and their relations to business management. First, how did the massive environmental change affect their livelihoods, social relations, identity, and cultures? Second, how did they articulate and defend their rights and interests? What did the land struggle—*a luta pela terra*—mean to the Indians? Third, did the communities expect certain CCR actions from the firms, and if so, what were these? How did they define what constitutes a "responsible" firm? Fourth, how did the communities perceive the influence of CCR initiatives on their lives? Did they benefit from social programs and other forms of corporate philanthropy?

My research approach was based on Indigenous knowledge, rather than starting from the usual top-down perspective. I used a qualitative research methodology among the Indians, combining a case study with Grounded Theory and field ethnographic approaches. The research materials also included a few interviews at the corporate level and analyses of corporate disclosures or reports. The companies'

CCR policies, mutual relations, and their subsequent impact were brought under closer scrutiny by juxtaposing corporate words with corporate actions. Since nearly 50 years of land conflict between the Tupinikim-Guaraní and Fibria Celulose (formerly Aracruz Celulose) was resolved in 2007, the entire Indigenous territory (18,070 ha) was finally formalized in Espírito Santo state. The third community, the Pataxó, was chosen in this study as a specific focus group in order to find out Indigenous views and expectations as to what constitutes responsible business practices, and what a good relationship entails. The Pataxó are affected by a multinational Veracel Celulose. The Pataxó Indigenous Territory was waiting for official registration at its total size (52,000 ha) in Bahia state. I used my earlier interviews among the Tupinikim and the Guaraní as a reference case. The field research sites and the Indigenous territories are in Espírito Santo and Bahia (see Myllylä, 2015, pp. 50-52).

The Finnish forest industry cluster is well established in Brazil: The Swedish-Finnish Stora Enso and the Brazilian Fibria Celulose each owns 50% of their joint corporation, Veracel Celulose in Bahia. In addition, consultants such as Pöyry and Metso, which supplies machines and equipment, are involved in both states. Considering the operational context of business (see United Nations, 2012, pp. 20-21) in Brazil, the Finnish companies' position becomes questionable: agribusiness on the Atlantic coast has benefited exceedingly well from a situation where the state has evaded its legal responsibility—officially recognizing the ITs—and therefore, industrial activities have been established on already disputed lands. In addition, agribusiness as a neighbor often creates side-effects for wider environments, diminishing local people's livelihoods. Hence, the Finnish firms were entangled to various degrees in the multifaceted land struggles of the Tupinikim, the Guaraní, and the Pataxó. As one Pataxó member described the development impact of agribusiness (Myllylä and Takala, 2011):

> The arrival of eucalyptus has created more poverty. It has not created jobs—nothing. Before, coffee, papaya, and cattle used to be grown here, all of which created employment. Instead of improving the socioeconomic situation, Veracel, on the contrary, has increased poverty.

Although the Finnish companies have duly outlined their CSR principles and the assumed societal benefits of their operations, they do not take into account local socioeconomic conditions among the Indigenous communities, namely poverty and the unequal distribution of economic and natural resources.

Yet the protection of Indigenous rights is not exclusively an issue of the Brazilian Government (Bier, 2005) as the country has signed certain international agreements: ILO Convention No. 169 (the Indigenous and Tribal Peoples Convention, 1989); the 1948 United Nations Declaration of Human Rights; the 2007 United Nations Declaration on the Rights of Indigenous Peoples (UNDRIP); the 1996 International Covenant on Civil and Political Rights; the 1966 International Covenant on Economic, Social, and Cultural Rights; and the 1972 Stockholm Declaration on the Human Environment. The ILO Convention No. 169 is the most important operative international law that is meant to guarantee the rights of Indigenous nations, and it is a legally binding international instrument that deals specifically with the rights of Indigenous and tribal peoples—Brazil ratified this in 2004. In addition to ILO Convention No. 169, the most critical international instrument is UNDRIP; these agreements are compatible and mutually reinforcing, as they define Indigenous peoples' rights to lands, territories, and resources under international law (see Myllylä, 2015, p. 29). One fundamental problem, however, with a large number of guidelines and conventions, is the fact that they are scattered across numerous, mutually uncoordinated regimes and documents. Indigenous peoples' juridical position is complex, delayed, and insecure in the country (Myllylä, 2014).

Since the state itself does not adhere to domestic laws—much less international agreements—it is one of the primary violators of Indigenous rights. Hence a power vacuum allows multinational corporations (MNCs) to step in and benefit from the unclear situation. The UN Guiding Principles (GPs) on Business and Human Rights (2011, pp. 5, 14, 20, 23, 27), implementing the United Nations "Protect, Respect and Remedy" framework, specifically outline the state's duty to protect human rights. The GPs emphasize that business should interact with governments in a way that affirms the state's duty to protect Indigenous peoples' rights. Furthermore, the GPs state that firms should pay particular attention to the rights, needs, and challenges of populations that may be at heightened risk of becoming vulnerable or marginalized due to business operations: the more extensive and severe the impact, the more a business needs to be aware of Indigenous peoples' rights, and respect them. Therefore, business enterprises may need to consider additional standards. The recommendation is particularly valid with regard to agribusiness that much resembles extractive industries. These sectors usually cause massive environmental problems, leading to diverse negative social, cultural, and livelihood changes among poor rural and forest-adjacent communities (see for example, Myllylä, 2010).

The concerns of the three Indian communities in this study, especially in territorial issues, reflect well on the Indigenous peoples' rights under ILO Convention No. 169 (see articles 7, 13-19) and the United Nations Declaration on the Rights of Indigenous Peoples (see Articles 25, 26, 29, and 40, Appendix, pp. 183-187). This is also the case with regard to the cross-cutting issue of self-determination as a holistic concept. In the case of the Tupinikim, for instance, Fibria (Aracruz) questioned the origins and identity of the Tupinikim during the land conflict (see Myllylä, 2010). The ILO Convention defines the *scope* of Indigenous peoples' lands: Indigenous peoples have rights over a broader territory, comprising the *total environments* of areas which these communities occupy or otherwise use, inclusive of natural resources, rivers, lakes, and coasts (see also International Labor Organization, 2013, pp. 21, 22, 23). However, these wider Indigenous territorial rights were not apparent in the Brazilian cases, since the companies restricted the Indians' movement and livelihoods.

The UN Declaration (Article 18, Appendix, p. 182) recognizes that Indigenous peoples have a right to participate in decisions that affect their rights. In Brazil, the Indigenous communities are excluded from decision-making concerning the arrival or location of foreign companies. The communities are not involved in the business decision-making on the more equitable benefits. In fact, they did not claim to be part of the decision-making, except concerning the Indigenous territory issue. I also found minimal assistance to Indigenous communities compared with the huge financial profits that the Finnish companies produced in the region (see Myllylä, 2014). The Indians were afraid to lose the small benefits, such as school kits.

The Business Reference Guide (BRG) to the UN Declaration on the Rights of Indigenous Peoples recommends that business should not force development on Indigenous peoples. This refers to modernizing or interfering with the local economic dynamics and making the community too dependent upon the company's presence (United Nations, 2013, p. 38). I found that the Finnish companies' developmental role in Brazilian society is not small and undetectable. Stora Enso and the associated firms and export credit agencies comprise a powerful political and economic actor group, critically influencing local and regional development processes. Thus I argue that the main corporate CSR approach here, *philanthropy*, is likely to create dependency and tensions among the community members, if the aspects of equality and Indigenous cultures are not properly taken into account (Myllylä, 2014). This raises the question of whether corporate philanthropy is always a "good thing" if there is no scrutiny of how firms are carrying out their activities.

The BRG encourages business to engage in meaningful consultation and partnership with Indigenous peoples on a local level. The BRG also suggests the use of a company ombudsman to deal with community grievances (United Nations, 2013, pp. 2, 11, 32). In Brazil the companies' attempts to create partnerships with Indigenous villages were lopsided since some villages received more assistance than others. For instance, several village chiefs discussed how to improve the partnership with Veracel, and as a result they received project funding. The other chiefs complaining of ongoing land disputes with the firm were excluded from philanthropic activities. A few villages preferred to avoid any contact with Veracel. Nevertheless, in corporate reports and media the firms treated and discussed their local stakeholders as consisting of a homogeneous stakeholder group. Some villages also complained that the company management visited them and consultations were organized, but this did not lead to any positive change; people felt they were not genuinely listened to and processes were selective.

The BRG acknowledges that businesses are reporting on positive engagements with Indigenous peoples and the resulting benefits (United Nations, 2013, p. 7). In light of my research, it is quite difficult to rely on corporate disclosures as they tend to prettify situations and report selectively, for the most part leaving out the drawbacks. For instance, Veracel does not much mention nor analyze its local incidents with the Pataxó, or reveal the undermining land dispute as the main cause for these. Instead, the company characterizes its relationship with the communities as harmonious. Furthermore, the actual corporate–community interactions are in stark contrast with the corporate disclosures assuring the public that the companies operate according to the regulations and guidelines. However, the reports never specify the principles that should govern the firms' relations to Indigenous peoples in multiple ways. The companies (Veracel, Stora Enso, and Fibria) in their reports do not refer to Indigenous rights, but more generally to human rights. On the other hand, it is difficult to ascertain whether keeping silent about the breadth of Indigenous rights is a chosen business tactic or just indicates their ignorance. Perhaps traditional pulp and paper production is such a field of industry that its growth logic is incompatible with local communities with little education that depend on their environmental resources. Hence, although the national and international regulatory framework protecting Indigenous rights is strong, these companies do not recognize it in its entirety. Therefore, it can be argued that if the most critical questions, such as Indigenous land titles, are not a priority in corporate–community relationships, firms may merely buy local acceptability via social programs and other philanthropic actions. The Brazilian experience illustrates how complex the situations can be, challenging the guidelines, which must balance between general and specific issues.

Firms can secure membership and respectable status in international institutions and national societies promoting responsible business, and even receive multiple awards for good CSR performance, while simultaneously violating the rights of their Indigenous stakeholders in diverse ways, as the Brazilian experience illustrates. At the time of the land dispute incidents comprising violations of human rights and Indigenous peoples' rights in Espírito Santo State in 2005/2006, Fibria (Aracruz) enjoyed membership within the United Nations Global Compact, whose basic principles include respect for the rights of Indigenous peoples (see United Nations, 2013, p. 38). Furthermore, Veracel was expelled from the Global Compact in 2010 because the company failed to communicate progress by the required deadline, unbeknownst to the Stora Enso Sustainability Communications group (personal communication, 2011). The UN Global Compact has 10 principles covering human rights, labor rights, environmental protection, and anticorruption (see p. ix). However, these principles can be considered too general and vague compared with the complex situations of the Brazilian Indians vis-à-vis the pulp industry. Therefore, the principles do not offer practical guidance for the firms to encounter Indigenous communities, and hence the firms make their own, free interpretations. Information from the local stakeholder situations does not reach these types of global institutions (such as the UN Global Compact) since they do not have the capacity or proper monitoring and feedback systems, and rely too much on lopsided corporate disclosures. How could we then improve national and global regimes promoting good corporate governance? The first step is to focus more specifically on *indigeneity* itself: What kinds of elements are involved, and how does corporate–community interaction differ from other stakeholder situations? What kinds of Indigenous knowledge systems emerge, and how does Western scientific knowledge communicate with them—how can these diverse knowledge systems encounter in a productive way?

By retrospectively assessing the Finnish companies' performance in Brazil, the Business Reference Guide to the UN Declaration on the Rights of Indigenous Peoples offers a concise package for the concerned companies' diverse management levels, and perhaps could result in a higher corporate responsibility performance. Various guiding principles on business and Indigenous rights in general could further improve by offering more detailed recommendations on how to act in respect to complex incidents and other situations, such as when the business operation sparks an Indigenous resistance movement, or how to recognize and deal with certain demographic, political, economic, and social chain reactions deriving from business operations. Such situations are, for instance, created when agribusiness requires large land areas, expanding onto unregistered Indigenous lands or their vicinity, and furthermore, creating the loss of livelihoods, forcing people to live in poverty pockets, or to migrate to urban slums or protected rainforests. In addition, we need more critical analyses on corporate philanthropy in the global South, relying more on independent and transparent evaluations rather than only the companies' self-assessments.

Lessons learned and the CCR model

The overall research target in the study was to identify a new CCR framework that would better take into account Indigenous peoples. The process started by deconstructing the ambiguous CSR concept and then bridging the disciplines of business ethics and development studies, both theoretically and methodologically, by subjecting the Indigenous communities' values in the study to literature analysis. The outcome was a **Concentric CCR Roadmap Model**, which outlines 22 principles and 49 sub-principles, organized in three hierarchical levels: binding, ethical, and philanthropic responsibilities. The model addresses that philanthropy should not be used as a major management strategy when initially approaching local stakeholders: firms should not have direct access to the "core" of the communities, i.e. to their internal dynamics, culture, and development. Instead, judicial and other binding issues ought to be tackled first. The model indicates how to plan and execute philanthropic activities so that ethical aspects are also considered. The model also calls for new "bottom-up" approaches and fieldwork in data collection in business ethics research concerning the global perspective (see Box 7.1 and Figure 7.1). The model emphasizes that if the most critical questions, the Indigenous land titles, are not resolved first, then the companies are just evading their fundamental responsibility and appear simply to be buying local acceptance through philanthropy. The study also pioneers bridge-building between business ethics and development studies. In addition, it scrutinizes business ethics in the context of the judicial system governing interaction between companies and Indigenous peoples.

The Concentric CCR Roadmap model is presented in two stages: as a box (Box 7.1) and as a concentric model (Fig. 7.1). The outer circle (i.e. binding responsibilities) is described here by "*in which frames*" questions, while the middle circle of ethical responsibilities refers to *how* something is done. In the inner circle, philanthropic responsibilities, it is basically a question of *what* is done, primarily regarded as government's sphere of responsibility. Cultural context in the global South forms the model's "meta-framework".

Box 7.1 **Cultural context in the global South**

Source: Myllylä, 2014

I Binding responsibilities: "in which frames" questions

(local, regional, national, and international laws, standards, regulations, certifications, constitutions, and conventions)

1. Territory
   - Investigate and respect officially registered host community's territory and its total environment.
   - Investigate and respect traditional land- and resource-related rights.
   - Refrain from operating in areas where physical demarcation is in process.
   - Avoid operations in disputed areas (e.g., with protracted legal battles).
   - Avoid land grabbing or large-scale land acquisitions in regions with many small farms and wide-scale poverty.
   - Avoid restricting people's traditional access to natural resources and their subsistence. Avoid destroying cultural sites and traditional pathways.
2. Self-determination
   - Respect the self-determination right of the community in regard to all aspects (e.g., avoid interfering with its cultural identity).
   - People have the right to participate in plans and decision-making, which may have impact on their lives and natural environment.
   - No contact or interference at any level, whenever indicated or claimed by the community.
3. Dialogue
   - Related to the community's self-determination right, pursue genuine negotiations with the community.
   - Arrange meetings on the community's own terms.
4. Human rights
   - Respect international human rights and Indigenous people's rights.
   - Acknowledge the complexity of these rights, which may exist as natural rights or as legal rights, in local, regional, national, and international law.
   - Use peaceful responses to local protests and resistance movements.
5. Working rights
   - Respect national and international working rights (e.g., avoid racial and ethnic discrimination).

- ○ Offer training and employment for the youth, if required by the community.
- ○ Avoid using child and slave labor.

6. Environmental and social impacts
   - ○ Respect environmental legislation, standards, and land zoning, irrespective of whether their implementation and control systems have severe deficiencies in the host country.
   - ○ Respect healthy local living environments. Avoid causing land degradation, environmental pollution, overuse of resources, and loss of biodiversity. Do not disturb local food security and potable water resources.
   - ○ Perform a high quality environmental impact assessment (EIA).
   - ○ Perform a high quality social impact assessment (SIA), whether or not it is mandatory. Link it to the EIA.

7. Partners
   - ○ Acknowledge and investigate direct and indirect corporate impacts.
   - ○ "Know your partners": Avoid supporting or cooperating with repressive companies, local institutions, and other actors, especially violence-prone security forces. Avoid business with land speculators inducing local conflicts.

8. Benefit-sharing
   - ○ Reasonable benefit-sharing with the community

9. Compensation
   - ○ If corporate operations have already taken place in the community's lands, withdraw and prepare for reasonable financial compensation and restoration due to land degradation and other possible livelihood losses to the community, added to the land recovery costs (e.g., reforestation and purification of water resources).

II Ethical responsibilities: "how" questions

10. Equality and respect
    - ○ Respect people's livelihoods and homeland.
    - ○ Understand prevailing, difficult political, social, and economic contexts of the (often marginalized) community.
    - ○ Respect and learn from culturally different worldviews and knowledge systems.
    - ○ Realize genuine "partnership."
    - ○ Avoid patronizing approaches.
    - ○ Treat community leaders, subgroups, and members equally, in order to avoid a divisive impact on the community. Give special attention to youth and women.

11. Trust
    - ○ Make relations and agreements official; institutionalize.
    - ○ Keep promised responsibilities.

12. Diversity
    ○ Support cultural, economic, and biological diversity among the community and its environment.

13. Sustainability
    ○ Target sustainability of actions. Assist in ways other than offering material goods. Avoid community dependency and encourage local ownership.
    ○ Maintain institutional knowledge on the community in spite of personnel changes in the firm.

14. Doing more
    ○ Avoid making the host government's unfulfilled obligations to the community the scapegoat for adopting lower level business standards.
    ○ Find alternative, innovative practices (e.g., to large-scale corporate farming).

15. Impact
    ○ Assess community impact instead of listing mere actions and outcomes.
    ○ Evaluate the impact of business practices, production, and CSR initiatives (e.g., in terms of project cycle)
    ○ Impact assessment is basically an overlapping element through which other ethical responsibilities can be viewed and analyzed.

16. Transparency
    ○ Pursue transparency of actions and corporate reporting.
    ○ Offer sufficient and understandable information for the community, as well as for the local, national, and international audience.
    ○ Openness concerning the impacts of business production, and CSR initiatives (e.g., social projects, benefit-sharing, local disputes, environmental or human rights violations, etc.).
    ○ Offer realistic and detailed information on local community relations and projects to the public.
    ○ Indicate corporate learning from drawbacks and criticism.
    ○ Use experts who are independent and whose fees are not disproportionate in comparison to the resources allocated to the community.

17. Credibility
    ○ Transparency increases credibility.
    ○ Seek collaboration with an independent, reliable third party.

18. Civil society
    ○ Take the claims (norms) of the supporting civil society seriously. Respect the independence of research institutions, schools, and media.

III Philanthropic responsibilities: "what" questions

19. Basic services support, particularly in health care.
20. Support in employment and other forms of subsistence, particularly for youth.
21. Assistance to educational institutions and cultural activities.
22. Support in housing and infrastructure development.

Figure 7.1 **Concentric CCR roadmap model**
Source: Myllylä, 2014

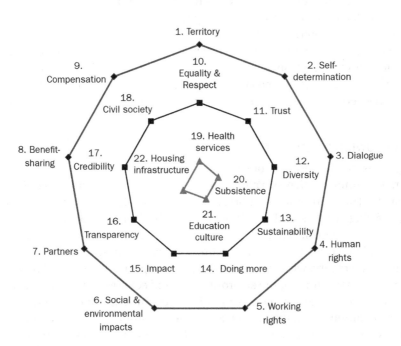

CULTURAL CONTEXT IN THE GLOBAL SOUTH

Several main recommendations for responsible corporate–community relationships can be addressed here:

1. Respect and listen beyond business rhetoric

Perceptions of the situations between the companies and the Indigenous communities tend to differ significantly. In Brazil, although company management and ombudsmen carried out numerous consultations and visits to villages, there seemed to prevail a communication gap: the business language ("the language of power", see Isaacs, 1999, pp. 208, 210, 211, citing Kantor and Lehr, 1975) did not meet all the expressions the Indigenous communities used ("the language of feeling"). The Indians felt the corporate management did not genuinely listen to their concerns. However, better mutual understanding can be found: "When the Indians say that the headwaters of a great river are sacred, and when the government of Brazil says they must protect their watersheds, they are essentially speaking the same language" (Boyle, 2013).

2. Monitor Indigenous rights in their entirety

Firms tend to speak of mere human rights, while there is a plethora of regulations protecting the rights of Indigenous communities. For instance, "land" ought to be seen as a holistic concept; not just land rights, but for instance, also the rights to the broader territory, referring to the *total environments* of the areas which these people occupy or otherwise use, inclusive of natural resources, rivers, lakes, and coasts (see for example ILO Convention No. 169, Article 13). This implies that despite Indigenous communities' need to use extensive land areas for their livelihoods, the companies tend to restrict their movement (see, for example, Myllylä, 2015, p. 76).

3. Acknowledge social diversity

Indigenous peoples do not constitute coherent and conflict-free groups, but they naturally comprise diverse values and perceptions, and mutual conflicts, also internally. Therefore, the definitions of a "responsible firm" varied from a company offering services and goods, to community isolation, avoiding any kind of contact with the firm. What was striking in the study, however, was the fact that all respondents prioritized the IT: before all else, the company should respect the Indigenous territory, withdraw immediately (also prior to the official registration), and pay compensation for the environmental and economic impacts it has caused. The overall challenge for management is to acknowledge and cope with the heterogeneity among its stakeholders, and generate strategies to adjust to these differences. The corporate CSR initiatives—if desired at all—should be selected by the communities themselves. Diversity ought to be acknowledged in the corporate reporting as well.

4. Learn from development work

A scarcely noticed issue is that the firms are not only responsible for the production impact but also for the CCR impact per se. Philanthropic activities may have a diverse and even counterproductive influence on local populations in terms of ownership, equality, and sustainability. Certain philanthropic actions—such as offering money or buying cars—entail a great risk of creating injustice situations in the communities. The lopsided business production impacts and corporate CCR activities can divide local communities—even at the micro- or family level—since people possess diverse interests and expectations vis-à-vis the company. These situations are very common for community projects in developing nations, from where lessons can be learned. Multinationals have also become gap-fillers for the public sector in nations that struggle with governance crises. The gap-filler situation, in turn, tends to create community dependency on corporations and allows local governments to evade their responsibilities. The end result may be that a firm's CCR activities support bad governance structures. The situation requires the clarification of the roles and responsibilities of corporations in the societies in which they operate.

5. Seek a realistic picture

Why do certain incidents repeat in stakeholder relations and what could be done differently to rectify the situation? In order to be seen as credible by the wider public, business performance assessments and corporate disclosures should be evaluated by a group of independent evaluators with broad expertise. Corporate reports often remain descriptive, trouble-free, selective, and lacking in in-depth analyses. Yet when comparing the stakeholders' experiences, the corporate words may not match corporate actions. Not the least, it is in the shareholders' and investors' interests to be informed of how the company actually performs, and what possible risks may be entailed in the business.

6. Be a trailblazer

Do more by creating new, proactive practices that indicate the firm's elevated consciousness of responsibility vis-à-vis vulnerable social groups, which also implies potential contributions to the business brand's improvement.

Finally, it would be worthwhile to pay special attention to ambiguous "gray" or border areas, where the limits of responsibility are encountered. How is corporate responsibility itself being "territorialized"; what and who are included and excluded, and why? Taking into account these aspects of uncertain terrains would also enhance the generation of new management practices.

References

Bier, S. (2005). *Conflict and Human Rights in the Amazon: The Yanomami.* ICE Case studies, 19. Retrieved from http://www1.american.edu/ted/ice/yanomami.htm

Boyle, A. (2013, January 23). *Amazon Indians go high-tech to map their land.* NBC News. Retrieved from http://www.nbcnews.com/id/3077244/ns/technology_and_sciencescience/t/amazon-indians-go-high-tech-map-their-land/#.VbZjy_nsEdU

Clements, E.A. & Fernandes, B.M. (2012, October 17-19). *Land Grabbing, Agribusiness and the Peasantry in Brazil and Mozambique*. Paper presented at the International Conference on Global Land Grabbing II, Land Deal Politics Initiative (LDPI), Ithaca, NY.

Escobar, A. (2015, June 11-13). *The Political Ontology of Territorial Struggles*. Paper presented at the 8th Conference of the Nordic Latin American Research Network (NOLAN), Helsinki, Finland.

Escobar, A. (2011). Sustainability: design for the pluriverse. *Development*, 54(4), pp. 137-140.

Feiring, B. (2013). *Indigenous Peoples' Rights to Lands, Territories and Resources*. Rome: ILC Scoping Study.

Gudynas, E. (2011). Buen vivir: today's tomorrow. *Development*, 54(4), pp. 441-447.

Instituto Brasileiro de Geografia e Estatística (2010). *Atlas do censo demográfico 2010*. Retrieved from http://loja.ibge.gov.br/atlas-do-censo-demografico-2010.html

International Labour Organization (2013). *Understanding the Indigenous and Tribal People Convention, 1989* (No. 169). Handbook for ILO Tripartite Constituents, International Labour Standards Department. Geneva: ILO.

Isaacs, W. (1999). *Dialogue and the art of thinking together. A pioneering approach to communicating in business and in life*. New York, NY: Doubleday.

Mitra, R. (2011). "My country's future": a culture-centered interrogation of Corporate Social Responsibility in India. *Journal of Business Ethics*, 106(2), pp. 131-147.

Myllylä, S. (2010). Ethnoterritoriality confronting multinationals: Indigenous Peoples' perceptions on eucalyptus plantation industries in Atlantic coastal Brazil. *Arctic & Antarctic: International Journal of Circumpolar Sociocultural Issues*, 4(4), pp. 97-145.

Myllylä, S. (2014). A Concentric CSR Roadmap Model for host community relations in the global South. *EJBO—Electronic Journal of Business Ethics and Organization Studies*, 19(1), pp. 27-51. Retrieved from https://jyx.jyu.fi/dspace/handle/123456789/43206

Myllylä, S. (2015). *Terrains of Struggle. The Finnish Forest Industry Cluster and Corporate Community Responsibility to Indigenous Peoples in Brazil*. Jyväskylä: University of Jyväskylä, Jyväskylä Studies in Business and Economics, 160. Retrieved from https://jyx.jyu.fi/dspace/handle/123456789/46643

Myllylä, S. & Takala, T. (2011). Leaking legitimacies: the Finnish forest sector's entanglement in the land conflicts of Atlantic coastal Brazil. *Social Responsibility Journal*, 7(1), 42-60. doi: 10.1108/17471111111114530

Parajuli, P. (1991): Power and knowledge in development discourse: New Social Movements and the State in India. *International Social Science Journal*, 127, pp. 173-190.

United Nations (2011). *Guiding Principles on Business and Human Rights. Implementing the United Nations "Protect, Respect, and Remedy" Framework*. New York & Geneva: UN.

United Nations (2012). *The Corporate Responsibility to Respect Human Rights. An interpretive guide*. New York & Geneva: UN.

United Nations (2013). *The Business Reference Guide to the UN Declaration on the Rights of Indigenous Peoples*. New York: UN.

8

Community–business dialogues

Natalia Aguilar Delgado
Assistant Professor in International Business, HEC Montreal, Canada

This chapter examines a project that tried to foster a new rights-based relationship between business and communities in the context of access and benefit-sharing. The pilot projects taking place in Peru, Brazil, and Madagascar were designed to try to transform the transactional relation between corporate and community partners through the use of participatory methodologies: one reflexive (where communities explore their own needs and aspirations, including procedures for free prior informed consent in accessing traditional knowledge); and one dialogic (where partners explore their shared values and commitments in a "biocultural dialogue"). In this chapter, I critically examine this initiative in trying to better understand what keeps community–business relations from being more transformative and beneficial to communities. In doing so, I contribute to the body of literature on community–business relations in emphasizing the importance of recognizing and respecting communities' needs and aspirations to promote their rights in practice.

Community–business relations, Traditional knowledge, Free prior informed consent

Introduction

Indigenous peoples and local communities have denounced the unfairness and the persistent inequality in community–business encounters in the context of biotrade (Wynberg, 2004). It is estimated that between 25,000 and 75,000 plant species are used for traditional medicine and only 1% of these are known to scientists and utilized for commercial purposes (Aguilar, 2001). Traditional knowledge plays an important role in the discovery of new leads for the development of drugs and also in the marketing argument for "exotic" products (Laird and Wynberg, 2008). However, few Indigenous peoples have ever received any kind of benefit from these technological developments and some have even experienced further exclusion in being denied access to knowledge or plants that have become privatized (Wynberg, 2010).

In 2010 a transnational regulation, the Nagoya Protocol, was created to regulate access and benefit-sharing (ABS) of genetic resources and associated traditional knowledge under the Convention on Biological Diversity (CBD). ABS initiatives recognize the rights of resource providers to free prior informed consent (FPIC) and promote the distribution of the benefits resulting from the exploitation of natural resources (Morgera and Tsioumani, 2010). This global regulation is relevant for Indigenous peoples because it recognizes their right to FPIC, as defined in the UN Declaration on the Rights of Indigenous Peoples (United Nations, 2008). Importantly, the Nagoya Protocol, in its article 12.1 requires countries to "take into consideration indigenous and local communities' customary laws, community protocols and procedures, as applicable, with respect to traditional knowledge associated with genetic resources."[1] Community protocols are a way for communities to engage with ABS processes determining the terms and conditions of access to their lands and knowledge by external stakeholders, in accordance with customary norms and values (Bavikatte *et al.*, 2015). Important to communities is that the right to FPIC and self-determination go hand in hand, since for Indigenous peoples to decide their own paths of economic, political, and cultural development, they should have the right to make informed decisions (Pimbert, 2012).

From the business side, the United Nations Global Compact (2013) suggests that business must try to create shared value when building relations with communities, building trust that increases the likelihood of obtaining FPIC.[2] In particular, the Business Reference Guide to the Declaration on the Rights of Indigenous Peoples specifies that businesses should "commit to obtain (and maintain) FPIC of Indigenous peoples for projects that affect their rights, in line with the spirit of the UN Declaration" (United Nations Global Compact, 2013, p. 25).

However, there are several challenges in ensuring a meaningful FPIC process. Buxton (2012) points out that FPIC processes rely heavily on Western bureaucratic norms, which do not reflect the knowledge, values, and practices of communities. Moreover, the urgency of the business world pushes communities to discuss and agree on complex issues in a timeframe that is aligned with the economic project, not necessarily with community needs and aspirations (Pimbert, 2012).

---

1 https://www.cbd.int/abs/text/articles/default.shtml?sec=abs-12
2 Importantly, several commercial banks adopting the social and environmental lending policies of the 2013 Equator Principles require FPIC for certain projects (Equator Principles, 2013).)

In 2011, the NGO Natural Justice and the Union for Ethical BioTrade (UEBT) implemented an initiative with the aim to test new participatory approaches to engage local communities in ethical biotrade supply chains that respect ABS principles. The idea was to support a biocultural dialogue between business organizations, members of the UEBT, and their community partners. First, communities were invited to reflect on their own needs, aspirations, and rights, including the right to FPIC. Then, in a second stage, communities and business partners convened in a dialogue to together define their shared values and commitments, in trying to create a new rights-based relationship. Despite the wealth of good intentions, the outcomes of the pilot cases did not achieve the expected objectives.

In this chapter, I critically examine this initiative in trying to better understand what keeps community–business relations from being more transformative and beneficial to communities. In doing so, I contribute to the body of literature on community–business relations in emphasizing the importance of recognizing and respecting communities' needs and aspirations to promote their rights in practice.

Literature on community–business relations

Banerjee (2000) and Whiteman (2009) note that organizational researchers pay little attention to the interactions between Indigenous peoples and corporations, despite the extensive empirical cases of corporate interests in natural resource development in regions of the world inhabited by Indigenous peoples and traditional communities. This phenomenon is even more accentuated in the case of extractive industries (Lertzman and Vredenburg, 2005), where communities are the most vulnerable to environmentally and socially adverse effects (Banerjee, 2000; Whiteman, 2009). Researchers generally characterize these relationships as hostile because of unequal power dynamics and worldview clashes (Bruijn and Whiteman, 2010; Kraemer *et al.*, 2013). Even when companies engage with Indigenous and local communities, it is mostly via CSR programs with a focus on stakeholder management serving to neutralize resistance to business activity (Murphy and Arenas, 2010).

Interestingly, much of this literature is centered on the corporate perspective, holding the assumption that exploitation is a given and it is just a matter of describing how this exploitation takes place. The literature is for the most part silent on the actual role local communities may play and how they may benefit from these encounters (Castro and Nielsen, 2001; Raufflet *et al.*, 2008). In fact, the constitutive aspects of these partnerships are important analytical dimensions to understand how they evolve and how they can actually benefit communities in the long term (Cornelius and Wallace, 2010).

Table 8.1 depicts Austin's collaboration framework (Austin, 2000; Austin and Seitanidi, 2012), in which relationships are characterized in four different stages: philanthropic, transactional, integrative, and transformational. These stages do not necessarily reflect a sequence in which relationships develop, but actually provide an indication of the extent to which value is exchanged or created between partners (Austin and Seitanidi, 2012). For instance, integrative collaborations are much more complex and organic than transactional arrangements because they entail more valuable resources, requiring a much deeper commitment (Austin and Seitanidi, 2012). In the case of transformational partnerships, the end beneficiaries take a more active role (Le Ber and Branzei, 2010) and the collaboration's transformative effects are felt at the individual level but also systemically, in more profound and structural ways (Austin and Seitanidi, 2012).

Table 8.1 **Collaboration continuum framework**

Source: Adapted from Austin (2000) and Austin and Seitanidi (2012)

Philanthropic	Transactional	Integrative	Transformational
Unilateral transfer of resources by a charitable corporate donor and a civil society organization recipient	Reciprocal exchange of valuable resources (e.g. sponsorships, sales, etc.)	Co-creation of value where missions, strategies, values, personnel, and activities experience organizational integration	Co-creation of transformative change at the societal level

Implicit in this framework is the importance of participation, but it is not clear how participation may affect the potential benefits of collaboration to communities. In what follows, I explore a case that exemplifies an effort to move a relationship from transactional to transformative through the use of participatory methodologies and examine the challenges that emerge.

A brief note on the methodology

The case explored here is based on secondary data, mainly on project reports and newsletters available on the internet[3] and case studies published in a book describing the initiative (Oliva *et al.*, 2012). The case was instrumentally chosen based on interviews conducted with the three staff members of the Convention on Biological Diversity that work with issues related to traditional knowledge. The interviewees agreed that this case is an original effort to include Indigenous and local communities' views in ABS agreements. Additionally, the author has conducted four interviews with the representatives of the organizations championing the implementation of the project, the UEBT and the NGO Natural Justice (Table 8.2).

3 An example is the newsletter entitled "Benefit sharing in practice: Biocultural dialogues" produced by UEBT (2012a).

Table 8.2 **Data collection**

Data source	Quantity	Pages
Documents		
Case study	1	7
Community protocols	2	48
Meeting/Project Reports/Presentation	3	35
Press release	3	4
Guide	1	30
Interviews		
Business association representatives	2	27
NGO representatives	2	22
CBD staff	3	31
Total	17	204

The community–business "biocultural dialogue" in ABS

In this section, I briefly present the actors championing the initiative: the private standard for Ethical Biotrade and the NGO Natural Justice. I then present the biocultural dialogue initiative.

The private standard for Ethical Biotrade

The UEBT is the organization overseeing the "Ethical Biotrade" standard that has promoted "sourcing with respect" since 2007. UEBT Trading Members commit to comply with the principles of Ethical BioTrade (UEBT, 2012b), which include, among other things, biodiversity conservation and fair and equitable benefit sharing.[4] The UEBT engages a third-party verification system that assesses company policies and their application to recommend gradual changes that ensure compliance with the standard. In addition, UEBT provides technical advice and support on CBD-related issues, including through training and practical tools on their website. The Union is financed by membership fees and contributions from donors. Currently there are 30 trading members and 16 affiliate members.[5]

---

4 Importantly, UEBT trading members should comply with fair and equitable sharing of benefits even if there are no relevant legislative or regulatory requirements at the national level.
5 Information available at the website: www.ethicalbiotrade.org, June 2016.

Natural Justice

Natural Justice is an NGO based in South Africa but with operations all around the world advocating conservation and sustainable use of biodiversity through the self-determination of Indigenous peoples and local communities. This NGO was one of the key actors promoting the concept of community protocol during the Nagoya Protocol negotiations and it has been developing many materials to guide communities in the process of crafting their own protocols (Delgado, 2016). Their approach is broad and flexible, which gives room for each individual community to design a unique protocol that is adequate for its own needs and aspirations (Box 8.1).

Box 8.1 **Structure of a community protocol**

Source: Based on Shrumm and Jonas (2012)

A self-definition of the group, its leadership, and decision-making processes
The links between their customary laws and biocultural ways of life
Their spiritual understanding of nature
Their conservation practices
The processes for sharing their knowledge
Their understanding of free, prior and informed consent to access their lands or traditional knowledge
Their local challenges
Their rights according to national and international law
A call to various stakeholders for respect for their customary laws, their community protocol and a statement of the various types of assistance needed by the community

The biocultural dialogues

In 2011, UEBT championed a project called "Biocultural Dialogues"[6] with Natural Justice, the NGO advocating the community protocol approach. The project sought to assess how the concepts of the community protocol approach could facilitate a dialogue between communities and companies engaged in biotrade activities.

> Community protocols are generally developed in the context of a community that wants to express, to have an internal discussion about their values their interest, with regards to biodiversity and wants to be able

---

6 The funding for this project came from the ABS Capacity Building Initiative, a multi-donor initiative that aims to support relevant stakeholders from the ACP countries (African, Caribbean and Pacific Group of States) in developing and implementing national ABS regulations, in particular to ratify and implement the Nagoya Protocol on ABS. More info at: http://www.abs-initiative.info/about.html

to express to other actors that it engages with ... So we were thinking what happens, how are these concepts and these lessons that have been learned useful when you don't just have a community but you have a relationship (Interviewee 4, UEBT staff member).

The project undertook three pilot cases in different developing countries with trading members of the UEBT:[7] in Peru, Brazil, and Madagascar. Each test case was intended to involve the selection of a facilitator, preparatory meetings with the community, and internal community workshops before the actual "biocultural dialogues" between communities and companies. In what follows, I present in more detail the pilot studies.

Pilot in Peru

This pilot in Peru (see Natural Justice, 2011a) involved an Indigenous forestry association in Madre de Dios (Asociacion Forestal Indigena Madre de Dios - AFIMAD) comprising seven Indigenous community suppliers of Brazil nut, and Candela, a fair trade organization and UEBT member specialized in commercializing products based on Peruvian biodiversity. After two workshops with community representatives, a first draft of a community protocol was put together. Afterwards, a meeting was held between the community and the company. To facilitate the dialogue a number of participatory methodologies were utilized (Oliva *et al.*, 2012). Among other things, the facilitators presented information in a format to encourage the participation of the communities. For instance, the facilitators would constitute mixed groups of representatives from the community and the company to explore the differences between "traditional" trade and "ethical" biotrade. One of the interviewees who took part in the project in Peru describes the process in detail:

> We had a first 2-day workshop with the representatives of the communities and we did a first exercise of getting to know what they wanted, how they wanted it and the thing that defined the community, based on the principles of the community protocols. One month later, we met again and after they consolidated this material and added things consulting their communities, we did a workshop including the company ... In this dialogue we explored things such as how do we want to work together, what are the roles and commitments to achieve success in this relationship. We did it based on the 7 principles of the UEBT (Interviewee 5, UEBT staff member).

Some challenges emerged. First, there were difficulties in involving the entire communities in discussions. Second, communities were keen to continue the

---

7 The project report points to the selection process of the cases in question. The test cases focused on communities and companies that used natural ingredients for biotrade-related value chains. Other criteria involved previous mobilization of the communities so that they could be readily engaged in discussions and an ongoing relationship with a commercial partner, in this case a UEBT trading member.

community protocol process beyond the subject matter of relevance to the company, raising concerns from the part of the company that was not willing to financially support the process. Later that same year, AFIMAD launched a Strategic plan,[8] with some of the elements discussed in the workshop.

Pilot in Brazil

In Brazil, the pilot project (see Natural Justice, 2011b) involved two actors: the local Amazonian community Nazarezinho and Beraca,[9] a Brazilian company specialized in health and personal care products extracted from the Amazon. The partnership between Beraca and Nazarezinho for the supply of açaí berries began in 2008 and has involved a number of activities including: the training of the community with respect to the importance of açaí trees and good practice on collection and harvesting; training on forest enhancement; meetings to discuss harvest (volume and price); and provision of ECOCERT organic certification for its products.

An initial meeting was arranged to present the pilot project to the community. A local NGO, Bolsa Amazonia, which was supposed to serve as a mediator, held additional meetings with the community. However, some problems emerged that impeded the community from fully engaging with the initiative. First, there was no internal reflection within the community because of a lack of trust in the association's leadership. Second, the dialogue with the company ended up being mediated by one staff member of the company, which raised questions about the neutrality of the process.

Pilot in Madagascar

In Madagascar, the initiative involved a community association of collectors and distillers of aromatic oils (called Manara-Penitra) and Man and the Environment (MATE), a NGO that created the company Aroma Forest, specialized in selling essential oils (see Natural Justice, 2011c). An independent consultant facilitated three community meetings to introduce the pilot project. Then, a two-day dialogue facilitated by the same independent consultant encouraged the community and MATE to share a joint vision of commitments and to clarify the role and responsibilities in the supply chain.

Natural Justice and the UEBT concluded in the final project report that in those meetings there was "excessive expression of the Association's needs, in turn raising concerns regarding expectation management" (Natural Justice and UEBT, 2012, p. 5). Among the things discussed in the meeting were: challenges the communities were facing with respect to administrative expenses and procedures, the need for child care facilities at different locations, and the willingness of the association to

---

8 The project was financed by the European Commission, under the Fund to Support Human Development.

9 Beraca is committed to the UN Global Compact principles and is also certified for organic products by ECOCERT.

become more independent from the NGO (Natural Justice, 2011c). As a result of this dialogue, the community decided not to go on with the process of building a community protocol.

Lessons learned and challenges

In terms of the lessons learned, from the business side, the dialogue was seen as an opportunity to improve their working relationship with the communities. In this context, the UEBT staff agrees that the initial internal reflection of the community was helpful in the sense that it allowed a broader discussion of the involved parties:

> In the context of a relationship where I'm selling you something, we could discuss price, we may discuss conditions, but we may not necessarily go into a lot of detail about why is it that I want to sell this, why is it that you want to buy it, what are you worried about … where do you think this relation will lead us to in 5 years … This biocultural dialogue was the basis for a value and rights-based discussion that I think was very useful in consolidating a relationship (Interviewee 4, UEBT staff member).

Speaking for the communities, the NGO staff point to some opportunities created by the dialogue, even outside the actual relationship established with the specific company:

> While it is true that the companies have more resources, more information … it is important that the community has its own space to think and discuss internally the different possibilities before sitting with the company to discuss "what are we going to build together?" (Interviewee 6, NGO staff member).

The final project report describes a number of challenges such as internal dynamics between the members of communities, financial constraints, and different expectations of the actors involved. Natural Justice and the UEBT suggest that each community is in a different stage of mobilization and for that reason the interest of communities in building community protocols may differ. None of the communities in the pilot projects followed up in a fully-fledged community protocol process, at least not in the proposed format. However, in the Peruvian case, after the dialogue took place, the community took a while before taking an extra step in building their own strategic plan financed by other organizations using some of the elements discussed in the dialogue. In addition, dialogues are usually time-consuming and costly because they involve a series of activities and meetings that must be facilitated by external organizations in order to be legitimate. The pilot undertaken in Brazil where the facilitator organization dropped out is an example of the importance of external actors conducting the dialogue process. Finally, communities naturally hold high expectations in these types of interventions because they see them as platforms to meet community needs that go beyond the economic relationship with a business partner. An example is in the Madagascar case, where the community brought up concerns with child care and a willingness to work with other partners. Conversely, the business organizations are willing to find processes enabling more "ethical" value chains, without heightening communities' expectations regarding other issues they may wish to resolve.

Discussion and concluding remarks

The pilot projects were designed to provide two participatory spaces for exchange that would transform the transactional relation between corporate and community partners. First, they were intended to provide a **reflexive space** for the communities to explore their own values, needs, and concerns. The goal was mainly to build internal cohesion in the community. In reaffirming their values and expectations while also deciding on how they want to interact with external actors, the community members were nurtured to reflect about their rights, needs, and aspirations. With the creation of this space for internal discussion, the expectation was that largely asymmetrical power would be somewhat balanced out through community empowerment. However, it is important to signal that the use of the community protocol concept was adapted to the circumstances of the initiative. The reflection considered more practical issues involved in the relationship between the partners, rather than constituting a more comprehensive exercise.

Second, the initiative tried to build a **dialogic space** between the community and the business actors in exploring their shared values and commitments. In the actual "biocultural dialogue," the idea was constructing a participatory platform to incentivize the interaction of the partners in a different attitude, from adversarial to more collaborative. In reconciling the different values and expectations under shared commitments, the partners were fostered, at least temporarily, to bracket power imbalances. Nevertheless, while it is true that the interaction moved beyond a strict price negotiation, the dialogue itself remained mainly focused on demonstrating the usefulness, for both parties, of following the principles of the business standard for ethical biotrade. This evidence points to a strong bias of the program in favor of corporate knowledge, which supports previous criticism directed at stakeholder management programs that consider local understandings and needs of communities only partially (Murphy and Arenas, 2010).

Based on the principles of fair and equitable sharing, the idealizers of the project believed that the participatory methodology fostered in the reflexive and dialogic spaces would catalyze community empowerment. Indeed, previous literature has pointed to the importance of redressing power imbalances in these types of partnerships and the role of empowering communities in achieving that (Murphy and Arenas, 2010). Nevertheless, the actual implementation of the project indicates that the process of transitioning from a transactional to an integrative or transformational collaboration (Austin, 2000; Austin and Seitanidi, 2012) demands more than applying participatory methodologies in situations where power is so asymmetrical and needs and aspirations are so dissimilar.

It is important to acknowledge that the project idealizers undertook a conscious effort to create more favorable spaces to bridge partners' different worldviews and to level the playing field. However, many difficulties and questions emerged when the program was implemented in practice. For instance, the methodology seemed to neglect previous internal local dynamics that hindered the cohesion building in the initial reflexive phase of the project and consequently harmed the establishment of a legitimate dialogue between parties. While the idea was to acknowledge the wider community context and discuss broader needs and aspirations of the community, a key question remained: how to balance community needs and aspirations that go beyond the scope of the relationship with the company? Another related challenge is the actual financial investment involved in establishing more collaborative interactions between community and business partners. In further replications, it is not clear where the funding should come from. Considering the possibility that the company funds the process, how could the legitimacy of the process be guaranteed?

So, the important question that remains is what are the community needs and aspirations in these processes? While benefit-sharing programs may be useful in providing funding for local development projects, they are often blamed for not properly reflecting community needs or culture (Whiteman and Mamen, 2002). Indeed, Western views would imply that Indigenous peoples are seeking economic gain as a primary concern, when in fact for many communities their close relationship with the natural environment ensures them food, shelter, and health care (Bavikatte *et al.*, 2015). Therefore, communities aspire to much more than profit from a relationship with a business partner: they want to ensure their right to keep their culture and traditional knowledge alive, which are so intertwined with biodiversity. This is why one of the key topics discussed in community protocol processes and in the dialogues is the meaning and procedures for FPIC. As noted by Ramdas (2012), Indigenous communities may wish to refuse to engage in an ABS agreement if it means commoditizing their resources and knowledge, which are sustained through a collective and spiritual relationship with nature. FPIC becomes then a tool for self-determination in this context because it enables the capacity of communities to decide whether to participate in negotiations with external actors (Pimbert, 2012).

In concluding, while there is no doubt that the right to FPIC is a critical step in helping to ensure more equitable relations, the pilot cases exemplified how challenging it is to achieve meaningful participation from communities. This might be the result of a lack of understanding of the real community needs and aspirations, which indeed go beyond the usual boundaries of a dialogue with a business partner. Therefore, it is critical that efforts aiming at integrative and transformative types of interaction respectfully recognize the political and cultural needs and aspirations of communities in order to promote community rights in practice.

References

Aguilar, G. (2001). Access to genetic resources and protection of traditional knowledge in the territories of Indigenous peoples. *Environmental Science & Policy*, 4(4), pp. 241-256.

Austin, J.E. (2000). Strategic collaboration between nonprofits and business. *Nonprofit and Voluntary Sector Quarterly*, 29, pp. 69-97.

Austin, J.E. & Seitanidi, M.M. (2012). Collaborative Value Creation: A Review of Partnering Between Nonprofits and Businesses. *Nonprofit and Voluntary Sector Quarterly*, 41(5), pp. 726-758.

Banerjee, S.B. (2000). Whose land is it anyway? National interest, Indigenous stakeholders, and colonial discourses. *Organization & Environment*, 13(1), pp. 3-38.

Banerjee, S.B. (2003). Who sustains whose development? Sustainable development and the reinvention of nature. *Organization Studies*, 24(1), pp. 143-180.

Bavikatte, K. & Robinson, D.F. (2011). Towards a people's history of the law: Biocultural jurisprudence and the Nagoya Protocol on access and benefit sharing. *Law, Environment and Development Journal*, 7(1), p. 35.

Bavikatte, K.S., Robinson, D. & Oliva, M.J. (2015). Biocultural Community Protocols: Dialogues on the Space Within. *IK: Other Ways of Knowing*, 1(2), pp. 1-31.

Bruijn, E. & Whiteman, G. (2010). That which doesn't break us: Identity work by local Indigenous "stakeholders." *Journal of Business Ethics*, 96(3), pp. 479-495.

Buxton, A. (2012). The spirit of FPIC: lessons from Canada and the Philippines. *Participatory learning and action*, 65, pp. 67-73.

Castro, A.P. & Nielsen, E. (2001). Indigenous people and co-management: implications for conflict management. *Environmental Science & Policy*, 4(4-5), pp. 229-239.

Cornelius, N. & Wallace, J. (2010). Cross-sector partnerships: city regeneration and social justice. *Journal of Business Ethics*, 94, pp. 71-84.

Delgado, N.A. (2016). Community protocols as tools for resisting exclusion in global environmental governance. *Revista de Adminitracao de Empresa*, 56(4), pp. 395-410.

Equator Principles (2013). *The Equator Principles*. Retrieved from http://www.equator-principles.com/index.php/ep3/ep3

Kraemer, R., Whiteman, G. & Banerjee, B. (2013). Conflict and astroturfing in Niyamgiri: The importance of national advocacy networks in anti-corporate social movements. *Organization Studies*, 34(5-6), pp. 823-852.

Laird, S.A. & Wynberg, R. (2008). Access and benefit-sharing in practice: trends in partnerships across sectors. In: Secretariat of the Convention on Biological Diversity. *Technical series*, 38.

Le Ber, M.J. &Branzei, O. (2010). (Re)forming strategic cross-sector partnerships: Relational processes of social innovation. *Business & Society*, 49(1), pp. 140-172.

Lertzman, D.A. & Vredenburg, H. (2005). Indigenous Peoples, Resource Extraction and Sustainable Development: An Ethical Approach. *Journal of Business Ethics*, 56(3), pp. 239-254.

Morgera, E. & Tsioumani, E. (2010). The evolution of benefit sharing: Linking biodiversity and community livelihoods. *Review of European Community & International Environmental Law*, 19(2), pp. 150-173.

Murphy, M., & Arenas, D. (2010). Through Indigenous Lenses: Cross-Sector Collaborations with Fringe Stakeholders. *Journal of Business Ethics*, 94, p. 103.

Oliva, M.J. (2012). Standards as a tool for putting the Nagoya Protocol in practice. *Business 2020: A magazine on Business and Biodiversity*, 7(1).

Oliva, M.J., Von Braun, J. & Lanao, G.S. (2012). Biocultural community protocols and ethical biotrade: exploring participatory approaches in Peru. *Participatory learning and action*, 65, pp. 166-174.

Natural Justice (2011a, July 26). First BCP in the Context of Ethical BioTrade. Retrieved from http://natural-justice.blogspot.ca/2011/07/first-bcp-in-context-of-ethical.html

Natural Justice (2011b, July 29). Second Pilot Study on Enhancing Community Dialogue with UEBT. Retrieved from http://natural-justice.blogspot.ca/2011/07/second-pilot-study-on-enhancing.html

Natural Justice (2011c, November 12). Third Biotrade Pilot in Vohimana, Madagascar. Retrieved from http://natural-justice.blogspot.ca/2011/11/third-biotrade-pilot-in-vohimana.html

Natural Justice and Union for Ethical BioTrade. (2012). *Project Review: The Use Of BCPs in The Context Of Ethical BioTrade.* Internal document.

Pimbert, M. (2012). FPIC and beyond: safeguards for power-equalising research that protects biodiversity, rights and culture. *Participatory learning and action,* 65, pp. 43-54.

Ramdas, S.R. (2012). Whose access and whose benefit? The Nagoya Protocol and customary rights in India. *Participatory learning and action,* 65, pp. 55-66.

Raufflet, E., Berranger, A. & Gouin, J.F. (2008). Innovation in business-community partnerships: evaluating the impact of local enterprise and global investment models on poverty, bio-diversity and development. *Corporate Governance,* 8(4), pp. 546-556.

Shrumm, H. & Jonas, H. (2012). *Biocultural community protocols*: A toolkit for community facilitators. Cape Town: Natural Justice.

Union for Ethical BioTrade (UEBT) (2012a). Benefit sharing in practice: Biocultural dialogues. Retrieved from http://ethicalbiotrade.org/dl/member-reports/UEBT.note2_.BioCultural.Dialogue.BenefitSharing.2012.pdf

UEBT (2012b). STD01 – Ethical BioTrade Standard. Retrieved from http://ethicalbiotrade.org/dl/STD01_Ethical%20BioTrade%20Standard_2012.04.11_Eng.pdf

United Nations (2008). *United Nations Declaration on the Rights of Indigenous Peoples.* Retrieved from http://www.un.org/esa/socdev/unpfii/documents/DRIPS_en.pdf

United Nations Environmental Programme (UNEP) (2013). In *Community protocols for environmental sustainability*: A guide for policymakers. Retrieved from http://www.unep.org/delc/Portals/119/publications/Community_Protocols_Guide_Policymakers.pdf

United Nations Global Compact. (2013). *Business Reference Guide to the Declaration on the Rights of Indigenous Peoples.* Retrieved from https://www.unglobalcompact.org/docs/issues_doc/human_rights/IndigenousPeoples/BusinessGuide.pdf

Whiteman, G. (2009). All my relations: Understanding perceptions of justice and conflict between companies and Indigenous peoples. *Organization Studies,* 30(1), pp. 101-120.

Whiteman, G., & Mamen, K. (2002). *Meaningful Consultation and Participation in the Mining Sector?* Retrieved from https://idl-bnc.idrc.ca/dspace/bitstream/10625/35236/1/127249.pdf

Wynberg, R. (2010). Hot air over Hoodia. *Seedling,* October, 22–24.

Section III
Modelling Success for Indigenous and Business Interests

9

A business quest for peace

Douglas Adeola
Ph.D. student, Peace and Conflict Studies, University of Ibadan; Program Manager, New Nigeria Foundation

Ogechi Adeola, D.B.A.
Lecturer, Lagos Business School, Pan Atlantic University, Nigeria

This chapter describes the conflicts and peace process in the oil-rich Niger Delta region of Nigeria with a focus on Chevron's initiatives aimed at changing the conflict dynamics. The region is home to Ijaws, Itsekiris, Ilajes, Ogonis, Andonis, and other Indigenous peoples. The chapter pays attention to how the Indigenous people advocated for their rights and how the company responded through its community engagement strategy.

Conflict management, Community engagement, Niger Delta

Introduction

Business cannot succeed in societies that fail (World Business Council for Sustainable Development, WBCSD).

The subject of business sustainability has drawn extensive attention from researchers and practitioners over a long period of time and has given rise to models such as the triple bottom line concept of "People, Planet and Profit" (also known as TBL or 3BL), a phrase coined by John Elkington in 1994 (*The Economist*, 2009). TBL highlights the social responsibility of businesses to pay close attention to social equity as well as economic and environmental factors when conducting business. Other concepts such as the UN Global Compact, Voluntary Principles Initiative (VPI), and the United Nations Guiding Principles on Business and

Human Rights (UNGPs) emphasize the need for a principled approach to doing business; preventing and addressing the risk of adverse impacts on human rights and maintaining the safety and security of business operations within an operating framework that encourages respect for human rights.

Corporations frequently confront sensitive, complex environments and varied expectations among stakeholders that pose serious challenges to their business operations. An example of such a business climate is the oil-rich Niger Delta area. This region is home to ethnic groups such as Ijaws, Itsekiris, Ilajes, Ogonis, and Andonis. International oil companies (IOCs) including Shell Petroleum, Exxon Mobil, and Chevron operate in this zone. The area is known as a conflict zone, given the incessant conflicts, particularly between oil companies and the Indigenous people. According to Forrer et al. (2012) "extractive companies are arguably among the most entrenched private-sector actors in conflict." Moreover, as pointed out by Gonzalez (2010), oil has created a fluid, dark foundation which has resulted in many of the world's wars, conflicts, and grievances.

In the Niger Delta, oil exploration and exploitation have created new conflicts or fueled old ones. "These conflicts are neither special nor unique to the Niger Delta. However, the intensity and dynamics of these conflicts have been affected by both the presence of and politics of oil" (Onuoha, 2005, p. 77). In particular, the activities of extractive companies that involve the use and possible degradation and pollution of land and water have had a negative impact on Indigenous people's human, economic, social, and environmental rights. Frequent clashes between companies and communities have led to loss of lives, properties, and livelihoods (Amadi and Tamuno, 1999; Falode et al., 2006; Odoemene, 2012; Olujimi et al., 2011).

Unfortunately, the Nigerian Government has failed to regulate the conduct of oil firms. The absence or inadequate enforcement of monitoring measures or policies aimed at checking on oil business activities has resulted in practices that defy efforts at greater transparency and best practices in business operations. Hence the constant friction between the Indigenous people and the multinational oil companies, which are generally considered complicit in the conflict context and surrogates of the Nigerian Government. Despite the cries of discontent by the people, the oil companies have capitalized on the government's lackadaisical attitude and taken the liberty to behave badly in their quest for profit. For instance, by 1984, flaring of gas with its attendant environmental consequences had been made technically illegal by the government. However, the oil companies could get around the law that required them to re-inject the gas into the earth rather than flare it by paying a penalty or fine, which was considered far less expensive. This angered Ken Saro-Wiwa, a Niger Delta indigene from Ogoni in Rivers state and an environmental rights activist, who wrote in 1992:

> As a final remark of their genocidal intent and insensitivity to human suffering, Shell and Chevron refuse to obey a Nigerian law which requires all oil companies to re-inject gas into the earth rather than flare it. Shell and Chevron think it cheaper to poison the atmosphere and the Ogoni

and pay the paltry penalty imposed by the government of Nigeria than re-inject the gas as stipulated by the regulations (Saro-Wiwa, 1992, p. 82).

The government's refusal to facilitate socioeconomic development in the area has aggravated the situation. The wealth derived from oil by the Nigerian Federation is not reflected in the socioeconomic life of the oil-producing communities and does not improve their standards of living (Human Rights Watch, 2002; Saro-Wiwa, 1992). In his remarks regarding globalization, Kaur (2014, p. 149) wrote that "the region remains grossly underdeveloped, pauperized, marginalized and largely a poverty zone. The basic facilities and infrastructure of a modern society like potable water, electricity, health care facilities are lacking in the area." The Niger Delta is also believed to be suffering from injustices based on minority status in the Nigerian Federation (Osaghae, 1995). The central government, which is controlled by the major ethnic groups, has absolute control of the distribution of revenues as well as the ownership of land and crude oil through the Land Use Act of 1978 and the Petroleum Act of 1969.

The implication of these injustices is that the Indigenous people are denied adequate development resources, the right to participate in the industry they host, and the right of compensation when their environment and livelihood are destroyed during oil exploration. The result is the rise of ethnic and minority-rights groups' demands for equity and justice for their people. Between 1990 and 1999 no fewer than 24 minority-rights pressure groups emerged (Obi, 2002), including the Movement for the Survival of the Ogoni People (MOSOP), Ijaw Youth Congress (IYC), and the Ijaw National Congress (INC). Some of these groups have made declarations and demands that call attention to the plight of their communities in a bid to promote social equity and achieve economic and environmental justice. These declarations include the Ogoni Bill of Rights, the Kaiama Declaration, Aklaka Declaration of the Egi people, the Oron Bill of Rights, the Warri Accord, and the Resolutions of the First Urhobo Economic Summit (Ekine, 2001). Militant groups sprang up and attacked oil facilities and anything that symbolized government and oil companies' presence. Between 2000 and 2007, over 12,000 cases of vandalism were recorded particularly relating to Nigerian oil pipelines and installations with most reports coming from the Niger Delta (Nwankwo and Ezeobi, 2008). Kidnappings of oil workers and expatriates for ransom became a regular occurrence. In just over one year, January 2006 to February 2007, there were 33 reports of kidnapping of over 200 people. Most of those victims were expatriate oil workers (Africa Masterweb, 2007).

As the spate of attacks on their facilities and the kidnap of their workers and service providers surged, oil companies declared *force majeure* on their operations, claiming they were unable to carry out their legitimate business activities. Disruptions of oil production took a heavy financial toll on the oil companies. Government coffers suffered with each attack as well. Income from oil production was the primary source of state revenues (80%), foreign exchange earnings (90%), and export revenues (96%) (Emuedo, 2014). This blow to the economy has been the basis of the government's response to the agitations and armed struggles by the Indigenous people of Niger Delta. As stated in *TELL* magazine (1995, p. 49), "threats by the local communities struggling for redress were mostly followed by intensified security siege." The hanging of Ken Saro-Wiwa[1] in 1995 was strongly connected with security reports that indicted him as the principal saboteur of Nigeria's oil industry.

Fracas, fiasco, and fall-outs

The oil companies, on their part, spent millions of dollars on security and in providing material support for security forces. However, the operations of these security forces employed by or acting in support of oil and gas companies were usually brutish and abysmally dismal in human rights records (Odoemene, 2012; Okolie-Osemene and Aghalino, 2011). Even peaceful protests by the Indigenous people were sometimes met with severe brutality. This was described by Michael Watts (2001) as "petro-violence"—security imposed jointly by the government and oil companies to police their installations and the environment of social unrest that surrounds petroleum extraction.

In addition to the deployment of security forces to quell the attacks by protesting Indigenous people of Niger Delta seeking attention, patronage, and redress for rights, oil companies used other strategies as part of efforts to secure a social license to operate (SLTO) in the region. They engaged in sparse social investments in an attempt to "buy peace." They also dispensed cash and inducement contracts to curry favor from Indigenous people who could assure and ensure access to their operations. For example, Chevron engaged in community assistance, community investment, and community development initiatives that included the provision of pipe-borne water, hospitals, and schools. Development projects were provided mainly on an ad hoc basis and often were not sustained because they did not get the input of the Indigenous people, neither did they address major concerns about social, economic, human, and environmental rights violations. Mostly, the implementation of these initiatives was based on Memoranda of Understanding (MoUs) entered into between Chevron and a particular Indigenous group or community. The company also engaged in large settlement of individuals and groups through the award of inducement contracts and large ransom payments meant to pacify potential trouble makers. Thus there emerged a group of benefit captors who

---

1 Ken Saro-Wiwa, a writer and popular activist in the forefront of the protest against environmental degradation by oil companies was tried by a military court under the military dictatorship of General Sani Abacha for masterminding the murder of some local chiefs at a pro-government meeting. The international outrage that followed his execution led to Nigeria's suspension from the Commonwealth of Nations for a period of about three years.

capitalized on the circumstances. Infighting regularly broke out on allegations of dishonesty, deception, corruption, compromise, self-centeredness, greed, and lack of transparency and accountability among groups and individuals championing issues that affected the rights of Indigenous people at the community level. As one respondent remarked, "even when we selected leaders, by the time they interacted with Chevron, they corrupted them with money. They did not represent us well." Because the Indigenous people felt dissatisfied with any intervention being carried out by Chevron, actions such as vandalism of company assets, occupation of oil platforms and flow stations, and disruption or shut down of operations continued unabated.

The quest for peace with the Indigenous people

As violence and instability persisted in most of the region and the trillions of dollars spent yearly on security and military activity were unsustainable and not yielding adequate results, alternative methods of fostering peace were sought (Forrer *et al.*, 2012). The experience of the 1990s specifically gave impetus to the need to seek drastic solutions to the unending crises in the Delta. While booming oil markets had allowed Chevron and the country to prosper despite difficulties associated with restiveness from rights advocates and militant pressure, beginning in the mid-1990s, the Niger Delta area became more charged and less conducive for business operations. There was a gale of discontent on the part of the Indigenous people stemming from unfulfilled promises, killings, unemployment, destruction of livelihoods, and so on, which both the government and the oil firms failed to address. Rising costs associated with continuous attacks on oil facilities, kidnappings, extortion, threats to staff, and destruction of assets, compelled some oil companies to explore other ways of addressing the seemingly intractable conflicts. In the case of Chevron, the quest to address the challenges in its sphere of operation followed the March 2003 occupation of Chevron's flow stations and Escravos export terminal by women, which led to the shutdown of its western production operations. The women's demands were that Chevron should upgrade members of the communities who were contract staff to permanent staff status, provide employment for their children on an annual basis, provide vital infrastructure, give monthly allowances for the elderly, and establish income generating schemes (Chevron/Texaco, 2003; Okon and Ola, 2002).

Managing the circumstances surrounding the shutdown involved engaging with oil-bearing communities; assessing the possible environmental, social, and economic effects of operations; and committing to transparency in addressing these concerns. Chevron formed a multi-disciplinary team drawing mainly from its operations, government and public affairs, health, environment, and safety departments with the mandate to review the operational situation around Chevron's operations in the Niger Delta. The team was to recommend plans for restoring operations in the western Niger Delta and establish a secure, stable, and sustainable operating environment throughout its operations. The need for this plan was underscored by a Chevron board member Peter Robertson in a 2004 position paper: "Petroleum, Poverty, and Profits: Changing Philosophies of Community Engagement."

> We need to build on our efforts to sustain equally successful community engagements. Our productive portfolios of long-term oil and gas leases must be matched by productive portfolios of long-term community projects—projects that improve lives and promote broad economic growth. … this isn't solely a moral or ethical imperative. It is a business imperative too—one that goes to the heart of our ability to prosper and survive (Robertson, 2004).

In 2004, Chevron introduced a community engagement initiative known as Global Memorandum of Understanding (GMoU). The GMoU is a tripartite agreement involving Chevron, the government, and clusters of communities of Indigenous people in Chevron's area of operation. However, its implementation involved other stakeholders such as non-governmental organizations (NGOs), agencies of government, and other interested development organizations and donors. These stakeholders are members of various GMoU committees offering technical support to the Regional Development Committees (RDCs) in the implementation of their community development programs.

The GMoU's deployment was preceded by extensive negotiations with clusters of communities on issues affecting corporate/community relations such as employment for Indigenous people, contracts and subcontracts for Indigenous contractors, and development projects in the communities. It was signed with over 425 communities in the Niger Delta, an estimated 850,000 Indigenous people clustered into eight RDCs defined by historical linkages, ethnic affinity, and local government geographical scope. These RDCs are given funds each year that are released in quarterly tranches. Up to 80% of the fund goes into a project account held in a special-purpose bank account, while the remaining 20% is for general administration. The fund is administered by community engagement management boards (CEMBs), which serve as the highest decision-making body for each RDC. The CEMB members include representatives from Chevron, Indigenous communities, NGOs, government (local and state), and other participating development agencies. Development projects implemented by the RDCs are chosen from prioritized projects in the community development plan (CDP). The CDPs are generated after a needs assessment or a sustainable livelihood assessment (SLA) is carried out by community experts.

The GMoU's stated objectives are to enhance community ownership of development, peace, and security. This is in line with what many scholars in the last decade considered a necessity for the private sector to act ethically. As stated by Rettberg (2004, p. 1), "emphasis on the private sector's contribution to fuelling armed conflict has neglected our understanding of business motivations operating in the opposite direction: building peace." Nelson (2000, p. 12) asserted that in today's global economy, businesses had a growing commercial rationale for playing this role "in order to avoid the direct and indirect business costs of conflict and to reap the business benefits of peace."

To date, oil corporations in the Delta seem not to have fully explored their peace potential to the benefit of the stakeholders. It was only in the last decade that some oil firms have begun to recognize the need for a more direct and practical approach to engendering peace. A key strategy adopted in doing this is the deployment of business initiatives (e.g., the GMoU) to address some concerns of the Indigenous people impacting on corporate–community relations. Such initiatives or interventions become tools for addressing rights issues and concerns, especially in situations where the government has abdicated its responsibility for addressing the concerns of its citizens, including the protection of their human rights. They can also be strong tools to minimize economic gaps, promote equity, harness social success, and bring about peace and stability.

Findings from observations and interviews held with about 60 randomly sampled respondents Indigenous to the Niger Delta area revealed varied views about the success of the initiative. Most respondents agreed that the GMoU established a new paradigm in corporate–community relations. It created a platform for involving critical stakeholders in discussions that affected the Indigenous people and their communities; it established a governance structure to manage corporate–community affairs; and it enhanced development by involving communities in the identification, design, and implementation of projects. According to a respondent, "the GMoU system involves people in the planning and implementation of projects unlike those initiated by Chevron without seeking the consent of the people." Respondents also noted that the GMoU aim to recognized Indigenous people as critical stakeholders in Chevron's operations. An essential component of the GMoU was an initial facilitated negotiation involving representatives of Chevron, communities, and government. One agreement reached with the Indigenous people was the provision of funds for community-owned and community-driven development; other agreements related to employment and contracts for the indigenes. In the 10 years following the deployment of the GMoU, over ₦18 billion (≈US$57 million) was committed to more than 400 communities, villages, and chiefdoms across eight RDCs in five states of the Niger Delta to fund approximately 620 projects including rural electrification, local and foreign scholarships up to the Ph.D. level, housing, transportation, health care, shoreline protection, and microcredit financing. These projects are implemented by Indigenous contractors after going through a bid process. Some of the Indigenous community representatives interviewed agreed that Chevron has implemented its side of the GMoU agreement by meeting its financial obligations to the communities.

Many respondents felt that some of the actions made possible through the instrumentality of the GMoU can be associated with the steady decline in the violent confrontations between Chevron and the Indigenous people in communities around its operation. Also, the GMoU has given the Indigenous people a sense of ownership and control of resources. Though the GMoU resources are generally considered to be grossly inadequate by the communities for implementation of community development projects, it is nevertheless a mini-realization of resource control and recognition of their rights to own and use the resources to drive their development. These issues align with the long-fought battle with the federal government by the Indigenous people for the control of their resources and the right to self-determination.

However, some respondents expressed a more negative view of the contributions of the GMoU. They noted the limited participation of indigenes in the industry via direct employment and contracts from the company. According to one respondent, "the major contracts are given to the Yorubas and other tribes, we are given slave jobs." Another remarked that "where there is no employment, there will be no development and no change, kidnapping will take place." Some respondents claimed that the GMoU has deepened inequality among the Indigenous people because not everyone has benefitted from contracts and other largesse from the initiative. In the opinion of these respondents, the GMoU is the worst thing that has befallen the oil-bearing communities. "Chevron is only postponing the evil day," according to one respondent and another felt that "Chevron just wants to make huge profit and forget the communities hosting them. They should drop the GMoU, it is a tactic to cheat us." However, this view was repudiated by some respondents who observed that those who were unhappy with the GMoU model were those who had benefitted from the old ways of doing things. They also affirmed that prior to the community development projects initiated in the decade 2005 to 2015, Chevron did little or nothing for the Indigenous people in the communities. In the words of a respondent, "the GMoU has brought physical development and the community people are happy—for what they are seeing in terms of physical development, though some still complain."

The lessons, way forward, and conclusion

The implementation of the GMoU has brought about a reasonable sense of fulfillment for both Chevron and the Indigenous communities regarding some of the issues that created the conflict context. In spite of the gap between the Indigenous people's aspirations and the fulfillment of same, the GMoU has altered the dynamics in the Niger Delta area. The major success of the GMoU is the achievement of the structure of expectations over rights and obligations of both Chevron and the communities. This has guided the parties and regulated their conduct, but when there are gaps in expectations, dialogue has been the main instrument for conducting corporate–community affairs and it has engendered cooperation, joint learning, and action. The GMoU has also addressed some fundamental issues leading to protests for rights. The Indigenous people have been able to use the GMoU resources through the RDC structures to engage Indigenous contractors and a local workforce to develop their communities, improve the local economy, and build their capacity to secure contracts with Chevron. The reward for Chevron is that these shared efforts have contributed to lessening violence in its areas of operation and generated local goodwill through which it has enhanced its production environment.

For years to come, Chevron and other oil companies will continue to be haunted by the recklessness in their operations. Likewise, the Indigenous people will carry the scars of the injustices and abuse they suffered at the hands of these firms. There-fore, measures being taken to remedy the past misdeeds and chart a new course must be broad in scope and scale. The GMoU seems very much a lofty social initia-tive by the fact of its modest success and its potential; however, business modus operandi must complement an initiative of this nature. There is still no convincing evidence that company operations are up to internationally accepted standards. Though Chevron has committed to environmental protection actions through its Escravos gas to liquid (EGTL) and other such projects, the problems of gas flaring and other environmental degradation occurring through sabotage and/or equip-ment failure continue to trigger environmental and economic rights violations.

The question of how to regulate and assure security and human rights continues to recur because of the kind of treatment usually meted out to rights agitators by security personnel acting on behalf of the government, Chevron, and other busi-nesses. Chevron Corporation has committed to voluntary principles on security and protection of human rights and Chevron Nigeria has deployed security per-sonnel who have been trained to man its facilities in line with those principles. However, some security personnel acting on behalf of Chevron and other oil com-panies have been quoted by respondents as saying that they are in the region to protect oil facilities and not human rights.

Beyond Chevron's social efforts the federal government must play a significant role in addressing the rights of the Indigenous people. The minority rights issues within the overall context of the Nigerian nation are beyond the GMoU or any cor-porate initiative. Nevertheless, the GMoU has provided a platform that can be used as a good starting point for a progressive realization of Indigenous people's rights and aspirations, and the pursuit of sustainable peace and development in the Niger Delta region.

Recommendations

Sustainable success will require a much stronger commitment to best practices and behaviors by Chevron and other oil companies. Two recommendations are foremost:

- Chevron operations and investments should be sensitive to the environment and the people through the use of improved technology and equipment in the exploration and exploitation of crude. There must be a balance between these two domains: production and profitability on the one hand and the right to environmental protections on the other hand. The import of this is that the quest for business growth and profit-making must not jeopardize the need to protect the planet and the people.

- There should be a redefinition of security operations by oil companies as they seek legitimate security goals. Adoption and implementation of the principles set out in business reference guides such as the Global Compact, the United Nations Guiding Principles on Business and Human Rights (UNGPs), and the Voluntary Principles on Security and Human Rights (VPs) can help companies work effectively with governments to reduce or eliminate the use of violence and encourage respect for and protection of human rights. One example of such an action would be for Chevron Nigeria to engage in the holistic implementation of the VPs in its operations.

References

Africa Masterweb. (2007). *Chronology of Nigerian militants' attacks*. Retrieved from http://www.africamasterweb.com/AdSense/NigerianMilitants06Chronology.html

Amadi, S.N. & Tamuno, S.O. (1999). Oil exploration in Nigeria: Its socio-economic impact on the oil-bearing communities. *Tiber*, 3(1).

Derr, K.T. (1997). In Nigeria, we have helped improve health care, schools and the infrastructure. *Africa Today*, 3(5), pp. 32-33.

Ekine, S. 2000. *Blood and Oil: Testimonies of Violence from Women of the Niger Delta*. London: Centre for Democracy and Development.

Emuedo, C. (2014). Oil and conflict nexus: The greed model and insecurity in the Niger Delta, Nigeria. *Global Journal of Human-Social Science*, 14(4). Retrieved from https://globaljournals.org/GJHSS_Volume14/2-Oil-and-Conflict-Nexus.pdf

Falode, O.A, Ogedengbe, K. & Bickersteth, T. (2006). Managing environmental conflicts in the oil producing areas of Nigeria. *Trends in Applied Sciences Research*, 1(3), pp. 259-272.

Forrer, J., Fort, T. & Gilpin, R. (2012). How business can foster peace. *United States Institute of Peace, Special Report*. Retrieved from http://www.usip.org/sites/default/files/SR315.pdf

Gonzalez, A. (2010). Petroleum and its impact on three wars in Africa: Angola, Nigeria and Sudan. *Journal of Peace, Conflict and Development*, 16(11), pp. 58-86.

Kaur, S. (2014). Role of globalization in generating conflicts in Niger Delta. *International Journal of Political Science and Development*, 2(7), pp. 147-150.

Nelson, J. (2000). The business of peace: The private sector as a partner in conflict prevention and resolution. *The Prince of Wales Business Leaders Forum, International Alert, Council on Economic Priorities*. Retrieved from http://www.international-alert.org/sites/default/files/publications/The%20Business%20of%20Peace.pdf

Nwankwo, C. & Ezeobi, O. (2008, May 15). Nigeria lost N150bn to pipeline vandals in eight years. The Punch: Nigeria.

Obi, C. (2002). Oil and the minority question. In A. Momoh and S. Adejumobi (Eds.), *The National Question in Nigeria: Comparative Perspectives* (p. 113). Ashgate: Aldershot.

Odoemene, A. (2012). The Nigerian armed forces and sexual violence in Ogoniland of the Niger Delta Nigeria, 1990-1999. *Armed Forces & Society,* 38(2), pp. 225-251.

Okolie-Osemene, J. & Aghalino, S.O. (2011). Interrogating the implementation of Niger Delta master plan and conflict transformation strategies of Obasanjo's Administration. *Journal of Intra-African Studies,* (5), pp. 253-265.

Okon, E. & O. Doifie (2002). *A report of the Niger Delta Women Justice (NDWJ) on the Delta Women Siege on the American Oil Company, Chevron-Texaco in Delta State of Nigeria.* Port Harcourt: Niger Delta Women for Justice.

Olujimi, J.A, Adewumi, E.A. & Odunwole S. (2011). Environmental implications of oil exploration and exploitation in the coastal region of Ondo State. *Journal of Geography and Regional Planning,* 4(3), pp. 110-121.

Onuoha, A. (2005). *From Conflict to Collaboration: Building Peace in Nigeria's Oil Producing Communities.* London: Adonis and Abbey.

Osaghae, E.E. (1995). The Ogoni uprising: Oil politics, minority agitation and the future of the Nigerian state. *African Affairs,* 94(376), pp. 325-344.

Rettberg, A. (2004, December). Business-led peacebuilding in Colombia: Fad or future of a country in crisis? *Crisis State Programme, Working Paper Series no. 1.* Retrieved from http://eprints.lse.ac.uk/28201/1/wp56.pdf

Robertson, P.J. (2004, December). *Petroleum, Poverty and Profits: Changing Philosophies of Community Engagement.* Paper presented at the Eradicating Poverty through Profit Conference, San Francisco, CA. Retrieved from https://www.chevron.com/stories/petroleum-poverty-and-profits-changing-philosophies-of-community-engagement

Saro-Wiwa, K. (1992). *Genocide in Nigeria: The Ogoni Tragedy.* Lagos: Saros International.

TELL Magazine (1995, December 4), p. 49.

Watts, M. (2001). Petro-violence: Community, extraction, and political ecology of a mythic commodity. In M. Watts & N. Peluso (Eds.), *Violent Environments,* pp. 189-212. Ithaca: Cornell University Press.

10

Everything is one?

Relationships between First Nations and salmon farming companies

Lars Huemer, Ph.D.

Professor, BI Norwegian Business School

Salmon farming is a controversial business activity in British Columbia. This chapter presents two types of relationship between First Nations and salmon farming corporations, focusing on how the relationships have developed from conflict and suspicion to what today appears as more collaborative and mutually respectful ventures. Concerns about sustainability and the possible role of corporations in facilitating the emergence of community-based enterprises are discussed.

Relationships, Salmon farming, Community-based enterprises

Introduction

Many First Nations along the Canadian west coast have relied on seafood and the catch of wild salmon to sustain their communities. Salmon farming could represent a commercial alternative to the traditional way of living, but this business has not been an obvious choice for First Nations, and interacting with corporations can be challenging for Indigenous peoples (see, for example, Peredo and Anderson, 2006). Conflict is common regarding goals, the use of resources, and the distribution of benefits (Gedicks, 2001; Calbucura, 2003).

Opposition to salmon farming has been particularly strong in British Columbia (B.C.), with common criticism from First Nation communities and external stakeholders alike. To illustrate, First Nation members—including heredi-tary chiefs—recently called for the eviction of multinational-owned fish farms. Salmon farmers were labeled "poison"—an environmental problem that harms wild fish, disrupts natural migration routes, and spreads disease—thereby threat-ening Indigenous people and their culture (Nikiforuk, 2016).

Other First Nations have started to accept salmon farming, and have developed partnerships with corporations. According to B.C. Salmon Farmers association, there are 19 economic and social partnerships with First Nations; close to 80% of the salmon raised in B.C. is done in partnership with First Nations. The industry provides jobs in remote coastal areas, making it possible for First Nations employ-ees to care for their families and stay in their traditional communities (BC Salmon Farmers Association, 2016).

This study focuses on two First Nations and their formalized relationships with two salmon farmers. Ahousaht has worked with the global fish farming giant Cer-maq for a number of years, and Tla-o-qui-aht has a more recent partner agree-ment with Creative Salmon, a small, local salmon farming company. Of interest is how these First Nations and their corporate partners have interacted in order to develop their relationships. An Ahousaht member stressed that "the West" and its corporations usually miss the idea that "everything is one; People and Ocean." But can this sense of unity and shared destiny be developed between First Nations and corporations? This is an interesting issue, since the meeting between corporations and Indigenous peoples concerns questions of how to make a living, how to make living itself meaningful, and may even challenge the conditions under which one makes a living (cf. Bebbington, 1999).

In particular, this chapter relates to the concept of community-based enter-prise (CBE) as one way of dealing with First Nation resource development. A CBE, according to Peredo and Chrisman (2006), aims to contribute to both local eco-nomic and social development, and is built on the collective skills and resources of the community. Of interest in this chapter is whether the pursuit of a common community good can be facilitated through corporate relationships.

The following section presents the design and methods of the study. This is fol-lowed by the main section, which is a description of the focal relationships. An analysis of Indigenous perspectives on salmon farming and whether relationships with corporations may influence the development of CBEs is presented thereafter.

Methods

This project is exploratory and builds on a longitudinal case study relying primar-ily on interviews and observation techniques. The advantage with a qualitative approach is that it embraces empirical nuances and is open for different points of view (e.g., Kvale, 1996; Denzin and Lincoln, 2000); that is, different people, with dif-ferent social and cultural outlooks, perceive reality in different ways.

Data sources and analysis

The focal relationships are the Ahousaht First Nation and Cermaq relation, and the Tla-o-qui-aht First Nation and Creative Salmon relation. Ahousaht is located on Flores Island, off the west coast of Vancouver Island. The Ahousaht First Nation has a population of over 1,000 people in the reserve and over 2,000 total members, and is the largest nation on the west coast of Vancouver Island. Cermaq is a global salmon farmer and the second-largest aquaculture company in B.C., with its head office in Campbell River. The company holds half of its operations in the Ahousaht territory, where it has been farming Atlantic salmon since 2000. Mitsubishi acquired the company in 2014; the previous majority owner was the Norwegian state.

The Tla-o-qui-aht First Nations (formerly referred to as the Clayoquot) live on different reserves on Vancouver Island. Their primary economic activities are fishing and tourism. Creative Salmon was established in 1990, and contrary to multinational Cermaq, Creative Salmon is a relatively small, local company farming Chinook (Pacific) salmon. All of its farming activities take place in First Nations' territory, and approximately 25% of its west coast crew are First Nation, including Tla-o-qui-aht. The company has been focusing on organic practices since 1995. The implications of organic practices are further addressed below.

The chapter builds on 24 interviews, the majority focusing on the Ahousaht–Cermaq relationship, which has been studied since 2010 (Huemer, 2014). The Tla-o-qui-aht–Creative Salmon relationship has been followed since 2015, and builds on interviews with the resource manager of Tla-o-qui-aht and the general manager and communications and human resource manager of Creative Salmon. Hereditary chiefs, elders, the operations manager, and previous fish-farm committee members were interviewed in the Ahousaht case, in addition to Cermaq Canada's CEO, the communications and sustainability manager, and the community liaison. A semi-structured interview technique was used. Main themes included understanding of the respective entities; First Nations and corporations; reasons for opposition and the process towards acceptance; and partner protocols.

Additional interviews were conducted with other First Nation leaders, including those opposing the business, as well as corporate representatives from other firms. Non-governmental organizations such as the Pure Salmon Campaign and the manager of Aboriginal Aquaculture Association (AAA) were also interviewed.

The interviews lasted between one and three hours. Participation in a two-day workshop focusing on "how to work with First Nations" was helpful in preparing for the interviews and in acknowledging the oral tradition of Indigenous peoples. In practical terms, this implied an awareness of listening without interrupting with additional questions. As a result, some replies lasted over 30 minutes, including rich descriptions of context, culture, and history. Finally, a field trip to Cermaq's farming sites took place in 2010. Members of Ahousaht's fish farming committee also took part in this trip.

During the comparative case analysis, particular emphasis was given to First Nation perspectives and opinions regarding salmon farming and corporate relationships.

Indigenous participation in salmon farming

The following text presents the two focal relationships: the relationship between Ahousaht First Nation and Cermaq, and the relationship between the Tla-o-qui-aht First Nation and Creative Salmon.

The Ahousaht–Cermaq relationship

Opposition and sustainability concerns

Coastal First Nations in Canada perceive salmon farming as a controversial activity. As Ahousaht's operation manager explains, "When fish farming came, our people was almost at war with them." The operations manager suggested there are three camps in the community today: those who oppose and have negative thoughts about the enterprise; those in favor; and a third group not knowing which side to choose. Those in favor appreciate the economic benefits and employment, whereas, according to this manager, those against tend to disregard information about sustainability improvements that have been accomplished over the years.

From Cermaq's perspective, it is clear that its business depends heavily on First Nation's support. Company representatives also claimed that the relationships between First Nation and the industry are changing. One example is a recent reception in Victoria, Vancouver Island, which Cermaq hosted for the government and industry representatives. A couple of Ahousaht members showed up with a drum, and one Cermaq manager, due to the conflicts over the years, jokingly asked "Are you going to protest?" The unexpected performance, conducted in Ahousaht language, was on the contrary an appreciation of their relationship with Cermaq. The Ahousaht members were there on the behalf of the hereditary chiefs to demonstrate their respect for the partnership. "They got up there, stole the show and ... said wonderful things" (Cermaq's communications and sustainability manager).

Partnership and support

The hereditary chiefs of the Ahousaht First Nation, the Tyee Hawiiih, have concluded that fish farming is replacing the prosperity that has been missing since the downturn of commercial fishing. Ahousaht and Cermaq have developed a common vision regarding salmon farming in Clayoquot Sound, a UNESCO Biosphere Reserve where anti-salmon-farming campaigns have been particularly strong. The intention is to meet or exceed existing environmental standards and that they will strive to be a progressive, innovative Aboriginal/industry partnership that seeks mutual long-term social, economic, cultural, and spiritual benefits for both parties (Huemer, 2014).

Ahousaht and Cermaq signed their first protocol agreement in 2002. It included an acknowledgment of the Ahousaht traditional land presence and rights, which was fundamental for the First Nation. A second protocol agreement was signed in

2010, and further established the principles for working together with sustainable and mutually beneficial salmon-farming operations. The protocol aligns Ahousaht's interests with Cermaq's performance.

The operations manager of Ahousaht mentioned that Cermaq has, for years, been supportive in good and bad times for the community by assisting in various events and functions. He continues:

> Norway was the only nation that recognized us, our people and our hereditary chiefs, our territory. The Norwegian government did a real good job; I feel that they helped identify who we are. That we are not just Indians, we are actually a community.

In 2015, a renewal of the protocol was signed, with a duration of five years. From Cermaq's perspective, Ahousaht's concerns were focused on financial rather than sustainability matters this time. Whereas it took several years to establish the previous protocol, the new version was completed in six months. The main change in the formalization of the partnership is, as expressed by Ahousaht's operations manager, that the First Nation wants to be "more business-minded." Ahousaht has dismantled the fish farming committee and created a smaller board to improve communications between Cermaq and the Ahousaht community. Moreover, the chiefs have established the Ahousaht Corporation in order to separate internal community politics from business. In other words, the First Nation desires a more clear-cut separation of funds coming from its own commercial activities and governmental funds. Cermaq also finds that other First Nations have started to create corporations for that same reason.

Both parties stress the necessity of improving communications. According to Cermaq's community liaison, "Communication is the biggest thing in our relationship. The corporate structure is very much a paper/email system that can be tracked. Looked back upon, recorded, it can be accessed. Combining that with a verbal culture can be difficult."

The company has continued to support scholarships intended to improve the employability of Ahousaht members. Cermaq organizes social events and holds open-house meetings and career-fairs in Ahousaht territory. In the current protocol, there is an intent to hire Ahousaht members based on qualifications and skills, but no fixed number has been established. Capacity building aimed at facilitating employment is a common concern. Education and training is a prioritized theme, and a recent program involving ten Ahousaht members resulted in three immediate hires, not only by Cermaq, but also by Creative Salmon. As the community liaison for Cermaq expressed, "We want a better-equipped community."

Managing the business with Ahousaht values and principles

As stressed above, one explanation for the creation of the Ahousaht Corporation is to separate governmental funding from commercial income. This also aims to return to pre-European organization style based on the hereditary system, as explained by the operations manager:

> I believe we are actively using the past and the old ways to reeducate people. A lot of people are so used to the elected system, the chief in council, a generation that really does not understand the hereditary system. Now the Hereditary chiefs explain their roles and responsibilities. I for my family had an event for my daughters ... this was witnessed by 1000 people. We did ceremonies that have not been done for 85 years.

Ahousaht's operations manager hopes this approach will influence the way they do business.

Cermaq is aware of these changes, acknowledging that Ahousaht intends to strengthen the hereditary tradition and old forms of resource management. Cermaq's main challenge here is to maintain a close relationship to the community, since the members of the First Nation are central in terms of future support. Good community relations that go beyond pure financial interactions with the Ahousaht Corporation are significant, according to Cermaq's managers: "How you blend the corporate culture and the First Nation culture is a dance, you have to give and take" (Cermaq community liaison).

Both Ahousaht and Cermaq representatives agree that it is essential for Ahousaht members to retain their cultural identity. At the same time, those employed in the business must be committed to the job. From Cermaq's perspective, it is argued that "not everyone can go to every funeral; we also need to run the company" (Cermaq communications and sustainability manager). Accordingly, the operations manager of Ahousaht argued that "we also understand that this is a business and people need to show up for work."

Mutual learning

There are different kinds of learning processes taking place in this relationship. The parties have spent a considerable amount of time learning about one another's cultures and practices. Cermaq continues to share the management teams' developed understanding with the entire organization, and the new protocol emphasizes cross-cultural awareness. According to the managers, Cermaq employees need to understand that First Nations represent distinct cultures. There is also a mutual recognition of Ahousaht's need to better understand Cermaq's business approach. Ahousaht has gained knowledge from working with Cermaq, not least in terms of protocol development. Education, labor, and business opportunities such as subcontracting are other sources of learning.

Cermaq has developed knowledge in different areas through its relationship with Ahousaht. In terms of salmon farming, this includes the location of sites, the Elders' cleansing ceremony after accidents, and traditional knowledge concerning fish routes. Moreover, Ahousaht represents Cermaq's initial engagement process, and this relationship has formed Cermaq's baseline for other First Nation relations. Therefore, Cermaq's managers stressed that they have developed some fundamental knowledge about how to interact with First Nations and how to create mutually meaningful partner agreements. Cermaq's managers argued that they now approach new relationships from a more equal position; it is no longer viable for them to enter a First Nation territory and "make an offer." This new approach is based on a desire to develop partnerships while acknowledging the needs of both the First Nation and the company. As expressed by Cermaq's community liaison,

> I think we have learnt a fair bit what works and not, how to approach in a way that achieves that transparency and clarity. No hidden agendas. We are very confident, we have shown that there can be long-term benefits to communities, it is a viable model.

The Tla-o-qui-aht–Creative Salmon relationship

Opposition and sustainability concerns

The Tla-o-qui-aht nation, including the resource manager, was not always in favor of salmon farming. Thoughts about evicting Creative Salmon existed, and concerns about the industry's sustainability are still present in the community. Moreover, the industrial activity did not always benefit the First Nation:

> You want pristine waters ... of course you want to be in our rivers ... We have great amount of fresh water which keeps salinity low and sea lice low. You want to be here and have nice waters, it is too expensive for you to be on land ... then you should pay a premium price (Tla-o-qui-aht's resource manager).

The general manager of Creative Salmon acknowledges that companies, including his own, entered the area without much thought about the First Nations: they just started farming fish. This has, of course, influenced First Nations' opposition. Since Creative Salmon wants to be in Tla-o-qui-aht territory, the general manager argues that some kind of consent is definitely better than the costs of conflict.

An interesting event took place in 2015, when the Annual General Meeting of the B.C. Salmon Farmers Association was held at Tla-o-qui-aht's traditional land. This was the first time that a partnering Nation hosted the association and its members, and corporate representatives view the invitation as an acknowledgment of the industry. The meeting began with a *Community Dialogue* session, followed by a *Partnerships Dialogue* session, which featured speakers from the Tla-o-qui-aht First Nation, the Ministry of Aboriginal Relations and Reconciliation, and the Aboriginal Aquaculture Association. Tla-o-qui-aht's resource manager acknowledged the relationship with Creative Salmon and emphasized that other companies operating in their traditional territory will also need to formalize relationships with them.

Partnership and support

Tla-o-qui-aht's vision is to have sustainable fish farming with year-round job opportunities in combination with vibrant seasonal fish runs. Creative Salmon's general manager also emphasized their desire to do no harm to the environment, a concern they share with the First Nation.

Reaching the Tla-o-qui-aht–Creative Salmon protocol was a time-consuming effort, as in the Ahousaht–Cermaq case. Creative Salmon hired a First Nation liaison in the late 1990s; this helped the company in understanding their First Nation employees better. The first version of the protocol agreement was primarily operational in focus, and it did not have the rigor of the dialogue the parties have developed in their current agreement regarding output and footprints including net density and feed content.

The parties had been discussing the protocol for about 10 years before the initial agreement. The current protocol took four more years to develop, and was signed in 2014. The parties met on a regular basis and the company continued to have council meetings and open-house meetings, which in combination with experiences by Tla-o-qui-aht employees changed the First Nation's perception of the company and its activities. The Tla-o-qui-aht's resource managers stressed that they spent a long time becoming educated on Creative Salmon's farming practices, and that justified the content of the final protocol agreement.

That Creative Salmon has historically been "in a decent spot regarding sustainability", according to the general manager, seems important to the relationship. Creative Salmon's business model is based on a number of practices which are regarded as being sustainable by both the firm and the First Nation; these include the farming of Pacific salmon and low-density production using seawater-washed, non-treated nets. Such practices reduced Tla-o-qui-aht's concerns and led to the initial approval of their leaders to engage in a dialogue with the corporation. As expressed by Tla-o-qui-aht's resource manager, "it is a lower return model. And we do so willingly … If you want a higher return, grow Atlantic. And then you get all the other concerns." The trade-off, according to the resource manager, is between economic benefits and the sustainability of the operations.

Creative Salmon's general manager's experience is that the First Nation essentially appreciated their way of working and that the protocol agreement did not imply any significant changes in how the company operates. The main difference today is that existing practices have been formalized and Tla-o-qui-aht has a say in future developments. From the First Nation's perspective, the fact that Creative Salmon has never farmed Atlantic salmon and historically has been focusing on sustainability is of great importance: "we are happy that it is not Atlantic. And if it had been … I probably could not have got the protocol signed" (Tla-o-qui-aht's resource manager).

The most significant change in the current protocol appears to be in terms of communication, such as conducting regular meetings, and in assisting the fish farm committee to become an expert entity in the business. Organizationally, three hereditary chiefs and three representatives from Creative Salmon make up the fish farm committee's formal structure. The particular business model is central in the current agreement, which was a request from the hereditary chiefs. In addition to the business dimension, the protocol agreement also includes funding, education, and salmon enhancement projects.

The company also made a predator management plan available to the committee, as well as benthic monitoring reports and information on feed content and fish density. The company is also expected to immediately notify Tla-o-qui-aht about fish health issues, and the parties have agreed to monitor developments and the feasibility of closed containment projects. Creative Salmon is further expected to make their best efforts to hire qualified Tla-o-qui-aht members.

Tla-o-qui-aht's resource manager pointed out that the relationship has been good and that there is a general support for the salmon farmer, which has already assisted the First Nation in fish stock restoration, a coho salmon project, and the refurbishment of one of Tla-o-qui-aht's hatchery decks.

Discussion

Ahousaht and Tla-o-qui-aht have come to consider salmon farming as one feasible way of developing their communities. Both First Nations have signed protocol agreements with salmon farming companies operating in their territories. Concerns about these agreements still exist among Ahousaht as well as Tla-o-qui-aht members. Nevertheless, a mutual willingness to learn—about corporate practices and modern salmon farming techniques, and about First Nation values and priorities—explains the development of these relationships.

The two First Nations' experiences are similar in certain ways. They both emphasize economic advantages including employment, salmon enhancement funding, and business opportunities based on training and educational programs. There is also a desire to increase work opportunities in the industry, in combination with vibrant seasonal fish runs.

Ahousaht and Tla-o-qui-aht both express pride in their agreements, as shown in comments by Tla-o-qui-aht's resource manager on their invitation to the Salmon Farmer Association's annual meeting: "We've just signed the protocol and would like to share the practices we are proud of."

From a corporate perspective, both firms acknowledge that their business depends on First Nations' support. Both corporations engage in various forms of community activities, and they have stabilized their operations within their respective First Nation partner's territory.

Combining First Nation values and corporate principles is, of course, challenging at times, and all parties emphasized the importance of communication and mutual understanding. The firms try to organize shifts and work practices so that their Indigenous employees can honor community traditions. At the same time, it appears that community members are asked to adapt to corporate productivity needs, both by corporate managers and First Nation leaders. Tensions do occur; however, these cannot be solved through written standards, but rather through ongoing dialogue and mutual adaptations.

There are also some noteworthy differences in these relationships, such as how the First Nations have approached the business activity and how sustainability is perceived. Ahousaht relates to the Cermaq Group, one of the largest salmon farming multinationals in the world. Cermaq is a world leader (in the salmon industry) in terms of certifications and transparency reports. Cermaq is also certified in accordance with the Aboriginal Aquaculture Association (AAA). They farm Atlantic salmon, which in volume is by far the most common species, and the most debated one in terms of sustainability. Tla-o-qui-aht interacts with a local producer that has differentiated itself from its large-volume competitors by farming Chinook salmon. Creative Salmon does not have the AAA certificate, but is nevertheless acknowledged for its organic profile. The two First Nations and their respective corporate partners thereby stress these aspects differently when arguing in favor of the sustainability of their operations.

These differences also explain some variation in farming practices. It is worth noting that Ahousaht explicitly and knowingly refer to one of Cermaq's official values—being "business-minded"—when referring to ongoing reorganizations to improve conditions in the community and its corporate relationship. Ahousaht has abandoned the fish farming committee structure and the managerial function of chiefs in council in favor of a corporate structure, the Ahousaht Corporation. Meanwhile, Creative Salmon and Tla-o-qui-aht continue with a fish farming committee.

First Nation–corporate relationships and community-based enterprises

Economic transactions are affected by the location of individuals and organizations in networks of personal relationships (Granovetter, 1985.) First Nation communities provide a particular boundary setting for such embedded relationships, where collective action based on trust and reciprocity may result in a strong community identity. Moreover, Indigenous peoples are ecologically embedded (Whiteman and Cooper, 2000).

The focal relationships of this study indicate that close relationships between First Nations and corporations may emerge; they become embedded. Recent research suggests that a community identity and an organizational (corporate) identity can cue each other and generate reciprocal actions that reinforce and coproduce identity (cf. Howard-Grenville *et al.*, 2013). To illustrate, the resource manager of Tla-o-qui-aht argued, in the official protocol agreement between the First nation and Creative Salmon, that stewardship of their land is fundamental. Moreover, he suggested that "Creating this harmonized operational environment with Creative Salmon is central to our Nation's work to manage our traditional territories using an approach that respects *Hishuk ish ts'awalk* (everything is one)."[1] The expression "everything is one" is arguably linked to environmental concerns and to a belief in interdependencies between different entities. The relationships studied in this chapter suggest that First Nations and corporations are interdependent in their joint attempts in making salmon farming sustainable and economically viable.

Such interdependence also indicates that corporations may play an interesting part in facilitating the emergence of "community-based enterprises" (CBEs). Peredo and Chrisman (2006) defined a CBE as a community acting corporately as both entrepreneur and enterprise in pursuit of the common good.

The Ahousaht and Tla-o-qui-aht First Nations have identified salmon farming as an economic opportunity and organized themselves in order to respond to it. Their approach is rooted in community culture, and natural and social capital are integral and inseparable from economic considerations. These CBE characteristics have shaped how the First Nations relate to the corporations and how they organize their own activities. In particular, the creation of the Ahousaht Corporation appears to be a modern governance structure that is rooted in cultural traditions.

According to Peredo and Chrisman (2006), CBEs are profoundly affected by the ability of the community to innovatively combine and adapt a variety of ancestral and new skills, experiences, cooperative practices, and values. Cermaq's managers explicitly stress the desire to work with a better-equipped community, and collective ancestral knowledge is being acknowledged in these relationships. However, it is also acknowledged, from a corporate viewpoint, that it is difficult to assess what the reaction from First Nations would be to salmon farming if they faced feasible alternatives in B.C. Whether different funding programs and sponsorships will make a long-term difference in the communities is a recognized concern. Moreover, the fact that community members leave their traditional land after a period of employment is an occurrence shared with remote non-indigenous areas.

Conclusion

First Nations and corporations are trying to combine business with sustainable community development. To what extent they succeed and how they influence one another in the salmon farming industry—for instance, in terms of developing CBEs—are topics for future research. The influence of First Nations in making

---

1 Creative Salmon and Tla-o-qui-aht First Nation protocol agreement July 4, 2014.

corporate strategy multigenerational and an understanding of "business minded-ness" that is long term and inclusive in terms of community and corporate devel-opment are worthwhile challenges.

The relationships presented in this chapter exemplify the UN Global Compact's emphasis on joint efforts in supporting a precautionary approach to environmen-tal challenges. Company managers emphasized the right to be different and to be respected as such. First Nation participants of this study confirmed this princi-ple, a cornerstone of the United Nations Declaration on the Rights of Indigenous Peoples. They also confirmed a corporate recognition and respect of the rights of Indigenous peoples affirmed in treaties. The companies showed recognition and respect for Indigenous knowledge and traditional practices, although commu-nity traditions and conventional "bottom-line" considerations do collide at times. Regarding the Business Reference Guide to the Declaration, it seems as if the guide assists companies and First Nations in establishing cooperative ventures. For instance, the adoption of a formal policy, consultation, and the role of language are pertinent issues in these relationships. To illustrate, Ahousaht language is used in the protocol agreement between the First Nation and Cermaq. Finally, the ILO Convention 169 declares the right of Indigenous peoples to retain and develop their political, economic, and social institutions, and to protect their traditions and customs. The development of the Ahousaht Corporation and the role of the heredi-tary chiefs are representative illustrations, as is the First Nations' role in identifying and protecting important cultural places when new farming sites are located.

References

BC Salmon Farmers Association (2016, June 21). Breeding success through partnerships. Retrieved from http://bcsalmonfarmers.ca/breeding-success-through-partnerships/

Bebbington, A. (1999). Capitals and capabilities: A framework for analyzing peasant viability, rural livelihoods and poverty. *World Development*, 27(12), pp. 2021-2044.

Calbucura, J. (2003). Investing in indigenous people's territories, a new form of ethnocide? The Mapuche case. In M. Bell & M. Fredrickse (Eds.), *Walking towards Justice: Democrati-zation in Rural Life* (pp. 229-255). Amsterdam & New York: JAI/Elsevier.

Denzin, N.K. & Lincoln, Y.S. (2000). Introduction: The discipline and practice of qualitative research. In N.K. Denzin & Y.S. Lincoln, (Eds.), *Handbook of qualitative research* (pp. 1-28). Thousand Oaks, CA: Sage.

Gedicks, A. (2001). *Resource Rebels: Native Challenges to Mining and Oil Corporations.* Cam-bridge, MA: South End Press.

Granovetter, M. (1985). Economic action and social structure: The problem of embedded-ness. *American Journal of Sociology,* 91, pp. 481-510.

Howard-Grenville, J., Metzger, M.L. & Meyer, A.D. (2013). Rekindling the flame: Processes of identity resurrection. *Academy of Management Journal,* 56(1), pp. 113-136.

Huemer, L. (2014). Creating cooperative advantage: The roles of identification, trust and time. *Industrial Marketing Management,* 43, pp. 564–572.

Kvale, S. (1996). *InterViews.* Thousand Oaks, CA: Sage.

Nikiforuk, A. (2016, August 31). First Nation protestors rally for fish farm evictions. *The Tyee.* Retrieved from http://www.thetyee.ca/News/2016/08/31/First-Nations-Fish-Farm-Eviction-Rallies/

Peredo, A.M. & Anderson, R.W. (2006). Indigenous Entrepreneurship Research: Themes and Variations. In C.S. Galbraith & C.H. Stiles, (Eds.), *Developmental Entrepreneurship: Adversity, Risk and Isolation* (pp. 253-273). Oxford: Elsevier.

Peredo, A.M. & Chrisman, J.J. (2006). Toward a theory of community based enterprise, *Academy of Management Review,* 31(2), pp. 309-328.

Whiteman, G. & Cooper, W.H. (2000). Ecological Embeddedness, *Academy of Management Journal,* 43(6), pp. 1265-1282.

11

Strong Indigenous communities

Indigenous worldviews and sustainable community development

Keith James, Ph.D.
Professor and Director of Tribal Initiatives, University of Arizona; Onondaga Nation member

Mark L.M. Blair, J.D., LLM, Ph.D.
Lecturer in American Indian Studies, University of Arizona; Saginaw Band of Chippewa member

A case study is presented of a multiple party (Indigenous and non-Indigenous; private, public, and non-profit) sustainable development collaboration in interior Alaska. Indigenous worldviews and values were used as the framework for a community-based participative research process that incorporated both traditional knowledge, and mainstream science and technology. The project yielded a strategy and tactics for achieving the "triple bottom line" of community health, environmental health, and economic health (World Commission on Environment and Development [WCED], 1987) for a regional group of Alaska Native communities.

Indigenous, Sustainable development, Alaska Natives

Overview

For our cultures to survive, we must become better stewards of water and land. Stewardship, not management (Alaska Native Elder).

The theme of this chapter is that Indigenous worldviews need to serve as the foundation of Indigenous/non-Indigenous negotiations over attempting sustainable economic development. A case study of an economic development and regional-planning project among a group of Indigenous communities in Alaska, some non-Indigenous non-profit and for-profit organizations, and representatives of non-Indigenous governments (i.e., the state of Alaska and the U.S. federal government) is presented and used to support the value of participatory partnerships based on Indigenous perspectives. The planning effort was successful for Indigenous communities in that it: 1) maintained their cultures and lifestyles while; 2) adding to the economic opportunities available to community members. Those outcomes occurred because the values and worldviews of the communities guided the planning, yielding results in accord with the UN's "triple bottom line" of economic development (World Commission on Environment and Development [WCED], 1987).

The legal context in which Alaska Natives operate creates uncertainty in their ability to assert their goals and perspectives over those of non-Indigenous groups who covet (or feel the right to control) Indigenous lands and resources. The UN Declaration on the Rights of Indigenous Peoples can, however, help counter the undermining of Indigenous rights created by national and state laws and policies, and economic globalization. The case illustrates how strong application of the UN Declaration by strong Indigenous communities can promote the triple bottom line of cultural preservation, environmental health, and economic development. It provides a model, for other parts of the world, for attaining economic development that is genuinely in accord with Indigenous rights.

Alaska Native history and legal context

Economics have always been part of Alaska Native life. The United States federal government role began with the 1867 "purchase" of Alaska from Russia. From then until after World War II, the U.S. government largely treated Alaska Native people as vassals from an inferior culture. U.S. policy toward American Indians and Alaska Natives (ANs) has oscillated between assimilation and tribal "autonomy" (Case, 2002). The Treaty Era came first and was marked by formal Nation-to-Nation military and trade agreements. The federal government never concluded treaties with ANs, though (Blanton, 1996; Getches *et al.*, 1993). Next, in federal policy, came the Allotment, Assimilation, and Termination Eras. During those years, white settlement was encouraged (e.g., free allocations of Alaska land were given to "settlers" who agreed to live on, mine, or farm it). At the same time, many AN people died from introduced diseases, and assimilation policies (e.g., boarding schools; forced use of the English language) were put into effect (Kawagley, 1995). Where access was easier (e.g., coastal areas) or where desirable resources were found (e.g., gold in the region of Fairbanks), greater AN dispossession of land occurred and greater assimilation pressures were exerted. In more rural and less (from an outsider perspective) desirable areas, traditional culture and lifestyles were significantly buffered.

World War II, the building of the Al-Can highway that connected the lower-48 U.S. States to Alaska by road by way of Canada, and the expansion of U.S. military operations in Alaska increased both settlement and resource development pressures. At the same time, AN people, like Indigenous groups around the world, were also pressing for legal rights and land controls (Bielski, 2000; LaDuke, 1997). As the non-AN population of Alaska grew and it moved toward statehood, pressure built to regularize and resolve the land claims and other rights of AN people that the U.S. had previously dealt with de facto, not *de jure*. Alaska became a state in 1958, and the Alaska Statehood Act (United States Code 2006) called for ANs and the State of Alaska to reach agreement on land claims.

Modern U.S. federal Indian Policy began with President Nixon's Native American "self-determination" (Congressional Record, 1970). Self-determination is a purported attempt to end paternalism and forced assimilation by giving AI/AN peoples greater control of administration of federal Indian programs and of tribal lands. While "self-determination" remains the core of United States federal Indian policy, in reality, the U.S. Government retains much power to influence (or veto) the plans and decisions of U.S. Indigenous groups (Clarkson, 2007; Summit, 1997).

Alaska Native Claims Settlement Act (ANCSA) of 1971

What follows is a greatly simplified version of the ANCSA and its amendments and regulatory and judicial elaborations. The ANCSA was the culmination of converging U.S. federal, state, and AN interests in legalizing AN status. From the non-Indigenous perspective, it was targeted at legitimizing federal, state, and settler rights. From the AN perspective, it was intended to provide legal and land rights, along with compensation for past land/resource losses and socio-physical abuses. The Alaska-Native Corporation model in the ANCSA creates a unique legal framework relative to other U.S. Indigenous peoples. As such, it provides a key context to ongoing AN/non-AN negotiations and disputes over land control, resource use, and economic development (Berry, 1975; Bielski, 2000; Summit, 1997).

The ANCSA allocated 44 million acres (18 million hectares) of land to ANs and created 12[1] regional corporations containing nearly 200 village corporations (Summit, 1997). The 12 corporations are substantially based on cultural/linguistic groups (e.g., Yup'ik versus Athabascan) within Alaska and were intended to impose

---

1 A 13th AN corporation, for urban and out-of-state ANs, was established, went bankrupt, was re-established, and is now headquartered in the state of Oregon, U.S.A.

a capitalistic (i.e., corporate) structure and system on ANs that differed from the collectivistic "federal trust relationship" that applied to other U.S. Indigenous groups (regional corporations hold surface and subsurface rights to the land, while village corporations within the regions hold only surface rights). The ANCSA allowed oil exploration and production to begin, though most AN land allocations did not include any substantial oil reserves (the lands of the AN North Slope Corporation being the major exception). Residents of a village (village corporation members) are also, though, shareholders in the regional corporation that encompasses their village. As shareholders, they receive dividends from the revenue (if any) of their corporation; most regional corporations have little or no yearly revenue. All but one "reservation" (the Annette Island Reserve in Metlakatla) in Alaska were terminated, the intent was to terminate Indigenous land claims and sovereign powers, while creating a mainstream, capitalist model for ANs (Bielski, 2000).

However, both subsequent court decisions and other (i.e., the ANSCA) Congressional acts support AN sovereignty and rights to allocated and traditional-use lands (see, e.g., Bielski, 2000; Federally Recognized Tribe List Act, 1994; Ford, 1997). Therefore, when corporations, mainstream society, and the state of Alaska desire (as they frequently do) some form of economic development within Alaska Native regions, Indigenous rights and sovereignty often become a point of contention. As part of waging that contest, Alaska Native groups have sometimes invoked United Nations' policies and resolutions on the rights of Indigenous peoples. We briefly review the UN policy on development and Indigenous rights below, and its relevance to Indigenous Alaska before describing a case in which it was the background to private business, the Alaska state government, non-profit non-AN organizations, federal agencies, and AN communities attempting to reach an agreement on economic development plans for a region of interior Alaska.

The Business Guide to Indigenous Rights

The *Business Reference Guide* (UN Global Compact, 2013) to the UN Declaration on the Rights of Indigenous Peoples (UNDRIP) entreats businesses to use practices and procedures that respect the rights of Indigenous peoples. The cultural, educational, identity, governance, and economic rights of Indigenous communities are outlined in the UNDRIP. So, too, are rights to traditional lands and associated natural resources. Some ideas for best practices by business are outlined for each area of rights. Related to land, businesses are enjoined to engage in collaborative decision-making and development in all actions that might affect Indigenous regions and peoples. The goal is to achieve "sustainable development," which the UN has defined (WCED, 1987) as attaining the triple bottom line of community (including cultural) health, physical-environment health, and economic success.

Self-determination and informed consent

The UNDRIP states that, in projects involving Indigenous communities and lands, companies have an obligation to attend to two fundamental elements regardless of local or national laws or presence or absence of "official" governmental recognition of an Indigenous group and its rights. The first element is the right of self-determination; and the second is the right to free, prior and informed consent. Self-determination rights mean that Indigenous communities should control their own land, territory (i.e., not just the land that they live on but also that crucial for gathering, hunting, and ceremony), and resources, as well as control their cultural, economic, and political materials and systems. Free, prior and informed consent (referred to hereafter as "informed consent") is the right of an affected Indigenous group to either agree to or decline a project or activity, based on a full understanding of the project's impacts and implications.

When it comes to business activity that will impact on cultural, natural resource, or other Indigenous rights, genuine informed consent necessitates that an Indigenous perspective be taken on defining and assessing costs, desired benefits, and potential unintended consequences. In other words, an Indigenous perspective has to be applied to determining the mechanisms and criteria of "free, prior and informed consent."

Because Indigenous and non-Indigenous peoples differ in their cultural values and norms, and because the non-Indigenous individuals who control, advise (especially, legally), and negotiate for mainstream corporations tend to have identities that lead them to dis-identity with Indigenous communities, true self-determination and informed consent are difficult to achieve. In the case that is presented below, a non-Indigenous corporation, multiple non-Indigenous non-profit organizations, and non-Indigenous governmental and university scientists were all involved in discussions with a group of Alaska Native communities over economic development of regional natural resources. The multiplicity of parties made for a complex range of challenges. The bulk of them, however, seemed to flow out of cultural differences between the (government, corporate, and non-profit) mainstream scientists/lawyers, and the Alaska Native community members. The key elements of cultural difference are outlined next.

The current case

The Alaska Native communities involved were a group of villages in the interior (i.e., non-coastal) area of Alaska. The region involved in the case was defined by a major watershed consisting of a large river valley, along with many creeks, streams, and other tributaries to the river. The majority of the Alaska Native villages in the valley were Athabascan, though the watershed spanned the boundaries of two Alaska Native corporations, so did include a minority of non-Athabascan villages and people.

At the outset of the project, almost all of the villagers were engaged in subsistence living based on fishing, hunting, and gathering of traditional wild plants. Subsistence was becoming more challenging for them, however, due to both climate change that was affecting fish, animal, and plant numbers and distributions, and to resource competition from outsiders. The desire of a non-Alaskan, non-U.S. corporation (supported by the state of Alaska) to extract mineral resources in the valley triggered the process of discussion about economic development in the region. Indigenous disquiet had been growing for some time before that, however, over smaller scale intrusions into the valley by non-Indigenous companies and individuals as well as over natural resource pressures due to growth of the Indigenous population itself and to environmental change.

A series of meetings between members of the regional Indigenous villages with the outside parties were organized by a non-profit environmental organization. The first author on this chapter consulted and collaborated with that non-profit. Most meetings took place in villages, but two were held at the headquarters buildings of U.S. Government facilities in the area. Village leaders and grassroots village members attended meetings, and all villages were represented to some extent even at the meetings that did not take place in their own community. More members of a particular village tended to be present, of course, when the meeting was held in their home community. At one meeting, a couple of representatives were also present from a Canadian Indigenous group whose lands abutted part of the watershed in question. The non-Indigenous parties consisted of multiple staff members of the convening non-profit group, multiple scientists and administrators from both the State of Alaska Government and from various U.S. Federal Government agencies, scientist/academics from a handful of different universities, representatives of the corporation interested in the minerals, representatives of the sport-fishing industry, and some non-affiliated, non-Indigenous individuals from the region. The two most common disciplines of the non-Indigenous participants were the physical sciences and law.

The first author of this chapter facilitated collaborative planning by the Indigenous and non-Indigenous participants aimed at achieving a comprehensive plan for regional sustainability that attended to the triple (or quadruple—Walters and Takamura, 2015—spiritual health being the fourth) bottom line of environmental health, cultural health, and economic health. Planning also incorporated both traditional knowledge and mainstream science approaches, and both qualitative and quantitative elements. A "strong" version of community participative action research was built into all projects.

Strong community-based participative research (S-CBPR)

Community-based participative research (CBPR) involves cross-education by community members and scientists about their knowledge, concepts, and approaches to knowledge and understanding (e.g., Chataway, 1997; Israel *et al.*, 1998). Community members are engaged as full partners in designing and executing all scientific data collection, analyses, interpretation, and interventions. Community/scientist teams collaborate on all phases of project execution.

A CBPR approach was used for this project. It is a "strong" version of CBPR, though, because the foci of all of the projects were the goals and needs of the Alaska Native communities involved. Community worldviews, in other words, defined the aims of the collaboration, but then the knowledge and techniques of both sets of participants were brought to bear to achieve those aims. S-CBPR focuses on cooperative design and execution of projects as a means of maximizing their S-CBPR outcomes, and uses the strategy of full collaboration and cooperation as a mechanism to combine direct efforts to address goals or concerns of participating communities, execution of scientifically sound research, and the education of community partners so that they will have the capacity to do similar projects on their own (Chataway, 1997; Israel *et al.*, 1998; Institute of Medicine, 2003). It also uses both mainstream science and Indigenous approaches to evaluating outcomes (e.g., LaFrance and Nichols, 2009).

The facilitated planning process began with presentation of the UN Declaration on Human Rights and its major principles as the framework within which planning would take place. Next came an effort to get all parties to understand the differences and similarities in the worldviews, as outlined below, and to then have them use that understanding to engage in an S-CBPR approach to planning. Example comments and disputes that occurred in the planning process are subsequently presented to illustrate how the Indigenous worldview as promulgated was the core starting point for planning goals and actions. The quotes and interpretations provided are based on meeting transcripts, as well as some survey/inventory data provided by the participants.

Worldview similarities and differences, Indigenous and mainstream

Figure 11.1 is a modification (by Keith James) of an original figure from Barnhardt and Kawagely (2004; cf. Kawagley, 1995). In the case summarized here, the figure and other interventions (outlined below) were used to help make explicit for both groups the differences and similarities in their underlying cultural principles. Such awareness set the stage for an effort to develop a collaborative plan for natural resource stewardship and economic development that met the goals of the Alaska Native communities involved. Moreover, when mainstream scientists become aware of their own (scientific) culture, and how it fits, in places, with Indigenous values, norms, and techniques, it helps them identify with Indigenous peoples and their priorities and goals. In addition, awareness of the *unique* aspects of traditional knowledge (TK) can also help mainstream scientist understand how TK and approaches to knowledge use in economic development can add value when combined with mainstream science. Finally, understanding the comparatively unique components of mainstream science (far right in Fig. 11.1) can help *Indigenous community members* see why science operates in some of the ways that it does and what value it might add, as well as be aware of potential pitfalls they may encounter in attempting collaborations with scientists.

Figure 11.1 **Mainstream science and indigenous science**

Source: adapted from Barnhardt and Kawagely (2004) (cf. Kawagley, 1995)

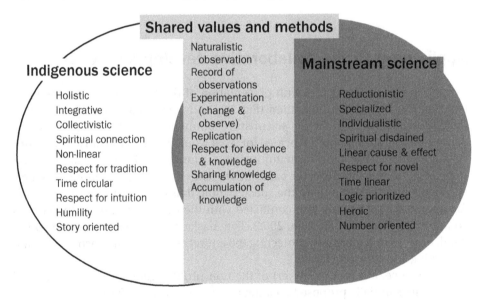

Development decision implications of worldviews

Table 11.1 presents an outline of the initial general disjunctions that seemed to exist between the AN communities and mainstream parties on the framework for a regional environmental and economic plan.

Table 11.1 **Development decision implications of cultural worldviews**

Development decision values and norms Mainstream participants	AN community members
Reductionism: Break complex topics into parts	Holism: Parts function as whole and can only be understood in context
"Nature" distinct from "human"	Goal of combined human, economic, and environmental stewardship
Short-term time frame	Long-term time frame
Develop goal(s) for each part; tailor application/law to goals for each part	Look for opportunities within whole context; tailor application/law to health of entire ecological system
Expert opinion, past experience, research results, cost-benefit analysis laws and regulations, linearity	Tradition, culture, life-experience, spiritual insights, intuition, "triple bottom line," consensus views, non-linearity
Design monitoring to assess goal effectiveness	Design monitoring to assess holistic health

Application to the collaborative development case

Despite the groundwork laid with presentation of the UN Declaration, the principles of CBPR, and the illustration (Fig. 11.1) on worldview differences, early in the discussions the mainstream scientists recommended micro-assessments. The private-sector participants advocated for what would bring in the most money (for them), at least in the short term: for instance, more sport-fishing or dredging for minerals. The non-profit sector participants tended to apply a monomaniac perspective that attended only to the specific topic that their organization has as its focus, and this frequently also conflicted with the broad interests of Indigenous communities (see, e.g., Dodson, 2002). The Alaska Native residents, on the other hand, focused holistically on protecting the entirety of the regional ecosystem, and protecting it for the long term.

For instance, a leader (a lawyer) of the non-profit organization that convened the meetings initially proposed creating a legal "water trust" for the region's central river. The private-sector representatives opposed that as anti-capitalistic. The scientists proposed reductionistic measurements that could either provide information about the effects of legal interventions, such as the "water trust" or assess the impacts of commercial exploitation/exploration. One Alaska Native participant, though, had this to say: "We support water quality, but that means maintaining everything—animals, people, subsistence lifestyle." A member of a different regional Indigenous community added: "(The river) is down and the fish quality has been changing for the worse over time—is that climate change?" A young (and assertive, relative to the "normal" reserved nature of Athabascan people) Alaska Native man added that land or water "trusts" often seemed to end up protecting a particular resource from Indigenous people. Laws and non-Indigenous agencies, he said, "box" pieces of the environment and "box" the people.

We see in the original project idea presented by the non-Indigenous participants, the reductionism, nature-separate-from-human, expert-opinion focused, quantitative-only view of mainstream society and mainstream science. In the cited comments that came back from the Native participants, though, we immediately get holism (and note that it's fish "quality", not just fish "quantity"), the idea that the people and culture are a part of nature, and both community and the natural world as part of AN identity. Worldview and identity are tied together; and identity is a mediator of goals and actions (Crompton and Kasser, 2010; James, 2006).

The congruence of the early stages of the different groups' ideas with Figure 11.1 was pointed out to the group, and points of potential congruence and the elements of the UN Declaration were reinforced, and the S-CBPR principles were again emphasized. Murry *et al.* (2013) describe an approach to bridging between the worldviews of the mainstream scientists and Indigenous community members to allow them to overcome their conflicts in priorities and form an effective partnership for action. That approach, supplemented by other strategies for building participative partnerships (e.g., Anderson and McLachlan, 2016; Chataway, 1997; Weaver and Cousins, 2004), was used in the current case as is summarized below.

Building community/mainstream science partnership

The UN Declaration on the Rights of Indigenous Peoples, the UN definition of community sustainability, and Figure 11.1 (common and divergent values and techniques) were shown to participants, described by the lead author of this chapter, and discussed by the participants. Next, AN community members and, separately, the non-Indigenous participants were put in teams to do "vision maps" for regional sustainability. Each (homogeneous, either all-AN or all non-Indigenous) team then presented their vision map to the full set of participants.

The preceding process reinforced differences in worldview and views of sustainability. In particular, the non-Indigenous parties learned about both TK and the values of the AN community representatives. One scientist stated, for instance, that: "we learned that they had salmon management knowledge and processes (before whites came ...) they had seasons for fishing, they had rules about keeping a clean camp, they knew different types of Salmon." (The individual quoted seemed astonished that Native folk knew anything before contact. Surfacing one's own ignorance, however, is an initial step in learning.) AN community members, on the other hand, both learned about the "culture" of science (and of non-Indigenous society), and that scientists had some knowledge that could be useful for advancing the sustainability of their local (AN) communities. For instance, one non-Indigenous team included a summary of a National Research Council report on causes of reductions in salmon numbers in the Columbia River in their presentation about their vision map, and the AN participants recognized the potential relevance of much of that information to their own region.

The differing (differing, that is between the scientist and AN community groups) statements of priorities or values that were presented were pointed out to the full set of participants and reflected on by them. They were analyzed for what they said about difference and similarities in the perspectives of the two groups and to produce a consensus on the worldviews and goals (i.e., in line with the UN Declaration, largely those of the AN communities) that would form the basis of collaborative planning.

Story-telling, visual presentations, and linear documents were all used to communicate perspectives, priorities, and goals. Native community members shared stories from oral tradition (the scientists were barred from repeating any story without community permission) to illustrate what they agreed and disagreed with within the analysis of worldviews and goals. Drawing of additional figures or pictures was encouraged. The scientists were encouraged to offer both personal experience and scholarly knowledge, while the whole group considered points of agreement and disagreement present in all inputs.

AN community member and non-Indigenous mixed teams were then formed to plan specific collaborative projects based on community worldviews and goals but ideally incorporating both TK and mainstream science. Those teams formed around one or limited-and-linked AN community goals, and were encouraged to seek limited-scale successes that the full group of participants could build upon.

Each team composed a collaborative vision map and prepared a verbal outline of their planned project. Each of those mixed teams presented their vision to the other attendees. All participants were encouraged to look for and call everyone's attention to places where different projects overlapped or could otherwise feed into each other. A visual network of projects and teams was constructed to support integration of projects. The results of all of the foregoing was a collaborative strategic plan tied to a collaborative set of action projects, all based on AN community views and goals.

Regional development outcomes

There were teams engaged in TK interviews and (separately) surveying of traditional and subsistence land/water information and uses, including information on sacred sites and other spiritual uses. Those teams' findings were then used, by the other teams, as guidance and input for their projects. For instance, a Water Quality team incorporated TK with soil surveys, measures of water flow, and water-quality testing (for both pollutants and fecal coliform). Another group used TK as a baseline for determining changes to vegetative complexes and their associated critters with the goals of preventing habitat damage and determining where removal of invasive species and natural biota restoration was needed. Another team charted sport-fishing boat counts and locations, and correlated them with water quality and fish (quantity, quality, and type) outcome effects. A legal approach to in-stream waterflow reservation was developed to ensure the continued viability of salmon-breeding grounds, subsistence fishing, and other community uses. Community members, however, were given decision control over the "water trust." Another team designed an approach to scientific examination of the "qualitative" fish-type differences that Alaska Native TK indicated. A multi-layered GIS system was used to integrate all of the information developed by all teams. In line with the S-CBPR framework, tribal members were trained on all of the scientific techniques employed, and had veto power over release of all data and analytic results. Alaska Native community members were trained on creating, updating, and using the GIS system; and the communities had control of what aspects of the GIS information would be made available to which groups.

Some cash economy development was planned, but with maintenance of traditional Alaska Native lifestyles always required. For instance, the communities decided to develop their own commercial fishing cooperative, as well as to offer sport-fishing trips, as part of a larger eco-tourism initiative. But maintaining and increasing subsistence fishing was always given priority over cash production.

A project of this sort is obviously challenging for everyone involved. Facilitators need great patience. Indigenous community members need to suspend their (justifiable) skepticism about partnerships with science. Scientists need to open their minds to the knowledge that community members have, and to the sustainable strategies that the two groups can collaboratively develop. Non-Indigenous peoples also have to open their hearts and spirits if they are to understand and resonate with Indigenous worldviews and Indigenous identities. With effort from all, partnerships are possible that may yet justify the label "*Homo sapiens.*"

References

Anderson, C.R. & McLachlan, S.M. (2016). Transformative research as knowledge mobilization: Transmedia, bridges, and layers. *Action Research*, 14, pp. 295-317.

Battiste, M. & Henderson, J.Y. (2000). *Protecting Indigenous Knowledge and Heritage: A Global Challenge*. Saskatoon: Purich Publishing Ltd.

Battiste, M. (2002). *Indigenous Knowledge and Pedagogy in First Nations Education: A Literature Review with Recommendations*. Ottawa: Indian and Northern Affairs Canada.

Berry, M. (1975). *The Alaska Pipeline: The Politics of Oil and Native Land Claims*. Bloomington: Indiana University Press.

Bielski, J. (2000). Judicial denial of sovereignty for Alaska Natives: An end to the self-determination era. *Temple Law Review*, 73, p. 1288.

Blanton, D. (1996). ANCSA corporation lands and the dependent Indian community category of Indian country. *Alaska Law Review*, 13, pp. 211-227.

Case, D. (2002). *Alaska Natives and American Law*. Fairbanks: University of Alaska Press.

Chataway, C.J. (1997). An examination of the constraints on mutual inquiry in a participatory action research project. *Journal of Social Issues*, 53, pp. 749-67.

Clarkson, G. (2007). Tribal bonds: Statutory shackles and regulatory restraints on tribal economic development. *North Carolina Law Review*, 85, pp. 1009-1085.

Congressional Record (1970). *116 Congressional Record* [record], 23, p. 131.

Cornell, S. & Kalt, J. (1998). Sovereignty and nation-building: the development challenge in Indian country today, *Harvard Project on American Indian Economic Development*, PRS 98-25, p. 2.

Crompton, T. & Kasser, C. (2010). *Meeting Environmental Challenges: The Role of Human Identity*. Surrey, England: World Wide Fund for Nature (World Wildlife Fund).

Dodson, M. (2002). Partnerships – a one way street? Partnerships between Indigenous Australians and the philanthropic and corporate community. *Journal of Indigenous Policy*, 2, pp. 22-25.

Federally Recognized Tribe List Act (1994). *Public Law No. 103-454* [public law], 108 Statute 4791.

Ford, M. (1997). Indian country and inherent tribal authority: Will they survive ANCSA? *Alaska Law Review*, 14, p. 443 & p. 451.

Getches, D., Wilkinson, C. & Williams, R. (1993). *Cases and materials on federal Indian law*, (3rd ed.). St. Paul: Thomson-West.

Giese, P. (1997). *Alaska Native Tribes*. Retrieved from http://www.kstrom.net/isk/maps/ak/aklinks.html

Hirschfield, M. (1992). The Alaska Native Claims Settlement Act: Tribal sovereignty and the corporate form, *Yale Law Journal*, 101, pp. 1331-1340.

Israel, B.A., Schulz, A.J., Parker, E.A. & Becker, A.B. (1998). Review of community-based research: Assessing partnership approaches to improve public health. In J.E. Fielding, L.B. Lave, and B. Starfield (Eds.), *Annual Review of Public Health*, 19, pp. 173-202. Palo Alto, CA: Annual Reviews, Inc.

James, K. (2006). Identity, values, and American Indian beliefs about science and technology: A first wave of data. *American Indian Culture and Research Journal*, 30, pp. 45-58.

James, K., Hiza, M., Hall, D. & Doppelt, R. (2008). Organizational environmental justice and community sustainability with a Navajo (Diné) case example. In S. Gilliland, D. Steiner & D. Skarlicki (Eds.). *Research in social issues in management*, 6, pp. 263-290. Greenwich, CT: Information Age Publishing

Kawagley, O.A. (1995). *Yupiaq world view: A pathway to ecology and spirit*. Prospect Heights, IL: Waveland Press.

Kendall-Miller, H. (2004). ANCSA and Sovereignty Litigation, *Journal of Land Resources & Environmental Law*, 24, p. 465.

LaDuke, W. (1999). *All our relations: Native struggles for land and life*. South End Press.

LaFrance, J. & Nichols, R. (2009). *Indigenous evaluation: Telling our story in our place and time*. Alexandra, VA: American Indian Higher Education Consortium.

Menzies, C.R. (2004). Putting words into action: Negotiating collaborative research in Gitxaala. *Canadian Journal of Native Education*, 28, pp. 15-32.

Murry, A., James, K. and Drown, D. (2013). From pictures to numbers: Vision mapping and sustainability collaboration between Native American community member and mainstream scientists. *American Indian Culture and Research Journal*, 37, pp. 1-24.

Summit, B. (1997). The Alaska Native Claims Settlement Act (ANCSA): Friend or foe in the struggle to recover Alaska Native heritage. *T.M. Cooley Law Review*, 14, p. 607 and pp. 626-27.

UN Global Compact (2013). *A business reference guide: United Nations declaration on the rights of Indigenous peoples* [compact]. New York: UN Global Compact.

Walters, F. & Takamura, J. (2015). The decolonized quadruple bottom line. *Wicazo Sa Review*, 30, pp. 77-99.

Weaver, L. & Cousins, J.B. (2004). Unpacking the participatory process. *Journal of Multidisciplinary Evaluation*, 1, pp. 19-40.

World Commission on Environment and Development (WCED) (1987). *Our common future: The world commission on environment and development* [report]. New York: United Nations General Assembly Report # A42/427 (alternate source: Oxford University Press).

12

Hupacasath First Nation
Roadmap to a sustainable economy

Judith Kekinusuqs Sayers, J.D.
Former Elected Chief of the Hupacasath First Nation
Adjunct faculty member, School of Environmental Studies, University of Victoria

Ana Maria Peredo, Ph.D.
Professor, Political Ecology, School of Environmental Studies, University of Victoria

Hupacasath First Nation in Vancouver Island, Canada, has become a symbol of integral community development and especially a model for clean energy development, having created the first aboriginal owned and operated run-of-the-river project. This chapter discusses the community processes behind the economic development plan and specifically explores two joint ventures. The chapter offers some insights from the experiences and lessons for success.

First Nations, Community development, Clean energy

Introduction

> We will give back to mother earth the respect and sanctity she rightfully deserves. We will make our lands, waters and air inviolable. We will spiritually cleanse the lands that have already been violated. We will take back our place as the rightful caretakers of our territory and far exceed the provincial and federal standards, for they are lax and inefficient (Jessie Hamilton, Hupacasath Treaty Main Table).

There is a complex and fractured relationship between the Canadian Government and Canada's First Nations. Historically, through a process of land dispossession undertaken by the British Crown, First Nations people were located on small pieces of land called "reserves". The Indian Act of 1876, which has been amended many times, still governs Canada's relationship with First Nations. The explicit purpose of the original Act, and of government policy behind it, was for many years to eradicate First Nations culture and assimilate their peoples in to colonizers' culture (Harrison and Parrott, 2016). The process of colonization took away the livelihoods of First Peoples on the prairies, mountains, rivers, and oceans, attempting to turn them into farmers in the process. Laws were imposed that impeded development, and First Peoples went from being resource wealthy to dependent on government funding, with severe restrictions on the use of their own resources. In the view of the First Nations, Canadian Governments became wealthy by exploiting First Nations' resources, leaving First Nations poor, with high unemployment and substandard social conditions. Those conditions continue to prevail in the current period (Sawchuk, 2015). It is in this context that, in 1995, the leadership of Hupacasath First Nation (HFN) directed its attention to the goal of economic independence:

> As the leadership in Hupacasath, we decided it was time to catalyze economic development to change the conditions we live in. We wanted to be economically independent so we could provide the services to our members that they needed. We knew that remaining on government funding would continue our pittance management as opposed to wealth management we desired (Judith Sayers, Elected Chief, 1995–2009).

Hupacasath First Nation Peoples (HFNP) are part of the larger Nuu-chah-nulth Nation on the West Coast of Vancouver Island, British Columbia (BC), located in the Alberni Valley. Their unceded traditional territory extends to 232,000 hectares, richly endowed with land, waters, and resources that had supported their way of life. Currently, their 350 members live on five reserves that occupy 232 hectares: 0.1% of their traditional lands. In 2001, the HFN launched a process aimed at reversing the forces that prevented their benefiting from the resources on their own lands. They began by setting out a roadmap toward sustainable community development.

Hupacasath people's aspirations: roadmap to a sustainable economy

Comprehensive Community Plan: working with members

The HFN leadership commenced by working with their community to develop a Comprehensive Community Plan that included an economic development strategy, a central tool for identifying economic development initiatives. Aboriginal rights and titles are collective in nature and belong to all HFNP. Given the collective ownership of the land and resources, a fundamental element in the planning process for economic development was the inclusion of all HFN members in the decision-making process.

Over a six-month time frame, there were extensive consultations with HFN members both on and off reserve to develop a plan. The consultations included surveys and workshops and achieved 95% involvement. The Comprehensive Community Plan emerging from consultation and the collective decision-making identified a number of fundamental starting points. Among these, the plan:

- Built the mission statement, goals, and strategies

- Identified economic development opportunities based on the resources available to the community

- Identified HFN strengths and weaknesses as well as an interest in employment

A fundamental aim for the Hupacasath was to build capacity and create employment and career opportunities for members, especially youth. The community recognized their young people as the community's hope for the future and was concerned about their leaving the community. The Plan's strategy called for diversification in the economy, as community members realized that they could not rely on government funding. The most immediate plans were to develop clean energy, construction aggregates, tourism, forestry, and fisheries, with long-range plans to move into manufacturing and other services.

Stewardship and sustainability

The Hupacasath people have inhabited their land for several thousand years, with a rich oral history and tradition transmitted by the Elders. A vital part of that history and tradition is a deep connection with the land. The Nation takes its stewardship responsibilities very seriously. During the consultations, protecting the land arose as the most important aspect to be maintained by Hupacasath peoples in planning economic development activities. Consequently, HFN engaged in building a Traditional Use Data base (TUS) to document any historic and current, cultural, or spiritual sites where members might exercise their rights. The information from the TUS was the basis for a Land Use Plan (LUP) in 2003 (Hupacasath First Nation, 2003). This plan set out where development could and could not take place, and set standards that were refined and made even more specific in phase two of the plan (Whitfield and Lem, 2006). The first objective for working with land, resources, and water is that Hupacasath must protect their rights with minimal impact. Through consultations, the members provided direction on balancing their way of life with environmental, social, cultural, and economic considerations.

Creating employment and training opportunities

One of the main goals for HPFN was to build capacity and create employment and career opportunities, particularly for young members. Hiring as many of their own members as possible was key to HFN community economic development. A database of members was established to map out the training, education, and experience existing in the community. This was used to compare members' qualifications with the businesses the HFN was developing, to identify skills gaps and determine the training needs to support the new ventures.

Financial transparency and stable governance

Sound financial management and stable governance were identified by the leadership as vital for the community but also for the lending institutions or potential partners that might consider investing in their Nation. Over the years, the HFN developed by-laws to facilitate transparency and allow members to understand how things worked. HFN members receive yearly audits and financial statements every two months. In 2008 a financial accountability policy was adopted.

Canada's Indian Act is not merely a body of law, but establishes concepts of Native identity and the conceptual framework that shapes First Peoples' lives in many ways (Lawrence, 2003). Under the act, Nations are required to hold leadership elections every two years. Given that political stability can be a challenge for any community attempting to implement an economic development project, the election of Chief Sayers over a period of 14 years contributed significantly to the steadiness the HFN needed in order to pursue their mid- and long-term economic development projects.

Hupacasath people: building business partnerships

Hupacasath leadership recognized that creating positive relations was important to build their businesses. Over the years, they worked to build relationships with governments, other First Nations, industry, and suppliers in their territory. Working with government at all levels—federal, provincial, and municipal—smoothed the way to dealing with licensing needs and dealing with regulatory complications. While the HFN has for some time run a number of small businesses such as a woodlot, canoe tours, and a gift shop, this chapter focuses on larger-scale economic development initiatives in which the HFN partnered with outside companies. We discuss two specific cases.

Case Study #1 Eagle Rock Materials (ERM)

Early in 2002, HFN was approached by Polaris Minerals Corp. The company sought to develop an aggregate quarry and had done a preliminary report that showed a significant granite hill in First Nations' territory. This area was located on the west side of the Alberni Inlet, some 15 km south of the city of Port Alberni. Polaris did not attempt to develop the project further until they met with the three First Nations who asserted territory in the area: Hupacasath, Ucluelet (UFN), and Tseshaht First Nations (TFN). They provided the First Nations with information on the proposed project and funding that allowed the Nations to execute their own due diligence.

Tseshaht First Nation claimed territory in the area but declined to enter the arrangement. Hupacasath and Ucluelet First Nations engaged a firm to review the preliminary report. Both Nations consulted with their membership and decided to negotiate an agreement in principle to explore how they might work together.

The two First Nations negotiated an operating agreement that set out the structure, decision-making, and ownership of two companies to be incorporated. Defining what to consider a material decision was key as that included the requirement that First Nations must give their consent to material decisions, mainly concerning the natural environment. The final agreement was signed at the end of 2002 with a grand celebration. It was then considered a new model for business in the province. It was precedent setting because it established a meaningful partnership and shared ownership involving First Nations. There was an exceptional degree of First Nation community consultation and participation, a practice that became the model for Polaris's mining agreement with the 'Namgis First Nation located in Port McNeill, BC.

The company: ownership and impact benefit agreement (IBA)

The company was incorporated as Eagle Rock Materials Ltd (ERM). It was owned 70% by Polaris Minerals and 30% by the two First Nations, with Hupacasath and Ucluelet First Nations each owning 10% and the remaining 10% held in trust.[1] The board had one member of each First Nation and Polaris had four board members. A company called Eagle Rock Aggregates (ERA) was incorporated in the US using the same board structure.

The agreements that Hupacasath and Ucluelet First Nations were able to negotiate were innovative. Polaris agreed to finance all work up to the construction decision. On the 25th anniversary of the project, each First Nation partner had a one-time right to increase its ownership in ERM by 50%, potentially increasing First Nations equity in the project to 45%. First Nations also had a right of first refusal if Polaris sold its share. If the land was granted to a First Nation in a treaty settlement, the First Nations would not impose a tenure or tax on ERM with terms less favorable than what would apply without such treaties.

An impact benefit agreement (IBA) was also negotiated that provided the First Nations with preferential opportunities for business development, employment, and training. A heritage fund was to be established after five years of business, funded by an assessment of C$0.10/tonne, with funds administered by a society on terms established by the First Nations.

First Nations role in regulatory regime

A project of the magnitude proposed needed to fulfill a number of social and environmental requirements. As partners, First Nations worked alongside Polaris to

---

1 Polaris Materials. About us. Retrieved from http://www.polarismaterials.com/about-us/

determine the studies needed, the terms of references, and who would do the studies. First Nations learned how to be a proponent in the Environmental Assessment Process. An Environmental Assessment Certificate, Mines Act Permit and re-zoning of land were completed in 2003. In 2004, ERM finalized the Crown Lease for land and the foreshore lease and completed the forestry designation change, and minor permits. Plans were discussed with every community group in the project area, to let them know the aim of the project and provide opportunities for people to have their questions answered. A memorable moment occurred in an open house consultation event in the process of obtaining the Environmental Assessment Certificate, where normally significant opposition can be expected. Instead, members of the local community said "let's get this business up and running." By the time plans were presented at the main open house there was no opposition. The people from the Environmental Assessment office had never seen such a phenomenon and congratulated the team on their achievement.

In the course of these consultations and negotiations, the leadership of the project, including First Nation Chiefs, became a cohesive team. Plans at all consultations were presented jointly. At consultations, the Ucluelet board member recounted how as young boy, aware of his poverty, he would kick the rocks and wish he could make money out of them. He mentioned that his wish appeared ready to come true.

Eagle Rock Materials production and markets

ERM was permitted to extract a maximum of 6 million tonnes of high quality construction aggregate per annum. There was a total mineral resource of 710,000,000 tonnes over an area of approximately 465 hectares. The aggregate would be exported to concrete and paving markets in California where there was a supply deficit in both the San Francisco Bay area and the Los Angeles basin. The site of extraction was located near deep water on a major shipping route. There would be state of the art technology and a high standard environmental management plan. The project life was for 118 years at full capacity and would create 60–80 full-time direct jobs.

Where is Eagle Rock today?

ERM began establishing ports in California after securing all the necessary permits in BC. Following the catastrophic events of September 11, 2001, however, demand for aggregates in California dropped while the country recovered from the disaster. This was followed by a collapse in the housing market, and the demand for aggregate in California never regained its former levels. The business was put on hold until such time as the demand for aggregates increased.[2]

2 http://www.polarismaterials.com/about-us/

Case Study #2: The China Creek Project: Upnit Power Corporation (UPC)

In 2001, British Columbia (BC) Hydro proposed the construction of a natural gas-fired generation plant in Port Alberni. The local population, including environmentalists, households, HFN, and others opposed the plan on the grounds of its environmental impact, and the plan was abandoned (Aboriginal Business and Investment Council, 2016). However, the region remained in need of power and Hupacasath began searching for an environmentally sensitive way to create energy in their region of Vancouver Island. The Environmental Assessment office in BC provided funding for HFN to undertake research on clean energy, including an inventory of resources then available in the territory. Ten possible run-of-the-river opportunities were identified, and HFN determined that China Creek was the best option for a new source that would respect environmental priorities.

Hupacasath engagement with clean energy?

Hupacasath was keen to explore clean energy as an alternative to fossil fuel power. A run-of-the-river project, which would not require water storage with its invasive consequences, was compatible with HFN ecological and cultural values. The generation plant would be non-consumptive and would not change the water temperature. The HFN also identified a number of economic advantages. The clean energy industry in BC was in its infancy, and the project would have a good possibility of winning a bid from the BC Hydro call for partnerships. Clean energy would diversify the economy of the region. One of the biggest pluses was the reduction of greenhouse gases (GHG) and the access to green credits. A 6.5 MW single cycle (i.e. turbine) natural gas plant would produce 31 kilotonnes of carbon dioxide equivalent GHG (CO_2e) per year, assuming best practices, with an equivalent coal plant yielding far greater emissions.

After due diligence and members' agreement to include alternative energy in the HFN community plan, HPF developed the China Creek Project. Hupacasath negotiated and obtained agreement and licenses, brought in equity partners in December 2004 and started to create power in December of 2005. The project is a 6.5 MW run-of-the-river generating plant. During peak operations it can power up to 6,000 homes (City of Port Alberni, 2016).

Why China Creek?

China Creek had an adequate flow of water for at least eight to ten months of the year to make the project economically feasible. The river was enough of a vertical drop for the water to fall and was close to a BC Hydro interconnect. HFN then look at the potential social, cultural, and environmental impacts.

China Creek did not have sacred sites. Given the geography, there were no issues that could affect the salmon. The project would make a very small imprint on the land. Roads were already in place for two private logging companies that operated in the area, and the HFN felt confident that they could negotiate right of way agreements with them. Finally, HFN determined that there was no public access to these areas of a kind that would permit vandalism to the facilities. There were also no concerns from the population living around the area. FNP determined that China Creek was the right project for them.

Partnership and ownership

HFN knew they needed finance for the project so they searched for partners. During the assessment process HFN had worked with Sigma Engineering, a small arm of a larger company known as Synex Energy. They had built several run-of-the-river projects and had the knowledge and expertise HFN was looking for. Synex became partners and assumed a 12.5% share in ownership of the project.

Ucluelet First Nation (UFN) was chosen as a strategically aligned partner. HFN already had experience doing business with them in ERM. HFN leadership was aware that having another First Nations as an owner made applications stronger for grants, equity, and capital. UFN assumed 10% ownership. The City of Port Alberni, major consumer of the power to be produced, became a partner as well. The city provided HFN with the water flow data for China Creek, worked with them on securing an agreement on water use, and was willing to allow use of its roads. Port Alberni was given a 5% ownership by HFN in the project. HFN maintained majority of ownership, at 72.5%.

Corporate structure

Following two years of discussion concerning partnership agreements, two corporations were created: Upnit Power Corporation (UPC) as a general partner, and the Upnit Power Limited Partnership (UPCL). "Upnit," which means calm place, is Hupacasath's name for China Creek.

The operating board has four Hupacasath members; Synex, Ucluelet, and the City have one each. Having a general partner and limited partner allowed the company to flow funds from the general partner to the limited partner and out to Hupacasath without fiscal implications, given that Hupacasath functions as a government. HFN has its own by-laws, provide services to its members, and has a sophisticated governance structure.

UPC purchaser of power

In response to BC Hydro's 2002 call for energy suppliers, Upnit Corporation made a bid, was short-listed, and then obtained an electricity purchase agreement (EPA) in March 2003. The final bid was accepted in September and signed in October 2003. UPC turned on the switch to start producing electricity in December 2005. Since that time, the partners have operated a 6.5 MW run-of-river hydro plant to supply power to the unified grid under the terms of a 20-year EPA. Getting an EPA was key to getting financial support and other permission and licenses. An EPA acts as guarantee to financial institutions, providing a signal of secure revenue sources.

Innovative financing

The fossil free fuel project gained the attention and support of local people. But Hupacasath had to be creative in finding funding for feasibility and development costs. HFN wrote many proposals and lobbied for grants. One grant came from Aboriginal and Northern Climate Action Program (ANCAP) for C$250,000. In the early 2000s, few banks were giving loans on renewable energy projects as they represented an unknown venture. Among the few progressive banks that did make such loans was the HFN's own bank, but the bank wanted HFN to secure an additional C$1 million in equity that the bank knew they did not have. Another bank made them an offer, but had it turned down by its own head office when it went for approval.

Sayers reflected:

> There was one critical time when we had to order our turbines and needed a year lead-time. We hadn't as yet secured our water license or our capital. We had a hard discussion as council and decided to get a loan from our Nuu-chah-nulth Economic Corporation.

Interest rates were high but the Corporation accepted HFN's financial transfers from Indian and Northern Affairs Canada (INAC) as security, which a bank would not have done.

> We knew if they didn't get their water license or capital loan they would have a couple of turbines sitting in their parking lot. But as a council, we believed in the project and knew the benefits it would bring and took the chance.

The enterprise was able to obtain a low interest loan of C$945,000 from the Western Diversification Canada, a government agency that disperses funds in support of projects that may strengthen the economy of western Canada. However, the project still needed further equity. INAC had a matching equity program at the time, which linked to Western Diversification funds to provide a matching equity grant of C$2 million. Vancouver City Savings Credit Union, commonly referred to as Vancity,[3] operated through its "Vancity Capital Corporation" to help supply the remaining C$8.9 million. The Corporation brought together a syndicate of credit unions and—after some educational meetings involving the values-based Vancity, HFN, and the syndicate members—the remaining equity was forthcoming.

---

3 Vancity. About Vancity. Retrieved from https://www.vancity.com/AboutVancity/

Regulatory requirements

Problems did not end with financial challenges. The company also had to prove that there was enough water for the project. Reliable water data has to be included in the business plan, specifying the production months and potential of power generation. One concern was the effect of global warming on the water flow in China Creek. UPC engaged in climate change modeling to conclude that there would not be significant impact. Hupacasath organized studies on aquatic and riparian habitat, fish population assessments, snorkel surveys, invertebrate sampling, water quality monitoring, instream flow monitoring, wildlife and migratory bird habitat, and discharge monitoring. The venture required permits or licenses to cut trees, build roads, transmission lines, powerhouse, and fisheries and meet requirements in the Navigable Waters and Species at Risk Act. A Canadian Environmental Assessment screening was also needed since the project had received federal funding.

Aspirations for jobs for Hupacasath members

HFN was able to create 8–10 jobs for Hupacasath members during construction, mainly in the areas of environmental monitoring, driving heavy equipment, and construction of the powerhouse and intake. For the actual operations of the project, there are two band members operating the plant.

Cultural aspirations

Several ceremonies around China Creek were performed. The first was to approach the creek and ask, ceremonially, for permission to undertake the activity on the waterway. HFN had a celebration to "turn on the switch" and thank everyone who helped along the way. Gratefulness and recognition are important in First Nations' culture.

Capacity building aspirations

Among its four members in the UPC board, HFN has been sure to include a young board member ready to learn. HFN has continued to build capacity in operations, including safety plans and maintenance. They have built capacity in their members: having them understand how a run-of-the-river project works and how any negative effects can be mitigated.

Capacity building is occurring at all levels. Reflecting on her experiences, former Chief Sayer stated:

> I have built my own capacity going from not knowing anything about clean energy to spending a lot of time in the field. Once we were operating our project, I became familiar with the issues in the industry. I sat on the Public Advisory Panel to the Canadian Electricity Panel for 5 years. I have been on Clean Energy BC Board for over five years. Last year, I finished a BC First Nations Clean Energy Toolkit. I continue to work with First Nations on issues that affect the clean energy industry and share the expertise I have developed that started with the China Creek project.

Rebuilding community: what worked and lessons learned

First Nations in Canada see economic independence from the state as a first step on the road to the self-governance and sovereignty that they deeply desire. HFN has never given up its rights to its territory, and has been active in exploring business opportunities that will allow it to benefit from the resources of those lands. The success of its projects lies in the processes by which those ventures have been evaluated and negotiated, gaining community support from the beginning and incorporating at every step the needs and aspirations of the Hupacasath First Nation.

The HFN economic projects combine cultural, social, and environmental needs with pressing economic considerations. Aspirations have not been limited to offering a certain amount of employment, but have extended to negotiating ownership, full partnership, and participating together in all the aspects of the business, consistently maintaining a voice for environmental priorities.

In the case of the ERA joint project, a decisive factor was the early initiative on the part of Polaris in connecting with HFN in a way that acknowledged First Nations' traditional rights and title. The company provided information as well as funding that allowed HFN to conduct its own independent analysis in order to determine whether they agreed with the venture. Polaris agreed to environmental standards that exceeded provincial standards and were in keeping with First Nations' values. HFN was a vital part of every decision in the formation of the company. The Polaris team spent a great deal of time in both First Nations and established solid, trusting relationships. Polaris referred to the relationship with First Nations in describing the company's approach to building an alliance: "Their history with our society has been very bad. We have historically mistreated these people, these communities. It was very difficult to earn trust" (Kwantes, 2014). Polaris was present at community events and fish days and took HFN members on field trips to the site. Representatives attended information sessions and explained potential training and employment opportunities. The company and its officials conveyed a belief that it was moral, ethical, and good business to consult and work with First Nations. Polaris proved patient with the time it took for the communities to come to decisions. The company appeared willing to learn and understand. First Nation concerns were incorporated, along with proposed solutions, in written agreements concerning Eagle Rock Quarry. While that enterprise is on hold until the demand for aggregates increases, there was a significant learning about business development and partnerships. Deciding to suspend operation of the business for the time being was also part of learning and joint decision-making.

The China Creek project was an even more significant accomplishment. This was the first run-of-the-river project in BC with a First Nation as initiator and majority owner, and its recognition as such had an important impact on First Nations as well as the wider public. The learnings there reinforced and added to insights gained from the experience with the ERA project.

A number of important lessons can be draw from the combined experience (Kekinusuqs Sayers, 2015). First and absolutely fundamental to both processes was patient and inclusive consultation with the membership of the Nation whom the project was meant to benefit. In its quest for economic independence and self-governance, HFN embarked on developing a Comprehensive Community Plan. Without the grassroots support that this process won, projects would not have left the ground, no matter how well they combined economic and environment benefits. Engaging the community in building a plan that recognized the rights and aspirations of all members as well as their duties toward stewardship of the land, and developing accountability policies and good governance practices all combined as essential elements in these processes. This provided the basis for the HFN to engage in joint ventures with private companies, governments, other First Nations, and financial institutions

A second and major contributing factor was building relationships with relevant organizations and sharing ownership with key partners. Establishing a trusting and collaborative relationship with other First Nations who might otherwise see undertakings as irrelevant or, worse, competitive was very important. Building respectful and trusting relationships with companies that recognized government permission was not enough to secure a successful venture on First Nations territory also proved vital. Identifying companies that combined technical experience with a respect for First Nations traditions and aspirations was extremely important. Even then, learning was needed on both sides to grasp more fully the aspirations of First Nations on the one hand and the technical and financial requirements of a successful undertaking on the other.

Third, building credibility with government at all levels as well as regional funding agencies was an essential strategy in moving the project forward. Easing potential blocks in bureaucratic procedures and obtaining support from various agencies were aided by conscious processes of alliance-building with government and regulatory bodies. A crucial element in this was identifying and convincing a financial institution that shared similar values and strategic focus and was willing to experiment in the new field of clean energy and share the risks in investing there. In Sayers' words "We found that people are more inclined to give you what you want, when they know you will make something out of it."

Fourth, the project's efforts to build a relationship with media were fruitful. Media wanted positive stories and China Creek, especially, was a welcome contribution on that front. The Hupacasath name became known, with the result that governments and companies were willing to work with them. HFN told a story that others needed to hear, and that helped motivate and inspire other First Nations to do their own projects.

Indigenous communities around the world are looking at HFN projects as examples of community-produced, environmentally respectful undertakings that produce community livelihood in keeping with First Nations values. This chapter is meant to suggest some ways that undertakings like these can be pursued success-fully, but also how pursing them can contribute vitally to advancing cultural, social, and environmental purposes. These are lessons everybody can profit from.

References

Aboriginal Business and Investment Council (2016). Hupacasath First Nation. Retrieved from http://www.bcabic.ca/success-stories/hupacasath-first-nation/

City of Port Alberni (2016). Upnit power. Retrieved from https://www.portalberni.ca/upnit-power

Harrison, W.B. & Parrott, Z. (2016). Indian act. Retrieved from http://www.thecanadianencyclopedia.ca/en/article/indian-act/

Hupacasath First Nation (2003). Territory land use plan. Retrieved from http://hupacasath.ca/wp-content/uploads/2016/03/LUP-Phase1-2003.pdf

Kekinusuqs Sayers, J. (2015). B.C. First nations clean energy toolkit. Retrieved from http://www.cleanenergybc.org/wp-content/uploads/2016/04/BC-FN-Toolkit.pdf

Kwantes, J. (2014). First Nations alliances give Vancouver island sand and gravel quarry a concrete foundation. *Vancouver Sun*. Retrieved from http://www.vancouversun.com/business/first+nations+alliances+give+vancouver+island+sand+gravel+quarry+concrete+foundation/10372488/story.html

Lawrence, B. (2003). Gender, race, and the regulation of native identity in Canada and the United States: An overview. *Hypatia*, 18(2), pp. 3-31.

Sawchuk, J. (2015). Indigenous people: Social conditions. Retrieved from http://www.thecanadianencyclopedia.ca/en/article/native-people-social-conditions/

Whitfield, T. & Lem, T. (2006). Hupacasath land use plan phase 2. Retrieved from http://hupacasath.ca/wp-content/uploads/2016/03/LUP-Phase2-2006.pdf

Conclusion
Making the case for responsible business and management

Ella Henry, Ph.D.
Auckland University of Technology, New Zealand

Ana Maria Peredo, Ph.D.
University of Victoria, Canada

Amy Klemm Verbos, Ph.D.
University of Wisconsin-Whitewater, USA

This volume is meant to encourage and support business educators in implementing the Principles for Responsible Management Education (PRME), and to stimulate business practitioners whether or not they are aware of and committed to the goals articulated in the UN Global Compact. It is also intended to motivate anyone interested in advancing Indigenous peoples' rights under the UN Declaration on the Rights of Indigenous Peoples (the DRIP) and helping them realize their aspirations attainable through the full and free exercise of those rights. The PRME initiative's mission is to inspire and champion responsible management education, research, and leadership thinking, globally. The six PRME Principles (p.ix), and the associated reporting requirement for signatory institutions, provide academic institutions with a comprehensive platform for developing programs that encourage responsible business leadership: leadership that will create and manage a more responsible, inclusive, and sustainable global economy. Including Indigenous peoples, on our own terms and in accordance with our aspirations and rights, will assist in fulfilling this vision of more socially responsible business, and a more inclusive, empowering, and sustainable society.

Section I: Learning not to repeat failures

This section highlights some of the tensions that Indigenous peoples and Indigenous businesses confront, tensions that more principled business and management, in corporate and government realms, could ameliorate. Together, these chapters reflect on Indigenous experiences, and failures, and the manner in which business and government intersect with Indigenous peoples. But all failure is nothing more than an invocation to do better, and to learn from these lessons.

In the cases outlined in this section, we find examples of business and government developing programs and policies that, in hindsight, can be seen to impede the rights and aspirations of Indigenous peoples. Further investigation suggests that a greater awareness and application of the DRIP would have facilitated these policies and programs with more positive outcomes for the Indigenous communities in question. In one case this relates to the use and control of culture, artifacts and design. DRIP Articles 11 and 31 (see Appendix) could well inform the strategic development of Pendleton Mills. Further, business and government have a role to ensure Indigenous peoples are able to protect their interests and environments, as articulated across a range of DRIP Articles, including Articles 8, 18, 19, 29, 32, and 37 through 40 (see Appendix). Acknowledgment of and adherence to these articles would surely have improved the outcomes for the people of Motiti Island. The tensions faced by Indigenous peoples, when they adopt Western models, especially in business and the pursuit of material wealth, suggest that greater awareness of the DRIP Articles focusing on self-determination (3) and wellbeing (Articles 7, 23, 32, and 45; see Appendix) might provide the foundation for more sustainable and enduring support programs, particularly for fledgling Indigenous economies and business. Finally, while one must applaud any company that adopts and incorporates corporate social responsibility (CSR), such a strategy must also acknowledge that labor issues (Article 17; see Appendix), participation in decision-making (Article 18; see Appendix), and rights with respect to traditional lands (Articles 28 through 30; see Appendix) could be incorporated into a CSR or political CSR (PCSR) program, to maximize benefits for all parties and minimize potential conflict.

The BRG (Business Reference Guide) provides additional support, calling on businesses to take concerted action, sometimes in conjunction with local and state governments, to meet their responsibility to respect Indigenous peoples and their rights. For example, the BRG advocates for adopting and implementing formal policies (whether on a stand-alone basis or within a broader human rights policy) that specifically address Indigenous peoples' rights and the commitment to respecting these rights. This could have been an important element of an improved PCSR strategy developed by the RNM company in Papua New Guinea. Instead, its efforts resulted in increased cynicism among the local Indigenous population, ultimately resulting in negative performance and outcomes for the company. The BRG also recommends that businesses working with Indigenous peoples conduct rigorous human rights due diligence to assess actual or potential adverse impacts on Indigenous peoples. Such an audit might well have better informed the Greek shipping company in its dealings with all the relevant tribes in New Zealand. Ultimately, these resources, DRIP, the Global Compact, BRG, and even PRME, encourage more and deeper relationships, communications, and consultation with Indigenous peoples, in relation to all matters that may affect them or their rights. Taken together they provide tangible support for businesses, and commitment to obtain (and maintain) the free, prior and informed consent of Indigenous peoples for projects that affect their rights and resources, including culturally appropriate grievance mechanisms (BRG, 2013, p. 11). This may mean employing experts or setting up specialist sections to ensure better understanding of these resources. The Global Compact also provides further management tools, resources, and programs to assist businesses, that "can help ensure that markets, commerce, technology and finance advance in ways that benefit economies and societies everywhere and contribute to a more sustainable and inclusive global economy" (UNGC, 2014, p. 1).

Indigenous peoples, working more collaboratively with UN, government, and business, can be empowered to better protect their people, culture, identity, and environments. Civil society, from government to business, NGOs, and the fourth estate (media), all have a role to play, building and contributing to sustainable, responsible societies. Enduring, resilient, and socially and culturally adept societies adopt "triple bottom line" accountability, integrating people, planet, and profit (Elkington, 1994). More recently, scholars have developed the "quadruple bottom line", which incorporates culture and spirituality (Scrimgeour and Iremonger, 2004). We all, Indigenous or otherwise, have a role to play, as individuals and communities. Those who are privileged to live in democracies have voting rights, and a responsibility to vote for people, parties, and policies that deliver to society, planet, prosperity, wellbeing, and spirit. These cases provide insights about ways we can all adopt more responsible behavior, strategies, policies, and programs, to result in more successful outcomes.

Section II: Meeting ongoing challenges by listening to Indigenous perspectives

There is an ongoing need to improve responsible business and management vis-à-vis Indigenous peoples. An overarching theme throughout this section is how to disseminate and support positive practices between Indigenous peoples and corporations around the globe respecting Indigenous peoples' rights under the DRIP. In the name of economic development, businesses, sometimes in collusion with government, silence Indigenous voices, ignore their aspirations, and violate their rights. Kayseas *et al.* (Chapter 5) and Verbos (Chapter 6) focus on both the historical and the present violations of Indigenous rights comprising the Articles of the DRIP, often enabled by and legitimized in law. Indeed, in the preamble to the Articles, the history, current situation, and futures of Indigenous peoples are set out before their rights are enumerated. This history and current situation are the key to understanding why it is important for business to become more responsible toward a future consonant with the rights set forth in the DRIP.

Kayseas *et al.* envision a way forward if there is the governmental will to redress past wrongs, maintain policies supportive of self-determination, and require corporations operating on Native territories or affecting Native Nations nearby to engage with them in a positive and mutually beneficial way. An overarching theme throughout this section is how to disseminate and support positive practices between Indigenous peoples and corporations around the globe respecting Indigenous peoples' rights under the DRIP. Verbos identifies human rights abuses that map to the DRIP Articles 1 (human rights under international law) and 7 (right to life) (see Appendix), and UN Global Compact Principles 1 and 2 (p.ix). Moreover, the murders discussed in Chapter 6 served to assist in the destruction of Indigenous sacred spaces and territories, forced relocation without consent, and impair self-determination and participation in matters that affect Indigenous peoples, violating virtually all of DRIP Articles. Both chapters deal with Indigenous peoples' human, land, environmental, and redress rights, Verbos most particularly with DRIP Articles 1 (human rights under international law), 28 (damage to land), 29 (environmental protection), 32 (rights related to extractive industries in their territories and mitigation of environmental damage), and 40 (effective remedies) (see Appendix), denied by Texaco and its successor Chevron through legal tactics. It is clear that there is a role for greater corporate responsibility and for the legal systems around the world to support rights to redress (DRIP Articles 38, 39, and 40; see Appendix).

Myllylä (Chapter 7) and Delgado (Chapter 8) make clear that a Western perspective on full, prior, and informed consent by Indigenous peoples is insufficient. Myllylä's chapter relates to DRIP Articles 3 (right to self-determination), 18 (participation in decisions that affect them), 20 (rights relative to economic activities), 23 (right to determine strategies for development), and 2–29 (land rights) (see Appendix). Delgado's community–business dialogues focus more on DRIP Articles 11 (rights to cultural and spiritual property), 24 (right to traditional medicines), 31 (right to control traditional knowledge), 32 (right to free, prior, and informed consent), and 40 (right to effective remedies) (see Appendix). These issues map to UN Global Compact Human Rights, Environmental, and Anti-Corruption Principles (p. ix), as well as the BRG. Both provide concrete ways for businesses to become more responsible, a second theme from this section.

An example playing out as this book goes to press involves the Standing Rock (Lakota) Sioux Tribe in North Dakota, U.S. and the Dakota Access Pipeline. From an Indigenous perspective, Native and non-Native people are gathered in *prayer* or *spirit* camps in the largest gathering of Native Nations in modern history, as water protectors, a sacred responsibility for Native peoples. Their credo is "Mni Wiconi," Lakota for "water is life" (Shilling, 2016). *Indian Country Today* reported on August 20, 2016, that the Tribe had appealed to four areas of the UN that deal with Human Rights and Indigenous Rights.

On September 9, 2016, the D.C. Federal District Court denied the Tribe's request for a preliminary injunction to enjoin the permit to place the pipeline beneath

Lake Oahe.[1] On September 22, 2016, Victoria Tauli-Corpuz, the UN Special Rapporteur on the rights of Indigenous peoples, called for a halt to the pipeline project (United Nations, 2016a). The water protectors' attempt to protect sensitive cultural sites from destruction were unsuccessful, even after the Army Corps of Engineers asked the pipeline companies to voluntarily stop construction on private land, because the Corps lacks legal authority to halt anything other than the river crossing.

The water protectors endured arrest and holding in inhumane conditions, police dog attacks, rubber bullets, water cannons in sub-freezing temperatures, and a militarized state police force working to quash demonstrations and any effort to restore the access road to the Standing Rock Sioux Reservation. On November 15, 2016, Maina Kiai, the UN Special Rapporteur on peaceable assembly cited violence against "protesters" (protectors), in asking for a halt to pipeline construction (United Nations, 2016b).

On December 5, 2016, the Corps denied the final permit for the pipeline, determining that a full environmental impact statement, including consideration of alternative routes is required. This Standing Rock Sioux's victory was a short-term reprieve. President Donald J. Trump, reportedly an investor in Energy Transfer Partners who sold his shares (Pramuk, 2016), received campaign support from the pipeline companies (Mufson, 2016), and signed an executive order on January 24, 2017 to the effect that the project be expedited to the extent permitted by law (White House, 2017). The conflict is not over.

These are not the only areas in dominant cultures where Indigenous peoples attempt to exercise their inherent sovereign human, cultural, environmental, land, and treaty rights contained in the DRIP against overwhelmingly powerful and politically connected corporate foes. The BRG's free, prior, and informed consent requirements are a starting point to avoid the breaches of inherent Indigenous rights. And, those rights include the right to say "no." This agenda may be furthered through the PRME (Principles 2, 3, and 4) (p. x), bringing justice denied into the classroom as a call to do better. It is also incumbent upon educators to work with companies to accept Indigenous rights around the globe (PRME Principle 5) (p. x) and to convene stakeholder dialogues (PRME Principle 6) (p. x), but not with the corporation and its interests at the center, rather the rights and aspirations of Indigenous peoples.

Section III: What counts for success?

Business is continually expanding and searching for new resources. Many of those resources are in Indigenous territories and exploitation affects their ways of life. Although some resulting conflicts are continually reported by the media, others

---

1 *Standing Rock Sioux, et al. v. United States Army Corps of Engineers*, 205 F.Supp.3d 4 (D.C. Dist. Ct. 2016).

are not. The four chapters in this section concern Indigenous communities engaged with some form of enterprise where the communities themselves see at least a measure of success in the outcomes. Drawing on longitudinal cases, the four chapters discuss the evolution of a process of tension and/or conflict into some kind of shared prosperity. They are rich with suggestions as to factors that seem associated in one way or another with what is seen as success from an Indigenous perspective, and we hope those suggestions will be harvested to generate further discussions on how to promote desirable results from business arrangements with Indigenous peoples. It is also worth reflecting, however, on how those chapters explicitly or implicitly understand the matter of success. Success, no doubt, is a complex matter and will be composed of numerous factors. What are the factors that make up a more or less satisfactory outcome? How are they weighted, and do they vary from community to community? Being clear about what sort of success we are aiming for will help us be clearer about the best means of achieving it.

Many Indigenous communities are interested in profitable business ventures to improve their quality of life in their communities and nations; but financial interests are typically embedded in, even subordinated to, other goals such as respect for traditional ways of life. Broadly based community development is an important goal in all the cases in this section. In Chapter 9, Adeola and Adeola point to an important provision in the agreement between Chevron and Indigenous communities that promises funding for community-owned and community-designed development projects. Huemer in Chapter 10 is clear that the goal of the First Nations working with fish-farming companies is not just profit, but community development: a goal the companies have come to align with. In Chapters 11 and 12, James and Blair, and Sayers and Peredo, respectively, attest to the same concern for community development. Traditional, subsistence forms of life need not be sacrificed in the interests of financial returns. Community development includes employment, recreational, and cultural facilities among other things. In these communities, financial returns are seen chiefly as a means to cultural and community benefit.

A fundamental factor in success that emerges is the sense of a full and respectful partnership between Indigenous people and the corporations they ally with in pursuing business opportunities. This factor resonates strongly with Article 18 of the DRIP (see Appendix), which highlights the rights of Indigenous people to participate in decisions affecting the rights. Huemer notes that in the case of both First Nations he writes about, full working partnerships emerge out of extensive and demanding negotiations with their potential business partners. James and Blair outline the way that Indigenous and non-Indigenous actors working on a development plan for an Indigenous area arrive at a working relationship that recognizes full Indigenous rights to contribute to decision-making, even including a *de facto* veto right in some matters. Sayers and Peredo likewise emphasize the full partnerships that emerge for First Nations in their relations with two outside companies, giving them full rights in business design and operation. Though this partnership is less well-developed in Adeola and Adeola's Chevron case, at the heart of the reconciliation process between Chevron and 425 Indigenous communities is the way it acknowledges the stake of Indigenous peoples as inhabitants, and includes communities in identifying, designing, and implementing projects.

The concept of partnership goes much deeper in the Indigenous context than the usual idea of a business relationship. Success occurs in each chapter in this section when non-Indigenous partners recognize and accept Indigenous peoples as stewards of traditional territories, with their own understandings and responsibilities with respect to the land. A commitment to Indigenous communities' environmental concerns is therefore essential to a successful understanding. The echo of DRIP Articles 25 and 29 (see Appendix) is unmistakable here. The recognition in those articles of Indigenous rights to their traditional, spiritual relationship to the land, and the stewardship this entails, is precisely what is borne out in what are seen as successful partnerships. Full partnership thus extends to accepting Indigenous worldviews as relevant to decision-making. James and Blair point to a "fourth bottom line": spiritual health. This concept is evidenced by including Indigenous ceremonies as an important part of carrying a project forward, a point Huemer, and Sayers and Peredo illustrate as well. DRIP Articles 11 and 12 (see Appendix), requiring respect for the right to practice spiritual traditions, are implicitly but clearly embodied in those practices. A further and vital element is the way that full partnership includes—as James and Blair, and Huemer, respectively, describe—businesses accepting traditional knowledge as fundamental to project design and conduct. These practices are a striking application of DRIP Article 31 (see Appendix): protecting the right of Indigenous people to maintain and protect their cultural heritage and traditional knowledge.

Sayers and Peredo clearly underscore two further aspects of success, which are arguably implicit in the other cases in this section. The first is achieving independence: a ringing endorsement of DRIP Article 3 (see Appendix). The right demanded there for Indigenous peoples to pursue freely their economic and social development is represented at several levels. Financial independence is an explicit goal of the Hupacasath Nation's enterprise activity. The Nation wishes to be free of the financial dependence established by Canadian statute, and enterprise that respects its status and priorities is a means to that end. But that independence is linked with authority over its own future: dominion over its own affairs that has been wrested from First Nations by colonization. In Canada, this is a battle for "sovereignty" and" self-governance." In other jurisdictions, the struggle may be known by different names. But it is hard not to see this as the most fundamental aspect of success for Indigenous peoples involved in business: clearly an application of DRIP, Article 3 (see Appendix). The standard view of the purpose of business undertakings is making a profit. For Indigenous peoples, it is different.

Conclusion

Taken together, the chapters in this volume urge business educators to be forerunners in developing inclusive and responsible business leadership (PRME

Principle 3) (p. x) by means of educational environments that foster genuine corporate responsibility (PRME Principle 2) (p. x). They also invite scholars to research and write in a way that positions Indigenous perspectives as equally worthy to those of non-Indigenous peoples (PRME Principle 4) (p. x). Further, these chapters highlight the importance of Indigenous issues for practitioners, helping them to begin dealing with such issues in ways that respect Indigenous rights and aspirations (PRME Principle 5) (p. x). By implication (and in keeping with PRME Principle 6) (p. x), they call for stakeholder dialogues to focus on more than simply gaining Indigenous peoples' acquiescence to a corporate agenda. This book is also a call to those interested in developing alternative corporate models to work together with Indigenous peoples to blend culture, spirit, and self-determination into new, hybrid, sustainable business models that may not only work better for Indigenous peoples, but provide inspiration to implement better corporate practices for non-Indigenous business.

There is a purported Chinese curse, "may you be born in interesting times." Whether Chinese, English, or apocryphal, the saying is relevant for 2017. Britain stands on the threshold of an exit from the European Union, which it joined in 1973. The "Brexit" decision ostensibly stems from a distrust of globalization by a slight majority of its citizens, along with objections to open immigration, low wages, deindustrialization, and a longing for what is seen as a return to British sovereignty. The decision is creating uncertainty in Europe, one of the world's largest economic markets. Uncertainty also accompanies the election of a new U.S. President, ongoing Middle East conflicts, millions of Syrian Civil War refugees, white nationalist movements, and growing terrorist organizations such as ISIS and Boko Haram.

The world seems besieged with conflict and uncertainty, when we also face many environmental crises. Climate change or global warming is not so much a matter of belief as fact, the planet is warming, ocean temperatures and sea levels are rising, and polar caps are melting at an unprecedented and rapidly accelerating rate. Alongside this we face air, water, and soil pollution, overconsumption in developed and developing nations, overpopulation, rapid natural resource depletion, loss of biodiversity, deforestation, and urban sprawl, combining to paint an apocalyptic picture of the future. This is the bleak and barren legacy that we may be leaving for our future generations. All of which are antithetical to Indigenous worldviews. Our cultures survived intact for thousands of years because we lived with and treasured our forests, mountains, rivers, lakes, oceans, and the creatures who share those places with us. We believe Indigenous peoples have something tangible to offer, solutions that have been tried and tested across time and tide, and we want to share this knowledge with the world, not to commodify and capitalize it, but to enable it to free us from the very commodification that causes these many crises. We open our arms and look forward to working with governments, businesses, and civil society, to make a meaningful contribution, to be seen as part of the solution, and not a problem to be eradicated. We hope this book makes a small contribution to an alternate envisaged future of peace, prosperity, and wellbeing for future generations.

One of the most gratifying aspects of editing this book has been working within a team of Indigenous women scholars, a Tallana from Peru, a Māori from Aotearoa/ New Zealand, and a Potawatomi from the U.S. Midwest. We think and write not only as researchers and academics but also as the descendants of ancient peoples, who walk the talk of our ancestors, who connect to spiritual realms and cosmology forged over millennia, who are passionate about our indigeneity, and who want to find, create, and share tools that will enable others to share and enjoy our worlds in a sustainable and inclusive way, without trampling the rights of the original peoples belonging to these places.

References

Elkington, J. (1994). Towards the sustainable corporation: Win-win-win business strategies for sustainable development. *California Management Review*, 36(2), 90-100.

Mufson, S. (2016, November 23). Trump dumped his stock in the Dakota Access pipeline owner over the summer. *The Washington Post*. Retrieved from https://www.washingtonpost.com/news/energy-environment/wp/2016/11/23/trump-dumped-his-stock-in-dakota-access-pipeline-owner-over-the-summer/?utm_term=.2904f935c7ce

Pramuk, J. (2016, December 5). Trump sells his stake in Dakota Access Pipeline developer. *CNBC*. Retrieved from http://www.cnbc.com/2016/12/05/trump-sells-his-stake-in-dakota-access-pipeline-developer.html

Ross, G. (2016, September 7). Dakota Access Pipeline resistance: Stay in the game. We're winning. *Indian Country Today*. Retrieved from https://indiancountrymedianetwork.com/culture/thing-about-skins/dakota-access-pipeline-resistance-stay-in-the-game-were-winning/

Scrimgeour, F. & Iremonger, C. (2004). Māori sustainable economic development in New Zealand: Indigenous practices for the quadruple bottom line. University of Waikato, Hamilton, New Zealand.

Shilling, V. (2016, November 17). Standing Rock Sioux Tribe releases documentary—Urge Obama to listen. *Indian Country Today*. Retrieved from https://indiancountrymedianetwork.com/culture/arts-entertainment/standing-rock-sioux-tribe-releases-documentary-urge-obama-to-listen/

UNGC (2014). *United Nations Global Compact: Corporate Sustainability in the World Economy*. New York, United Nations.

United Nations (2016a, September 22). *UN human rights expert calls on US to halt construction of North Dakota oil pipeline*. Retrieved from http://www.un.org/apps/news/story.asp?NewsID=55154#.WHVCfFMrJ0w

United Nations (2016b, November 15). *UN experts back call to halt pipeline construction in North Dakota, citing rights abuses of protestors*. Retrieved from http://www.un.org/apps/news/story.asp?NewsID=55560#.WHU_-lMrJ0w

White House (2017, January 24). Executive Order Expediting Environmental Reviews and Approvals for High Priority Infrastructure Projects. Retrieved from https://www.whitehouse.gov/the-press-office/2017/01/24/executive-order-expediting-environmental-reviews-and-approvals-high

Appendix

The Articles of the United Nations Declaration on the Rights of Indigenous Peoples

Source: http://www.un.org/esa/socdev/unpfii/documents/DRIPS_en.pdf

Article 1

Indigenous peoples have the right to the full enjoyment, as a collective or as individuals, of all human rights and fundamental freedoms as recognized in the Charter of the United Nations, the Universal Declaration of Human Rights and international human rights law.

Article 2

Indigenous peoples and individuals are free and equal to all other peoples and individuals and have the right to be free from any kind of discrimination, in the exercise of their rights, in particular that based on their indigenous origin or identity.

Article 3

Indigenous peoples have the right to self-determination. By virtue of that right they freely determine their political status and freely pursue their economic, social and cultural development.

Article 4

Indigenous peoples, in exercising their right to self-determination, have the right to autonomy or self-government in matters relating to their internal and local affairs, as well as ways and means for financing their autonomous functions.

Article 5

Indigenous peoples have the right to maintain and strengthen their distinct political, legal, economic, social and cultural institutions, while retaining their right to participate fully, if they so choose, in the political, economic, social and cultural life of the State.

Article 6

Every indigenous individual has the right to a nationality.

Article 7

1. Indigenous individuals have the rights to life, physical and mental integrity, liberty and security of person.

2. Indigenous peoples have the collective right to live in freedom, peace and security as distinct peoples and shall not be subjected to any act of genocide or any other act of violence, including forcibly removing children of the group to another group.

Article 8

1. Indigenous peoples and individuals have the right not to be subjected to forced assimilation or destruction of their culture.

2. States shall provide effective mechanisms for prevention of, and redress for:

   (a) Any action which has the aim or effect of depriving them of their integrity as distinct peoples, or of their cultural values or ethnic identities;

   (b) Any action which has the aim or effect of dispossessing them of their lands, territories or resources;

   (c) Any form of forced population transfer which has the aim or effect of violating or undermining any of their rights;

   (d) Any form of forced assimilation or integration;

   (e) Any form of propaganda designed to promote or incite racial or ethnic discrimination directed against them.

Article 9

Indigenous peoples and individuals have the right to belong to an indigenous community or nation, in accordance with the traditions and customs of the community or nation concerned. No discrimination of any kind may arise from the exercise of such a right.

Article 10

Indigenous peoples shall not be forcibly removed from their lands or territories. No relocation shall take place without the free, prior and informed consent of the indigenous peoples concerned and after agreement on just and fair compensation and, where possible, with the option of return.

Article 11

1. Indigenous peoples have the right to practise and revitalize their cultural traditions and customs. This includes the right to maintain, protect and develop the past, present and future manifestations of their cultures, such as archaeological and historical sites, artefacts, designs, ceremonies, technologies and visual and performing arts and literature.

2. States shall provide redress through effective mechanisms, which may include restitution, developed in conjunction with indigenous peoples, with respect to their cultural, intellectual, religious and spiritual property taken without their free, prior and informed consent or in violation of their laws, traditions and customs.

Article 12

1. Indigenous peoples have the right to manifest, practise, develop and teach their spiritual and religious traditions, customs and ceremonies; the right to maintain, protect, and have access in privacy to their religious and cultural sites; the right to the use and control of their ceremonial objects; and the right to the repatriation of their human remains.

2. States shall seek to enable the access and/or repatriation of ceremonial objects and human remains in their possession through fair, transparent and effective mechanisms developed in conjunction with indigenous peoples concerned.

Article 13

1. Indigenous peoples have the right to revitalize, use, develop and transmit to future generations their histories, languages, oral traditions, philosophies, writing systems and literatures, and to designate and retain their own names for communities, places and persons.

2. States shall take effective measures to ensure that this right is protected and also to ensure that indigenous peoples can understand and be understood in political, legal and administrative proceedings, where necessary through the provision of interpretation or by other appropriate means.

Article 14

1. Indigenous peoples have the right to establish and control their educational systems and institutions providing education in their own languages, in a manner appropriate to their cultural methods of teaching and learning.

2. Indigenous individuals, particularly children, have the right to all levels and forms of education of the State without discrimination.

3. States shall, in conjunction with indigenous peoples, take effective measures, in order for indigenous individuals, particularly children, including those living outside their communities, to have access, when possible, to an education in their own culture and provided in their own language.

Article 15

1. Indigenous peoples have the right to the dignity and diversity of their cultures, traditions, histories and aspirations which shall be appropriately reflected in education and public information.

2. States shall take effective measures, in consultation and cooperation with the indigenous peoples concerned, to combat prejudice and eliminate discrimination and to promote tolerance, understanding and good relations among indigenous peoples and all other segments of society.

Article 16

1. Indigenous peoples have the right to establish their own media in their own languages and to have access to all forms of non-indigenous media without discrimination.

2. States shall take effective measures to ensure that State-owned media duly reflect indigenous cultural diversity. States, without prejudice to ensuring full freedom of expression, should encourage privately owned media to adequately reflect indigenous cultural diversity.

Article 17

1. Indigenous individuals and peoples have the right to enjoy fully all rights established under applicable international and domestic labour law.

2. States shall in consultation and cooperation with indigenous peoples take specific measures to protect indigenous children from economic exploitation and from performing any work that is likely to be hazardous or to interfere with the child's education, or to be harmful to the child's health or physical, mental, spiritual, moral or social development, taking into account their special vulnerability and the importance of education for their empowerment.

3. Indigenous individuals have the right not to be subjected to any discriminatory conditions of labour and, inter alia, employment or salary.

Article 18

Indigenous peoples have the right to participate in decision-making in matters which would affect their rights, through representatives chosen by themselves in accordance with their own procedures, as well as to maintain and develop their own indigenous decision-making institutions.

Article 19

States shall consult and cooperate in good faith with the indigenous peoples concerned through their own representative institutions in order to obtain their free, prior and informed consent before adopting and implementing legislative or administrative measures that may affect them.

Article 20

1. Indigenous peoples have the right to maintain and develop their political, economic and social systems or institutions, to be secure in the enjoyment of their own means of subsistence and development, and to engage freely in all their traditional and other economic activities.

2. Indigenous peoples deprived of their means of subsistence and development are entitled to just and fair redress.

Article 21

1. Indigenous peoples have the right, without discrimination, to the improvement of their economic and social conditions, including, inter alia, in the areas of education, employment, vocational training and retraining, housing, sanitation, health and social security.

2. States shall take effective measures and, where appropriate, special measures to ensure continuing improvement of their economic and social conditions. Particular attention shall be paid to the rights and special needs of indigenous elders, women, youth, children and persons with disabilities.

Article 22

1. Particular attention shall be paid to the rights and special needs of indigenous elders, women, youth, children and persons with disabilities in the implementation of this Declaration.

2. States shall take measures, in conjunction with indigenous peoples, to ensure that indigenous women and children enjoy the full protection and guarantees against all forms of violence and discrimination.

Article 23

Indigenous peoples have the right to determine and develop priorities and strategies for exercising their right to development. In particular, indigenous peoples have the right to be actively involved in developing and determining health, housing and other economic and social programmes affecting them and, as far as possible, to administer such programmes through their own institutions.

Article 24

1. Indigenous peoples have the right to their traditional medicines and to maintain their health practices, including the conservation of their vital medicinal plants, animals and minerals. Indigenous individuals also have the right to access, without any discrimination, to all social and health services.

2. Indigenous individuals have an equal right to the enjoyment of the highest attainable standard of physical and mental health. States shall take the necessary steps with a view to achieving progressively the full realization of this right.

Article 25

Indigenous peoples have the right to maintain and strengthen their distinctive spiritual relationship with their traditionally owned or otherwise occupied and used lands, territories, waters and coastal seas and other resources and to uphold their responsibilities to future generations in this regard.

Article 26

1. Indigenous peoples have the right to the lands, territories and resources which they have traditionally owned, occupied or otherwise used or acquired.

2. Indigenous peoples have the right to own, use, develop and control the lands, territories and resources that they possess by reason of traditional ownership or other traditional occupation or use, as well as those which they have otherwise acquired.

3. States shall give legal recognition and protection to these lands, territories and resources. Such recognition shall be conducted with due respect to the customs, traditions and land tenure systems of the indigenous peoples concerned.

Article 27

States shall establish and implement, in conjunction with indigenous peoples concerned, a fair, independent, impartial, open and transparent process, giving due recognition to indigenous peoples' laws, traditions, customs and land tenure systems, to recognize and adjudicate the rights of indigenous peoples pertaining to their lands, territories and resources, including those which were traditionally owned or otherwise occupied or used. Indigenous peoples shall have the right to participate in this process.

Article 28

1. Indigenous peoples have the right to redress, by means that can include restitution or, when this is not possible, just, fair and equitable compensation, for the lands, territories and resources which they have traditionally owned or otherwise occupied or used, and which have been confiscated, taken, occupied, used or damaged without their free, prior and informed consent.

2. Unless otherwise freely agreed upon by the peoples concerned, compensation shall take the form of lands, territories and resources equal in quality, size and legal status or of monetary compensation or other appropriate redress.

Article 29

1. Indigenous peoples have the right to the conservation and protection of the environment and the productive capacity of their lands or territories and resources. States shall establish and implement assistance programmes for indigenous peoples for such conservation and protection, without discrimination.

2. States shall take effective measures to ensure that no storage or disposal of hazardous materials shall take place in the lands or territories of indigenous peoples without their free, prior and informed consent.

3. States shall also take effective measures to ensure, as needed, that programmes for monitoring, maintaining and restoring the health of indigenous peoples, as developed and implemented by the peoples affected by such materials, are duly implemented.

Article 30

1. Military activities shall not take place in the lands or territories of indigenous peoples, unless justified by a relevant public interest or otherwise freely agreed with or requested by the indigenous peoples concerned.

2. States shall undertake effective consultations with the indigenous peoples concerned, through appropriate procedures and in particular through their representative institutions, prior to using their lands or territories for military activities.

Article 31

1. Indigenous peoples have the right to maintain, control, protect and develop their cultural heritage, traditional knowledge and traditional cultural expressions, as well as the manifestations of their sciences, technologies and cultures, including human and genetic resources, seeds, medicines, knowledge of the properties of fauna and flora, oral traditions, literatures, designs, sports and traditional games and visual and performing arts. They also have the right to maintain, control, protect and develop their intellectual property over such cultural heritage, traditional knowledge, and traditional cultural expressions.

2. In conjunction with indigenous peoples, States shall take effective measures to recognize and protect the exercise of these rights.

Article 32

1. Indigenous peoples have the right to determine and develop priorities and strategies for the development or use of their lands or territories and other resources.

2. States shall consult and cooperate in good faith with the indigenous peoples concerned through their own representative institutions in order to obtain their free and informed consent prior to the approval of any project affecting their lands or territories and other resources, particularly in connection with the development, utilization or exploitation of mineral, water or other resources.

3. States shall provide effective mechanisms for just and fair redress for any such activities, and appropriate measures shall be taken to mitigate adverse environmental, economic, social, cultural or spiritual impact.

Article 33

1. Indigenous peoples have the right to determine their own identity or membership in accordance with their customs and traditions. This does not impair the right of indigenous individuals to obtain citizenship of the States in which they live.

2. Indigenous peoples have the right to determine the structures and to select the membership of their institutions in accordance with their own procedures.

Article 34

Indigenous peoples have the right to promote, develop and maintain their institutional structures and their distinctive customs, spirituality, traditions, procedures, practices and, in the cases where they exist, juridical systems or customs, in accordance with international human rights standards.

Article 35

Indigenous peoples have the right to determine the responsibilities of individuals to their communities.

Article 36

1. Indigenous peoples, in particular those divided by international borders, have the right to maintain and develop contacts, relations and cooperation, including activities for spiritual, cultural, political, economic and

social purposes, with their own members as well as other peoples across borders.

2. States, in consultation and cooperation with indigenous peoples, shall take effective measures to facilitate the exercise and ensure the implementation of this right.

Article 37

1. Indigenous peoples have the right to the recognition, observance and enforcement of treaties, agreements and other constructive arrangements concluded with States or their successors and to have States honour and respect such treaties, agreements and other constructive arrangements.

2. Nothing in this Declaration may be interpreted as diminishing or eliminating the rights of indigenous peoples contained in treaties, agreements and other constructive arrangements.

Article 38

States in consultation and cooperation with indigenous peoples, shall take the appropriate measures, including legislative measures, to achieve the ends of this Declaration.

Article 39

Indigenous peoples have the right to have access to financial and technical assistance from States and through international cooperation, for the enjoyment of the rights contained in this Declaration.

Article 40

Indigenous peoples have the right to access to and prompt decision through just and fair procedures for the resolution of conflicts and disputes with States or other parties, as well as to effective remedies for all infringements of their individual and collective rights. Such a decision shall give due consideration to the customs, traditions, rules and legal systems of the indigenous peoples concerned and international human rights.

Article 41

The organs and specialized agencies of the United Nations system and other intergovernmental organizations shall contribute to the full realization of the provisions of this Declaration through the mobilization, inter alia, of financial cooperation and technical assistance. Ways and means of ensuring participation of indigenous peoples on issues affecting them shall be established.

Article 42

The United Nations, its bodies, including the Permanent Forum on Indigenous Issues, and specialized agencies, including at the country level, and States shall promote respect for and full application of the provisions of this Declaration and follow up the effectiveness of this Declaration.

Article 43

The rights recognized herein constitute the minimum standards for the survival, dignity and well-being of the indigenous peoples of the world.

Article 44

All the rights and freedoms recognized herein are equally guaranteed to male and female indigenous individuals.

Article 45

Nothing in this Declaration may be construed as diminishing or extinguishing the rights indigenous peoples have now or may acquire in the future.

Article 46

1. Nothing in this Declaration may be interpreted as implying for any State, people, group or person any right to engage in any activity or to perform any act contrary to the Charter of the United Nations or construed as authorizing or encouraging any action which would dismember or impair, totally or in part, the territorial integrity or political unity of sovereign and independent States.

2. In the exercise of the rights enunciated in the present Declaration, human rights and fundamental freedoms of all shall be respected. The exercise of the rights set forth in this Declaration shall be subject only to such limitations as are determined by law and in accordance with international human rights obligations. Any such limitations shall be non-discriminatory and strictly necessary solely for the purpose of securing due recognition and respect for the rights and freedoms of others and for meeting the just and most compelling requirements of a democratic society.

3. The provisions set forth in this Declaration shall be interpreted in accordance with the principles of justice, democracy, respect for human rights, equality, non-discrimination, good governance and good faith.

About the editors

Amy Klemm Verbos, J.D., Ph.D., is an enrolled citizen of the Pokagon Band of Potawatomi, Dowagiac, Michigan, and an Assistant Professor of Business Law at the University of Wisconsin-Whitewater. She was an Assistant Professor of Management from 2009 to 2012 (University of South Dakota) and from 2013 to 2014 (Central Michigan University). Her writings, many co-authored with Native American scholars, on Native American business and management education issues, the Principles for Responsible Management Education and Indigenous inclusion, and relational ethics have been published in the *Journal of Business Ethics, Journal of Management Education, American Indian Culture and Research Journal, Equality, Diversity and Inclusion: An International Journal, Business and Society Review, Journal of Management Development, Leadership* (forthcoming), and several edited volumes.

Ella Henry is an Indigenous Maori woman, a Senior Lecturer in Te Ara Poutama, the Faculty of Maori Indigenous Development, at Auckland University of Technology. Her Ph.D. thesis focused on Maori entrepreneurs in the creative sector, and her Master's thesis on Maori women and leadership. Ella has been involved in the evolution of the Maori screen industry in New Zealand, in tribal development, and in environmental issues on behalf of Maori for many years.

Ana María Peredo is a *mestiza* from Peru and Professor of Political Ecology in the School of Environmental Studies at the University of Victoria, Canada. Her research focuses on ways that communities can address poverty by constructing rewarding and sustainable livelihoods out of resources in their distinctive cultures and environments. She draws on her academic training in anthropology and management, as well as extensive experience living among Indigenous peoples, to explore alternate economies and their impact on the social and environmental aspects of community. Her research has been published in a range of journals, including *Academy of Management Review* and the *Journal of Entrepreneurship Theory and Practice*. Ana María has received several research, education, and knowledge mobilization awards, and has held visiting engagements at various universities, including a year-long fellowship at the University of Oxford, UK.